CONTENTS

INTRODUCTION   PAGE 14

WONDERS OF ITALY   PAGE 26

*THE BEAUTY AND THE DIVERSITY
OF THE ITALIAN LANDSCAPE*   PAGE 28

THE SPLENDOR OF THE PEAKS   PAGE 44

FRESHWATER REFLECTIONS
AND DROPS OF LAND   PAGE 76

RICE FIELDS AND VINEYARDS   PAGE 82

A LAND GENTLE BY NATURE   PAGE 90

WHERE THE PO EMBRACES THE SEA   PAGE 94

A CLIFF CRESCENT-MOON FILLED
WITH THE SEA   PAGE 96

THE HEART OF ITALY, NATURALLY   PAGE 106

GREEN PROMONTORIES
AND SHINING BAYS   PAGE 124

A STONE'S THROW FROM AFRICA   PAGE 134

WILD LAND, ENCHANTING SEA   PAGE 144

*ONE COUNTRY
FOR A THOUSAND CITIES*   PAGE 154

ROME: THE ETERNAL CITY   PAGE 176

TURIN: THE "LITTLE OLD LADY'S"
DRAWING ROOM   PAGE 196

AMONG RICE FIELDS AND ANCIENT
CHARTERHOUSES   PAGE 202

MILAN: THE CITY THAT NEVER SLEEPS   PAGE 204

BERGAMO AND BRESCIA: CLASSICAL
PASTS, MODERN PRESENTS   PAGE 214

MANTUA: THE CITY OF THE
GONZAGA FAMILY   PAGE 216

RAVENNA: A BYZANTINE ATMOSPHERE   PAGE 218

THE NORTHEAST: LAND OF ART
AND WORK   PAGE 220

VERONA: TRANQUIL BEAUTY   PAGE 222

VENICE: THE CITY OF THE DOGES   PAGE 224

LIGURIA: PORTS OF ART
AND COMMERCE   PAGE 240

BOLOGNA: IN THE HEART OF EMILIA   PAGE 244

LUCCA: THE WALLED CITY   PAGE 246

PISA: MIDWAY BETWEEN ART
AND UNIVERSITY   PAGE 248

FLORENCE: THE HEART
OF THE RENAISSANCE   PAGE 250

SIENA: A PEARL AMONG THE HILLS   PAGE 256

SAN GIMIGNANO: CITY
OF THE TOWERS   PAGE 258

AREZZO: IN THE LAND OF GOLD   PAGE 260

UMBRIA AND MARCHE: THE GREEN
HEART OF ITALY   PAGE 262

ORVIETO: THE CITY THAT
STANDS ON TUFA   PAGE 266

PERUGIA, ASSISI AND NORCIA:
ON THE TRAIL OF ST. FRANCIS   PAGE 268

NAPLES: THE QUEEN OF THE BAY   PAGE 274

BARI, BRINDISI AND LECCE: IN THE
HEART OF BAROQUE PUGLIA   PAGE 276

SICILY: FROM MAGNA GRECIA
TO THE THIRD MILLENNIUM   PAGE 278

SARDINIA: THE TREAUSURES
OF THE PROUD ISLAND   PAGE 284

*FESTIVALS, TRADITIONS
AND FOLKLORE OF AN
ANCIENT PEOPLE*   PAGE 286

**MASTERPIECES
OF ITALIAN ART**   PAGE 316

A GENIUS FOR PORTRAITURE   PAGE 320

LIGHT AND DETAIL IN GOTHIC
PAINTING   PAGE 330

THE FASHIONABILITY
OF PORTRAIT BUSTS   PAGE 336

DEVOTION IN THE WORK
OF FRA ANGELICO; THE BATTLES
OF PAOLO UCCELLO   PAGE 340

THE WORK OF PIERO
DELLA FRANCESCA   PAGE 346

THE ARRIVAL OF LEONARDO
DA VINCI   PAGE 352

MATER DOLOROSA   PAGE 354

THE DOMINANCE OF LINE   PAGE 358

TELLING STORIES   PAGE 366

THE CITY AS BACKDROP   PAGE 370

STRENGTH AND EMOTION   PAGE 374

THE IDEALIZATION OF CLASSICAL
ANTIQUITY   PAGE 382

A WORSHIP OF NATURE   PAGE 388

MOVING BEYOND MATERIAL
LIMITATIONS   PAGE 392

THE DIVINE MICHELANGELO   PAGE 394

THE PRIVATE ROOMS
OF JULIUS II   PAGE 396

TITIAN'S WOMEN   PAGE 402

MEDITATIONS ON DEATH   PAGE 406

THE MOVEMENT TOWARD
MANNERISM   PAGE 408

GUIDO RENI AND SENSUALITY   PAGE 414

TWO DESCENTS FROM
THE CROSS   PAGE 416

AMONG LEAVES AND FLOWERS   PAGE 426

LIGHT AND SHADE IN VENETIAN
PAINTING   PAGE 430

NEW WAYS OF SHOWING LIGHT   PAGE 438

STATUES FOR THE CARDINAL   PAGE 444

NEOCLASSICAL TASTE   PAGE 450

THE APPEAL OF THE SACRED   PAGE 454

LIGHT EXPRESSED IN STONE   PAGE 470

THE CHARM OF THE BYZANTINE
EAST   PAGE 476

REMEMBERING THE NORMAN KINGS   PAGE 482

FROM ROMANESQUE RIGOR TO
THE BEGINNING OF THE GOTHIC   PAGE 486

RELIGIOUS STORIES   PAGE 494

MIRACULOUS PISA   PAGE 502

THE CHURCH TRIUMPHANT   PAGE 504

THE SUPREMACY OF FLORENCE   PAGE 514

THE NOBLE FABRIC
OF THE CATHEDRAL   PAGE 522

TITANS AND GIANTS   PAGE 526

A THANKFUL OFFERING
FROM VENICE   PAGE 532

THE EMBRACE OF THE CHURCH   PAGE 534

INDEX   PAGE 540

© 2004 White Star S.p.a.

This edition published by
Barnes & Noble Publishing, Inc.,
by arrangement
with White Star S.p.a.

2004 Barnes & Noble Books

M109876543
ISBN 0-7607-5792-5

Library of Congress
Cataloging-in-Publication
Data available

Printed in China

Originally published in two volumes,
Wonders of Italy and
Masterpieces of Italian Art

*1 Michelangelo, Sistine Chapel, details of
the vault, 1508-12, Vatican City.*

*2-3 Courmayeur, a famed ski resort at
the foot of Mont Blanc.*

*4-5 The soft morning light strokes the
Tuscany's Chianti hills.*

*6-7 Budelli is part of the Maddalena
archipelago to the north of Sardinia.*

*8 Orvieto's cathedral is a masterpiece of
Italian Gothic architecture.*

*9 The façade of Milan's Duomo was begun
in the 16th century and finished in 1813.*

*10-11 The island of San Giorgio seems to
brush St Mark's square in Venice.*

*12-13 Spoleto, Piazza del Duomo, one of
the most charming squares in Italy.*

Introduction

taly has always been "il bel Paese," a beautiful country *par excellence* which the famous medieval encyclopedia created by Pierre d'Ailly described as "the most beautiful country, favorable for the fertility of its soil and the richness of its pastures." Italy was like a dream: "Once you have been to Italy, you will forget other lands. If you have been to Paradise, you no longer need Earth. (...) Europe compared to Italy is like a cloudy day contrasted with a sunny day," wrote Russian writer Nikolai Gogol after a stay in Italy. It is clearly a country that, once discovered, you no longer wish to leave. There is "everything necessary for life and which renders it so delightful," according to Bruzen de la Martinière in the 18th century, and the German poet Heinrich Heine declared, "it is a wonderful thing just to live in Italy."

But what is it that makes Italy beautiful? What is it, seen through the eyes of foreigners, and by those smitten in particular, that has made Italy the ideal setting where one can abandon oneself to pure emotions and violent passions? There are many answers even today and of the

14 The results of Michelangelo's anatomical research, previously evidenced in the statues of David (1501) and the Pietà, are clearly illustrated in his Moses in the church of San Pietro in Vincoli, in Rome.

15 These famous bronzes are a masterpiece of Greek art; they show two warriors or possibly two kings. They were found in Riace in Calabria and are kept in the National Museum of Reggio Calabria. The artist was certainly of prodigious talent but his identity is unknown; experts have dated the work to 460-450 BC.

16-17 Piazza Navona stands in the heart of Rome. Its oval shape occupies the space once covered by Diocletian's stadium. The square is especially popular after sunset and offers a beautiful all-round view of the three glorious Baroque fountains standing in line, as well as the surrounding churches and palazzi built in the 15th–16th centuries. They use the ancient stands of the stadium as foundations.

16 bottom Siena, still largely surrounded by its ancient walls, is full of beauty and history. Seen from high up on the outskirts of the city and lit up to show off its most important buildings and monuments, the center of the Tuscan city is resplendent. Easily recognizable are the cathedral and slender bell-tower with its black and white marble bands, and the tall Torre del Mangia.

most varied nature. First, Italy's countryside undergoes enormous variations as one travels from north to south and east to west: within relatively small areas one can see an extraordinary multiplicity of landscapes unfold one after another, sometimes within the space of just a few miles. For example, it is often enough to pass over the brow of a hill or to round the bend of a river to find oneself in completely different natural scenery. When one travels from the mountains to the hills and then to the sea, the contrast is even more obvious. When travelers enter Italy through the Alps, on leaving the peaks and valleys behind, they will be enchanted by the vast lakes at the feet of the mountains. They will be struck by the radiance of the new setting, the pleasantness of the temperate climate and the exuberance of the Mediterranean vegetation.

Visitors who travel the length of Italy will certainly not be disappointed by the magnificence of the hilly scenery through Romagna, Marche and Abruzzi with their thousand hill-top villages like terraces overlooking the long, sandy beaches of the Adriatic coast. They will likewise be captivated by the many islands and marinas that decorate the Tyrrhenian coastline from the Gulf of Naples down to Sicily where the mountains tumble steeply into the sea and the high cliffs are riven by clefts and small bays. The violent beauty of the land is intensified the length of the peninsula by the disquieting presence of volcanic phenomena like the curious blow-holes of Lardarello, the sulphurous baths of Saturnia, the Solfatura of Pozzuoli and Mount Vesuvius in Naples which make the beauty more real.

The coastline, especially in Liguria, made a deep impression on Vidal de la Blanche,

17 top The church of Santa Giustina is one of the oldest churches in Padua. It is unmistakable for its layout in the form of a tripartite Latin cross and for its eight oriental domes that cover the barrel vaults. The original church was built in early Christian times but destroyed by the earthquake at the beginning of the 12th century. The only remains of the building that replaced it are two marble griffins on the façade.

17 bottom The Duomo, the Baptistery and Giotto's bell-tower in Piazza San Giovanni are the universal emblems of Florence. The use of green and white marble and chiaroscuro to lighten the mass of the buildings, together with the daring designs that enabled the dome and bell-tower to be built, are magnificent examples of the engineering skill and imagination of artists like Brunelleschi, Giotto, Pisano and Ghiberti.

founder of modern human geography, during a trip in 1918. This is part of his description of Liguria: "The mountains stand right over the coastline, one might almost say enveloping it. On the hillsides sloping down to the water's edge, we see the main village emerge from the 'plantations' and olive trees, connected to the beach by stepped paths that are traversed daily by donkeys. Closed between two promontories, stretches out the sandy arc of the shore ... onto which the boats are beached."

Italy's rich and varied land is also heavily but harmoniously populated. "The Tuscan countryside simply could not be better kept," wrote Goethe after his trip to Italy, "every clod of earth seems as though it had been passed through a sieve." Indeed, Tuscany, the subject of so many paintings by Botticelli, Leonardo da Vinci and Giotto, seems the perfect example of nature benign to humans and their works, that assists and harmonizes civilization rather than contrasting it. For this very reason, Tuscany is one of the regions of Italy—but certainly not the only one—in which the city-countryside relationship seems especially harmonious, in which these two elements complement one another even aesthetically. The English poet Percy Bysshe Shelley painted an idyllic portrait of Florence describing the city set in a radiant setting which both illuminated it and was illuminated by it. He wrote: "It is surrounded by cultivated hills and from the bridge that crosses the wide channel of the Arno, the view is the most lively and elegant I have ever seen. One can see three or four bridges,

18 top There are thousands of traditions to be found throughout Italy. The carnival masks of Venice are an exhilarating example: the carnival is now a multimillion dollar business for the city which in February and March is besieged by tourists from all over the world who come to enjoy the enchanting atmosphere of the canals.

18 bottom Twice a year, on July 2nd and August 16th, Siena goes wild. The entire population of the city and the surrounding area is caught by the fever of the Palio, the horse race in Piazza del Campo which, in just a few minutes of horses, jockeys and excitement, is the culmination of months of impassioned preparations.

18-19 In Sardinia the Sartiglia, a carnival show dating back to the 17th century, is still a very popular and beloved festival. The main protagonist is the cumponidori, *a masked horseman (accompanied by more horsemen contending among themselves), who is must center a hanging iron star. If he succeeds, peace and health will be enjoyed by all for the following year.*

20-21 Temple G of Selinunte in Sicily was a building of gigantic proportions (370 x 177 feet) begun in 530 BC but never completed. It is one of the three temples of which remains are found at Selinunte, the Greek colony which was destroyed and abandoned after a bloody war with Segesta.

20 top The Greek theater of Taormina was in fact rebuilt by the Romans—as can be seen today—on top of the original building and dates from the 2nd century BC. From its cavea in the rock there is a wonderful view over the bay, the city and, in the distance, of Etna.

21 top The massive pediment of the Temple of Neptune at Paestum frames one of the most impressive structures of ancient times to have survived intact to the present day. It dates back to 450 BC and is one of the numerous important buildings to be found in the archaeological area in Campania enclosed by Roman and Lucan walls from the 4th century BC.

one of which appears to be supported by Corinthian columns, white sails on the boats that stand out against the green depths of the forest that reaches down as far as the edge of the water, and the slopes of the hills covered in every part by splendid villas. Cupolas and bell towers rise on every side and everything is surprisingly neat and clean. On the other side, the Arno valley curves into the distance with hills of olive trees and vines in the foreground, then chestnut trees, and finally one glimpses the smoky-blue pine forests at the feet of the Apennines."

Italy is above all an ancient land with a history of different civilizations that have overlapped, united and been transformed throughout the ages, contributing to give a "cultivated" look to the countryside. Italy is like a large, open history book that details the events of thousands of years, from the rock engravings in Val Camonica to Etruscan remains, from the Greek ruins of Magna Graecia to their Roman equivalents, from Byzantine monuments to glorious Renaissance buildings, up to the present time. To all this should be added a human touch that makes Italy a particularly active and interesting region to all: its folklore, its traditions and its multifaceted popular culture. This is a culture comprising ancient rites transformed and revisited throughout the centuries, that are not "archaeology" but which continue to constitute one of the richest and most appreciated aspects of the soul of the Italian people.

21 bottom Villa Adriana was built near Tivoli between AD 118 and 133 by Emperor Hadrian. He made it into a sort of imperial city which covered an immense area of over 300 acres.

22-23 This aerial photograph shows the large loop of the river Tiber in front of Castel Sant'angelo. Behind the river it is possible to see 16th century Rome, and then past the Forum, the Colosseum and ancient Rome.

24-25 St. Peter's Basilica, Vatican City, interior of the dome.

WONDERS OF *Italy*

A JOURNEY INTO ITALIAN ART, TRADITIONS AND NATURAL WONDERS

Wonders of Italy combines the natural splendors of the "Bel Paese"—beautiful country—with manmade treasures of art, architecture, and design in an all-encompassing tour of Italy's boot-shaped peninsula and associated islands. The book explores the incredible variety of Italian landscapes, from Tuscany and the Po valley to the wild beauty of the south with its volcanoes; from the majesty and might of the highest mountains in Europe to the vitality and beauty of the islands and coastlines.

TEXT BY ANNIE SACERDOTI

26 The gold, winged lion set in a lunette of St. Mark's Basilica is perhaps the most famous of the many symbols of the city of Venice.

27 One of Antonio Canova's best known masterpieces, Paolina Borghese, *sculpted between 1805-08, is now in the Borghese Gallery.*

The beauty and the diversity of the Italian landscape

In little more than 116,000 square miles, Italy contains an extraordinary diversity of terrain and nature. In contrast to the permanently snow-capped Alpine and Apennine mountains, there are long coastal strips in Calabria and Sicily that enjoy a temperate-subtropical climate and which are the kingdoms of palm and olive trees. Not far from the large, continental and intensively cultivated Paduan plain traversed by the river Po, stretch broad areas of hills covered with vineyards, and the many north Italian lakes with their own micro-climates. In the south, bare clay valleys, traversed by dry river beds and surrounded by land burnt by the sun, exist alongside the coastal regions with their promontories, flatlands, elevations and valleys. The granite plateaux of northwest Sardinia contrast with the Milanese plain and the gorges of Puglia. Each of these environments, sometimes no more than a few dozen miles from one another, has its own vegetation, colors, sky and light. Combined with the peaks of Sicily and Sardinia, the Alps, that enclose the country to the north, and the Apennines, that run the full length of the peninsular, cover almost 40% of all Italy; of the rest, approximately 20% is flat and 40% is hilly, so, by their very extent, the mountains are an essential part of the Nation. The 620 mile span of the Alps divides Italy from the rest of Europe while the Apennines, running northwest to southeast for 830 miles, cut Italy into two parts. The cut is so clean that it is difficult to pass from the Adriatic to the Tyrrhenian side even though the distance is short.

The forests that cover the Alps and Apennine mountains are Italy's green "lung," but unfortunately they have been decimated over the centuries. Humans have always

28 top The Matterhorn (known as Monte Cervino in Italy) in the Pennine Alps is a little over 14,690 feet high. Its pyramidal shape makes it unique. It dominates the Valtournenche on the Italian side and the valley of Zermatt on the Swiss side.

28 center Mont Blanc (known as Monte Bianco in Italy) is 15,780 feet high and the highest mountain in Europe. Its summit is formed by a succession of peaks and pinnacles and is marked by a number of glaciers.

28 bottom The Catinaccio, or Rosengarten, stands in the eastern Alps between the Fassa and Tires valleys. Its highest peak is the Catinaccio d'Antermoia at 9849 feet. Like the Dolomite mountains, it is formed by numerous pinnacles such as the Towers of Vaiolet.

drawn on these resources without thinking about the future, without considering what would happen once the woods and trees were all destroyed. When the damage caused by deforestation was understood, indiscriminate felling was prohibited and reforestation was introduced but it was often too late. Consequently, the original species of tree was often replaced by another, more resistant, type, conifers in particular, or perhaps species that are not even part of the natural Mediterranean habitat, such as the Australian eucalyptus, that have transformed the natural scenery of many areas.

Italy's mountains have always been inhabited although discontinuously and unevenly. There are still some mountains that have large populations and others that are almost empty. Settlements are often composed of groups of farmhouses, as in Sardinia, or by sizeable villages as in

southern Italy. In these locations, the populations have formed groups since time immemorial to defend themselves from bandits or to escape from malaria which, until after World War II, still existed in swampy areas.

Neither the Alps nor the Apennines have been closed worlds and have never constituted insurmountable barriers to the outside world. Roads, tracks and paths have always cut through them in all directions to allow man to pass. Even if sometimes difficult to use, the crossing points on the mountain passes have always been numerous. Hannibal's army crossed the Alps in 218 BC taking elephants and horses with it; the Romans knew and used seventeen Alpine passes, some of which they built themselves; in the Middle Ages, the barbarians descended on the north Italian plains without any particular difficulty.

28-29 The Brenta range stands to the west of the River Adda in the eastern Alps. The group is not part of the Dolomites but is considered with them because of the similarity of its bare sides and pinnacles. Numerous ledges mark horizontally the rocky walls, deeply eroded by wind and rain. The central part is characterized by true natural architectural works.

30 top The slopes of the Gran Sasso are covered with chestnut trees, oaks and conifers. Higher up, small lakes are commonly found, like Filetto seen here.

30 bottom The pastures of Gran Sasso are home to grazing animals like this horse in a meadow at the foot of Camosciara in the National Park of Abruzzo.

30-31 The mountain Gran Sasso stands in the middle of the Abruzzese Apennine mountains; its highest peak is the Corno Grande at 9560 feet. Its slopes are covered with vegetation right up to the snowline. Grains and fruits are cultivated on the mountainsides, and cattle, sheep and goats are raised in the meadows for the production of cheese and other dairy items.

Series of foothills slope gently down to the plains from the Alpine and Apennine chains so there is no sudden physical separation of the mountains from the flatlands; on the contrary, the two share an integrated economy. The mountain slopes are used to cultivate grains and fruit while the pastures allow cows, sheep and goats to graze for milk and cheese production. Further up there are mulberries and chestnuts, then oaks and conifers, and finally, where the cold makes vegetation sparse, there are only low bushes, moss and lichen below the snowline. When speaking of mountains, it is natural to think of the highest peaks, Mont Blanc, Monte Rosa, the Gran Sasso or the Maiella and to forget that plateaux and foothills are also included. For example, Lucchesia is part of the Apuan Alps and owes its prosperity to the waters that descend from them but the highest peak there is a little lower than 6500 feet. The mountains in Campania are not restricted to Vesuvius and the Lattari chain that separates the Gulf of Naples from the Gulf of Salerno; they also comprise the area formed by the curve of calcareous peaks at the foot of which are Caserta, Nola and Nocera, and that a rocky spur separates from Salerno. In the foothills of the Alps and Apennines, nature is gentler, the light brighter and the vegetation richer, especially where there are lakes.

31 top left The Apennine mountains in Abruzzo run in successive parallel chains down the Adriatic coast of the region. One group, in this section, the Maiella, reaches 9170 feet in height.

31 top right The Sibillini range in the central Apennine chain is a watershed between the Tyrrhenian and Adriatic seas. The highest point is at Mount Vettore at 8123 feet. At the foot of these mountains, wide plains open out where a carpet of brightly colored flowers appears as soon as the snows melt; they are in full flower at the start of summer.

Italy abounds with lakes, many of which were created by the actions of glaciers during the Quaternary period. The largest number of lakes is found at an altitude of 5900—9180 feet in the Alps: there are over 400, some of them large like Misurina near Cortina d'Ampezzo which is over half a mile long, and others small, like the Blue Lake in Valtournanche at the feet of the Matterhorn and lake Carezza in the heart of the Dolomites. Lakes are the dominant feature in

two areas in Italy: at the foot of the mountains between Piedmont and Veneto, and in the volcanic zone between Lazio and Campania.

Lake Orta, or Cusio, as it was called by the Romans, is the westernmost of the pre-Alpine lakes and lies entirely in Piedmont. It is perfectly sized: small enough to be seen all at one glance but also large enough to contain all the natural features of the larger lakes, even if on a smaller scale. On the island of San Giulio in the middle of the lake stands a church dedicated to St. Julius.

Lake Maggiore, or Verbano, spreads across the boundary between Piedmont and

Lombardy. It covers 80 square miles and is 1220 feet deep. One of its shores is in Swiss territory. The lake is fed by the Ticino and Toce rivers and is connected to Lake Lugano by the river Tresa. The overall shape of the lake is complex; it receives an abundance of water from the mountains that keeps the vegetation luxuriant on the steep slopes that tumble into the water and around the little bays and pebbly beaches. Villa Taranto, near Pallanza, and Villa Pallavicino, near Stresa, are two of the magnificent residences with Italian gardens that hosted aristocrats and nobles from all over the world until the 19th century.

Floating just in front of Stresa, the three islands of Borromeo are like precious gems set in the water. Palazzo Borromeo and its Italian garden stands on Isola Bella; the original village with its twisting alleyways is built on Isola dei Pescatori; and in the center of its park on Isola Madre there is a 16th century palace that has been transformed into a botanical garden for exotic plants and flowers. These are favored by the mild climate and sheltered by the surrounding mountains. The lakes of Monate, Comabbio, Biandronno and Varese are situated near to the southern bank of Lake Maggiore; they were formed in the same manner and at the same time as their larger neighbour. Lake Como, also known as Lake Lario, is in Lombardy. The surrounding mountains alternate steep, tree-covered gorges with shores lined with gardens and flowers. It covers 56 square miles. The lake was loved by author Alessandro Manzoni whose novel, "I Promessi Sposi," was set here. The northern tip is separated from the main body of the lake by the bottleneck at Colico; further down, the lake forks at Bellagio, one stretch leading to Lecco and the other to Como. Lake Como is fed by the Mera river and the Adda, the second of which continues its journey at Lecco. During the 19th century it was chosen to be the seat of country residences for aristocratic families. Still standing today between Como, Tremezzo and Bellagio are some of the most beautiful mansions built on any of the lakes, all of them boasting extensive Italian gardens: Villa d'Este, Villa Pliniana, Villa Serbelloni and Villa Carlotta. Lake Iseo, or Sebino, is formed

by the river Oglio running down from Valcamonica on its journey across the Po Valley. This Lombard lake boasts the largest lakebound island in Europe, Montisola, flanked on either side by two tiny islets, Loreto and San Giorgio. A few miles from the lakeshore at Cislago, there stand what the locals affectionately call the "wood fairies." These are extraordinary natural towers of earth and stone each topped by a large rock so that it looks a little like a hat. These "pyramids"have been created by the erosive forces of water washing away the surrounding soil to leave the towers standing up to 98 feet tall.

Further east we find Lake Garda, called Benaco by the Romans. The river feeding it from the north is the Sarca which changes its name to the Mincio when it leaves again from the southern shore. It is the largest lake

in Italy, covering 143 square miles, and it is almost considered a sea especially by the Austrians and Germans who are frequent visitors there. Because of its size, the various shores of Lake Garda are very different. They are lined with castles (like the Scaliger forts at Sirmione and Malcesine), sumptuous villas (like Villa Bettoni at Bogliaco on the Brescian side or Villa Albertini at Garda on the Veneto side) and gardens of Mediterranean vegetation (oranges, lemons, citrons, olives and vines are grown on its banks thanks to its extremely mild climate but also exotic plants as in the Hruska botanical garden at Gardone Riviera). The lake touches on three regions: Lombardy to the west, Veneto to the east and Trentino to the north east. The Sirmione peninsula, so loved by the Roman poet Catullus, stretches out into the lake on the south shore separating the two gulfs of Desenzano and Peschiera.

32 top Paleological finds have shown that Lake Como has been inhabited since time immemorial. Its strategic position between Italy and Switzerland has made it a transit point for centuries on the descent to the Po Valley.

32 bottom On the island of San Giulio, in the center of Lake Orta, stands the church of the saint of the same name. A 15th century bas-relief tells the story of the miracle of his arrival on the island which was infested with snakes and monsters at that time. When Giulio spread his cloak on the water, it turned into a raft. On reaching the island, he cleared it of the unfriendly creatures and built the church. This episode marked the beginning of his life as a preacher.

32-33 During the 19th century, Lake Como was chosen as a place to holiday and relax by the aristocracy, and beautiful residences were buit. The picture of the small port of Pescallo with its boats at anchor is typical of the tranquillity of this lake, still a popular holiday destination.

33 top The Lake Garda's waters up the territories of three regions: the western shore is in Lombardy, the eastern in Veneto and the northeastern in Trentino. The shores differ markedly but all boast castles, like this Scaliger stronghold at Malcesine.

34 top Lake Bolsena in Lazio (left) fills the main crater of the volcanic area in the Volsini mountains. Two islands sit in the center of the lake, Martana and Bisentina. Lake Corbara (right) in Umbria is surrounded by old farmhouses and acres of meadows.

34-35 Lake Vico in Lazio fills the crater of the volcanic Cimini mountains. The shores of the lake are surrounded by ancient forests.

35 top Lake Trasimeno in Umbria has no outlet. It is shallow and fed only by rainwater. For centuries it has been a center of meditation and is surrounded by Franciscan and Benedictine monasteries.

35 center The houses of Anguillara Sabazia face onto Lake Bracciano in Lazio. The name either derives from eels (anguille) that live in great numbers in its waters or from the aristocratic family, Anguillara.

35 bottom Algae and aquatic grasses are harvested in Lake Posta Fibreno in Lazio and are dried and used for cattle feed or fertilizer.

Lake Trasimeno is the largest lake in central or southern Italy. It was formed by floods and tectonic action and is fed by no river; it is shallow and the waters are supplied almost exclusively by rain so that its level is subject to extreme alteration from one year to the next. In the 15th century, Fortebraccio da Montone, the nobleman of Perugia, tried to dig an outlet from it to the Nestore basin but to no avail. The lakes' flat sides lined with poppies and marsh grasses have been the sites of many battles, the most famous of which was in 217 BC when the army of the Carthaginian general, Hannibal, overcame the Romans. The battle was so cruel that it is still recalled today in local place names: Sanguineto (bloody), Ossaia (charnel), Sepoltaglia (burial ground). Moving further south, close to Rome, another lake district is found with an unusual formation. These lakes exist in dormant or collapsed volcanic craters on Mounts Volsini, Cimini and

Sabatini and in the Alban hills. The lakes are named Bolsena, Vico, Bracciano, Albano and Nemi. Romans visited them frequently for their proximity to Rome, especially during summer when the heat becomes unbearable. They built castles and country residences or they went, just as they do today, for outings. The surrounding countryside is of fields, vineyards and pastures for the many herds of sheep. Different surroundings are to be found at the two coastal lakes, Lesina and Varano, on the edges of thick forest on the Gargano promontory in Puglia. These are more lagoons than lakes. Lesina is separated from the sea by a strip of land half a mile wide and is only 5 feet deep; it has brackish water and is infiltrated by the sea. Varano is Italy's seventh largest lake and separated from Lesina by Mount Elio, a small hill on which prehistoric remains have been found.

Sicily is a separate world from the mainland although its mountains are, from a geological point of view, a continuation of the heights of Calabria despite being on the other side of the Strait of Messina. Sicily's northern chain is divided into various groups: the Peloritani, the Nebrodi and the Madonie which are all in fact part of the same structural unit. Along the north west side of the island, the mountains of Palermo that surround the Conca d'Oro extend as far as Trapani with similar features: they are calcareous and dolomitic massifs from the Mesozoic period, mainly isolated, that overlook gently sloping clay and sandstone hills. The center of the island is a succession of undulations interrupted by Mount Cammarata (5177 feet) and ten or so other peaks (all over 3280 feet) which form the Sicani group of mountains between Corleone and Cammarata. In all directions as far as the Mediterranean there is a sea of modest mountains and valleys: to the east as far as the Erei, to the northeast as far as the Madonie, to the north as far as the

Busambra rock, and to the west as far as one of the euphemistically named "Montagna Grande" (the last western peak in Sicily, to the west of Calatafimi, and just 2460 feet high).

In ancient times the island was covered with forests of chestnut, oak and beech trees except for the coasts, the alluvial plains and the more recently created lava areas. All eastern Sicily is dominated by Mount Etna which, with good reason, can be considered a world apart from the rest of the island. It is a huge mass of black lava and tufa which contrasts vividly with the snow white peak and the green vegetation of its slopes. It is the largest active volcano in Europe and one of the largest on Earth. It is formed by a central cone and two hundred groups of occasionally active small side cones able to spew forth fluid lava which can then spread for huge distances.

The terrain of Sardinia is completely different to that of the Alps, the Apennines or Sicily. Arriving by sea, then moving inland, the visitor soon realises that this is a very unusual mountainous environment made up of isolated massifs—Gallura, Nurra, Gennargentu, Iglesiente and Sulcis—connected by plateaux of different heights and environment or by variably sized tectonic depressions such as those of Campidano and Cixerri. The long geological history of this island, more similar to France than to Italy, has shaped it into an utterly original environment. Its elevations are the result of the tectonic dislocation of an ancient granite massif which has been gradually smoothed over the centuries by erosion.

36 top The large Campidano plain in Sardinia stretches from the Bay of Oristano to the Bay of Cagliari and separates the Inglesiente-Sulcis mountains from the hills of Trexenta and Marmilla. It is a typical tectonic depression bordered by faults sometimes in the shape of rounded hills like those at Pula (see photograph) and hot water springs, like those at the spas of Sardara and Villasor.

36 center The huge mass of Mount Etna dominates eastern Sicily. Its flanks were once covered by copses of chestnut and oak trees and broom.

36 bottom The visitor in Sardinia is often confronted by bare, treeless countryside as far as the eye can see, like this one at Barbagia.

36-37 The Sinni is one of the few rivers that run through Basilicata. It has its source on Mount Sirino and runs through a long valley before reaching the bay of Taranto near Nova Siri, 58 miles later. The rivers in this region— the Bradano, the Basente (the longest at 95 miles), the Cavone, the Agri and the Sinni—are all torrential rivers, i.e., they are powerful during the winter rains but nearly dry during the summer drought.

38 *Portofino promontory is a nature reserve that extends 2 miles between Paradise and Tigullio bays. Portofino is a corner of Liguria famous for its natural beauty, the multicolored houses that surround it like a ring and for the richness of vegetation on the hill behind it.*

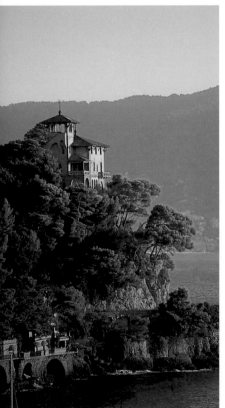

38-39 *Oltrepò Pavese occupies the huge province of Pavia from the right bank of the River Po east to the border with Emilia and west to the border with Piedmont. In all it covers 425 square miles. The vineyards that produce the famous red wines, Bonarda and Barbacarlo, are the most characteristic feature of the*

countryside of rounded hills topped by old villages, many of which hold works of great artistic value. Agriculture is the main income-producing activity (besides wine, cereals and livestock are produced) but there are also factories operating in the food, textile and iron and steel industries.

39 *These three views of the different sections of the Italian countryside show the diversity of the country's landscapes: Argentario (top) used to be an island but has now become a promontory with typically marine flora; Garfagnana (center) is mountainous in the center gradually giving way to hills; the Po Valley (bottom left) is utterly flat and this province, of Vercelli is flooded for many months of the year for the cultivation of rice.*

Italy's flatlands are not so extensive as either the hill or mountain areas and cover only approximately 20% of the country. These are nearly always alluvial valley formed by detritus deposited by rivers over millennia. The most important and the largest, covering 70% of Italy's flatlands, is the Po Valley through which the river Po and its tributaries run. The Po Valley has been greatly transformed by man during his history in north Italy. Its forests were cut down to make room for agricultural land, it was divided up into lots and several marshy

areas have been drained. The northern section of the plain is calcareous so that water is easily drained into the subsoil but the southern section contains layers of clay which does not let the water pass and creates pools on the surface. This is the so-called "springs" strip which divides the drier areas cultivated with cereals and vines from the "wet" zones used for rice and irrigated meadows. This farming area stretches from the tip of Veneto in the east to Emilia Romagna in the south west and has been profoundly altered by man in his slow transformation of nature. The same process has taken place in other small plains throughout the mainland and the islands: for example, on the Tyrrhenian side of the Apennines there are the lower Arno valley and Maremma in Tuscany, the Roman countryside in Lazio and the plain in Campania; on the Adriatic side there are the tablelands of Puglia and the zones around Bari and Otranto; in Sicily there is the Catanian plain and in Sardinia, the Campidano. Italy has 5360 miles of coastline, half of which are represented by Sicily and Sardinia. The Ligurian coast starts at the French border and is divided into the eastern and western rivieras by the Gulf of Genoa. At its deepest point, the Ligurian sea reaches 9180 feet. The western riviera is covered with olive groves and greenhouses which are not only attractive to look at but represent a huge industry.

From Ventimiglia to Genoa, the coastline is made up of sandy beaches separated by promontories with terraced hills behind. From Genoa to La Spezia on the eastern riviera, the scenery changes: the coast is high and rocky with frequent coves and projections like the Promontory of

Portofino which encloses the Gulf of Tigullio, or the point at Porto Venere which ends the bay of La Spezia. This stretch of coast has one of the richest vegetations in Italy and the maquis on the Portofino promontory is protected.

The coastline that runs down Tuscany and Lazio (from La Spezia to Rome), to where the river Tiber reaches the sea, resulted from alluvial formation. The Tyrrhenian coast is low with sandy ridges, called "tomboli" in Tuscany and "tumoleti" in Lazio, which create coastal pools like those on the Orbetello promontory. This zone typically consists of maquis along the coast itself with a long strip of pine trees behind, at one time quite dense. Some of this area, like the Maremma, used to be marshland but were drained at the start of the century. Just off the Tuscan coast stand the islands of an archipelago of which the largest is Elba. They too are covered with typical Mediterranean flora but unexpectedly lush for its geographical position. This is due to climatic conditions (high temperature, clear skies, little rain) more akin to Naples or Palermo than Pisa or Livorno.

40 top The coastline of Terracina on the Bay of Gaeta boasts a wide sandy beach. The town of Terracina stands at the feet of the Ausoni mountains at the edge of the Pontine plain near the Roman road, the Via Appia. It is both a fishing port and an agricultural center besides being a seaside resort. From the hill where the remains of the temple of Jove Anxur are found, there is a wonderful view over the Circeo promontory and the islands of the Pontian archipelago.

South of Rome, what was once a large swamp is today a highly cultivated area of Lazio. The Pontina plain has kept some of its original coastal lagoons at Sabaudia, Fogliano, Caprolace and Monaci and offers a natural environment that is unique to the mainland: there is an area of dunes covered with maquis, lakes behind (as in Circeo park), with forests of oak, ash, hornbeam and elm, mixed with eucalyptus. From Circeo promontory to the Cilento peninsula, the coastline forms a series of arcs to create the gulfs of Gaeta, Naples and Salerno.

The Ponziane islands sparkle in the sunshine in front of Gaeta while the islands of Ischia, Procida and Capri are in the Gulf of Naples. This is where the Tyrrhenian sea, maximum depth 12,240 feet, is the dominant theme in the local scenery with its range of intense blues. All the hillsides here are terraced with orange, lemon, fig and almond trees and vegetables and flowers which have replaced the original maquis.

The rather squat Cilento peninsula has its furthermost point at Cape Palinuro, where a species of primrose grows that dates back to the Tertiary period. This is followed by the Policastro gulf, with its high coastal land, and the two Calabrian gulfs of Sant'Eufemia and Gioia. Here the beaches are low and sandy in short stretches. The Strait of Messina is only 2 miles wide. It is the body of water that connects the Tyrrhenian sea to the Ionian, that washes the long Calabrian and Pugliese coasts as far as Santa Maria di Leuca and the Strait of Otranto, where the Adriatic begins. The Ionian coast is high and rugged with mountains that fall

straight into the sea and furrowed by river beds that are dry all summer and which rage after the winter rains. There are few ports in this area dominated by the gulfs of Squillante to the west and Taranto to the east. Across the wide Salentina peninsula and Puglian tablelands, the countryside changes completely. The coast of the Adriatic sea (which only reaches a maximum depth of 3953 feet) is straight and has few ports due to its geological formation. The Gargano peninsula is the only projection, bordered

by coastal lakes and confronted by the Tremiti islands. Mount Conero stands on the coast overlooking the port of Ancona. North of Ravenna we find the stretch of low, marshy coastline, lagoons, islands and cane-brake in the valleys of Comacchio and in the wide Po estuary. These are continued in the lagoons of Venice, Marano and Grado which have been greatly transformed by the hand of man. After the Gulf of Venice, the coast is flat and traversed by a series of parallel rivers as far as the Gulf of Trieste where the rocky and jagged coastline is covered in a

40 center The crags of Pizzomunno in Puglia, eroded by the action of water and wind, stand out boldly in front of the cliffs on the shoreline. They are without doubt among the most fascinating creations of marine erosion.

40 bottom The three famous crags of Capri in the Bay of Naples rise massively out of the water; their round bases rise to pointed tips on a horizontally layered column.

40-41 Amalfi stands in the center of the Amalfitana coast which stretches from the Bay of Naples to the Bay of Sorrento. Today Amalfi is a tourist resort and fishing port but in the 8th-9th centuries it was a sea-faring republic. The main part of the town is centerd around the port; the houses in the typical Campanian style are generally colored white or in pastel shades. The roofs are built

to an ancient design that allows rainwater to be collected and acts as insulation against the heat. The coast is dotted with more colored houses, Saracen towers, and citrus orchards. The view from the coast road over the clear waters of the sea is simply stupendous and, in the air, the Mediterranean smells of rosemary, oregano, strawberry bushes, honeysuckle, cluster pines and holm oaks linger.

42 top The island of Vulcano is part of the Eolian archipelago and lies off the north of Sicily. Its name is a clear indication of its origin: it is formed by a crater with three cones that are still active. Near to the Gran Cratere, a depression more than 500 yards in diameter, the Piano delle Fumarole can be seen from which sulfurous vapors continually escape. Legend has it that the island, called Thermessa in ancient times, was the home of Eolo, the "lord of the winds."

42 center Lampedusa is the largest island in the Pelagian archipelago and is closer to Tunisia than Sicily. The Isola dei Conigli in the photograph is a favorite place for sea turtles to lay their eggs.

42 bottom Cape Teulada is the southernmost point in Sardinia between Sant'Antioco and Cagliari. The history of Sardinia influenced the look of the island itself: the towers built along the coast in Medieval times were used as lookouts against attacks by Saracen pirates.

42-43 *The Maddalena archipelago, to the north of Sardinia and between the coasts of Palau and nearby Corsica, comprises seven islands: Maddalena, Caprera, Santo Stefano, Spargi, Budelli, Santa Maria and Ràzzoli. The magnificent island of Budelli (see photograph) has some of the best beaches of the whole group. Its coral depths color the sand and give the waters that bathe the island the transparency of a tropical lagoon.*

wealth of vegetation. Once again the two large islands, Sicily and Sardinia, are worlds unto themselves. The high and rocky Tyrrhenian coast of Sicily is lined with gulfs; nearby the Eolian (or Lipari) volcanic islands of which two, Stromboli and Vulcano, still host active volcanoes. Other islands, like Ustica to the west near Palermo, and the Egadi group at the western tip of Sicily, are like small gems set around the larger island. Sicily's southern coastline is completely unlike the others. It is flat with slight curves and washed by the shallow Sicilian sea (only

5416 feet deep) with Pantelleria and the Pelagian islands not far from the coast. The western coast faces onto the Ionian sea and is split into two: the center opens onto the Gulf of Catania while the north is straight.

The Sardinian shores are very different: jagged to the northeast with rocks eroded by the wind and, not far away, the Maddalena archipelago; with the wide Gulf of Cagliari on the south side, facing the islands of San Pietro and Sant'Antioco; and high on the long western coast that faces Spain.

44 top Classic and alluring, this view of the Dente del Gigante shows how the vertical layering of the granite, combined with the effects of wind and water, have created a sort of jagged monolith.

44 bottom The Aiguille Noire spears the soft white clouds which partially cover the south crest. Mistakenly considered a "minor" pinnacle on Mont Blanc, it is and always has been one of the most elegant and sought after peaks by mountain climbers.

THE SPLENDOR
OF THE PEAKS

44-45 The enormous bulk of Mont Blanc, is here seen from the wall of Freney, recognizable by the large glacier where the Bonatti expedition made its dramatic attempt at a descent in 1961.

45 top left The contrast between the intense blue sky and the whiteness of the ice of the Grandes Jorasses, seen from Courmayeur, enhances the magnificence of these famous peaks which, at over 13,120 feet, dominate the central section of the Italian-French border behind Val Ferret.

45 top right The summit of Mont Blanc, rightly nicknamed the "King of the Alps," was climbed for the first time in 1786, by Balmat and Paccard.

46-47 The Courmayeur side of Mont Blanc; on the left is the top of the mountain, on the right the Brenva wall is clearly identifiable. A little lower down, it is possible to see a part of the Brenva glacier whose southern tip stretches toward Val Veny.

48 top Valsavarenche is one of the six tributary valleys that feed into the Dora Baltea river from the south side. It is covered with woods of beech, maple, linden and pine trees and, on the increase, spruce and larch. Crowning this thick vegetation are the snow-sprinkled peaks.

48-49 The region of Valle d'Aosta is enclosed by the Graie and Pennine Alps. It covers over 1,150 square miles, many of which are covered permanently by snow and ice, like the walls of extraordinary mountains such as Mont Blanc, the Matterhorn, and Mount Rosa.

49 top left It is not unusual to find glorious scenery at the foot of Mont Blanc, as in the picture. The small church at Entrèves, a stone's throw from Courmayeur, shyly peeps over the snow dunes while the amphitheater of mountains behind makes for one of Europe's most spectacular settings.

49 bottom left The village of La Thuile stands at 4,728 feet on the French border in the extreme north-west of Valle d'Aosta on the road that leads to the Colle del Piccolo San Bernardo. La Thuile is not only famous for its summer and winter tourism but also for the presence of layers of anthracite in the rock nearby.

49 right Pointed like the church spire, the unmistakable trunk of the Matterhorn, (Monte Cervino to Italians,) rears up against the blue of the sky. The massive block of granite 14,691 feet high was climbed for the first time in 1865.

50 top The ibex, a hoofed mountain mammal, owes its survival in Europe to the creation of the Gran Paradiso National Park. The last specimens not to have been hunted or poached were able to increase in number in the protection of the park and now this magnificent creature has been returned to much of the Alps.

50 center The Monviso massif stands in the Cozie in the western part of the Piedmont Alps. It features a series of peaks, the highest of which is the Bric di Monviso at 12,600 feet. It overlooks the Po valley and is the source of the river.

50 bottom Gran Paradiso National Park can be reached by road either from the south in Piedmont or from the Valle d'Aosta valleys to the north, like the Valle di Rhêmes seen here. Chamoix are one of the two hoofed species that live in the park where they are protected like the rest of the fauna and flora.

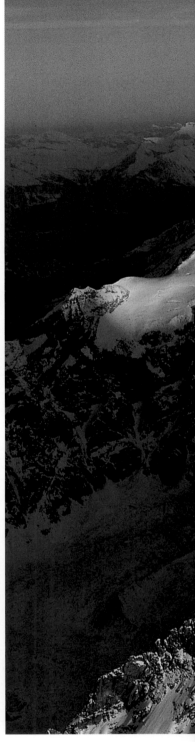

50-51 The unique and stunning outlines of the Matterhorn in the foreground, the mountain that rises over Cervinia, on the Italian side, and Zermatt, in Switzerland. Mont Blanc can be seen in the background.

51 bottom Gran Paradiso
National Park covers the Graie
Alps on the border between
Piedmont and Valle d'Aosta. It
was established in 1922 and
protects many species. There are
roughly sixty glaciers in its 280
square miles.

52-53 The Mount Rosa massif
stands on the border between
Valle d'Aosta and Piedmont. The
highest observatory in Europe is
found on Gnifetti Point. Although
the peak is tinged with pink at
sunset (rosa is Italian for pink),
the name comes from a German
term—the area has many ancient
walser settlements—which means
"glacier."

54-55 Two parallel valleys run down the side of Mount Rosa that overlooks Valle d'Aosta: Valle d'Ayas (see photograph) is the western of the two. Having wider spaces than the Valle di Gressoney to the east has made it one of the most popular summer and winter tourist destinations.

55 top left The medieval Fénis castle is probably the most resistant to the rigours of the weather in Valle d'Aosta. It was built from 12th–15th centuries near the village of the same name in the Dora valley. Still standing are the solid rectangular towers, the more slender circular tower and the crenellated walls.

55 bottom left Down the valley toward Aosta, the ruins of the castle of Châtelard can be seen near La Salle. The best preserved section is undoubtedly the tall circular tower which stands out against the snow-topped Mount Berrio Blanc.

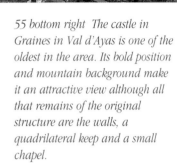

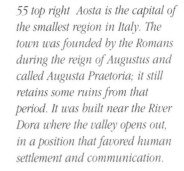

55 top right Aosta is the capital of the smallest region in Italy. The town was founded by the Romans during the reign of Augustus and called Augusta Praetoria; it still retains some ruins from that period. It was built near the River Dora where the valley opens out, in a position that favored human settlement and communication.

55 bottom right The castle in Graines in Val d'Ayas is one of the oldest in the area. Its bold position and mountain background make it an attractive view although all that remains of the original structure are the walls, a quadrilateral keep and a small chapel.

56 top left The district of Alagna comprises a number of smaller, decentralized administrative areas. The traditional wooden houses scattered around the Alpine valley have covered balconies or loggias for drying and storing hay.

56 bottom left Bardonecchia, close to the Fréjus tunnel, is one of the most famous winter sports resort in the province of Turin.

56-57 A thick white blanket covers the walser style houses in Alagna, in Valsesia. This style was brought to the valley at the foot of Mount Rosa by people moving south from the Swiss valleys.

57 top left Limone Piemonte stands in the southernmost area of Granda, the province of Cuneo, in Val Vermegnana. A famous tourist resort in the Maritime Alps, Limone boasts a fine Gothic church built in the 14th century.

57 top right One of Piedmont's top winter resorts, Sestrière was built by the Agnelli family in the 1930s. During the summer, the mountain is wrapped in thick foliage but in winter, it changes its covering to the white cloak that attracts thousands of skiers.

56 top right Sestrière takes its name from Lapis Sixtra, the milestone placed sixty miles from Turin. The town's main income is earned from winter skiing. The resort in the Val di Susa has had the World Ski Championships in 1997.

56 bottom right The fairy-tale, white-snowed Rimasco, in Val Sermenza, rises next to a tributary of the River Sesia.

58 top Livigno's typical wooden houses dot the snow that covers the town's main road and also the valley of the same name. Livigno is situated near the Swiss border at a height of 5,900 feet in a Customs-free zone.

58 bottom left Near the boundary between Lombardy and Trentino-Alto Adige in the central Alps, stands Mount Cevedale in the Ortles group. Glaciers and the effects of glaciation from the Pleistocene epoch are common to the whole massif.

58 bottom right The River Adda runs through Valtellina, the valley that divides the Ortles group of mountains in its upper stretch, then separates the Retiche Alps on the northern side from the Orobie Alps to the south farther down. It is one of Lombardy's largest valleys covering over 1500 square miles.

58-59 Mount Presanella, 11,666 feet, is one of the peaks that make up the Adamello range in Trentino-Alto Adige. The Tonale Pass is the point at which one passes into the Val di Sole on the northern side. Areas of Mount Presanella are permanently snow-covered.

59 bottom left The Bernina range on Lombardy's border with Switzerland is made up of a series of peaks around 10,000 feet high. One of these, Pizzo Roseg at 12,913 feet, is shown in the photograph. Rifugio Martinelli stands in the foreground at an altitude of 9,228 feet.

59 bottom right Situated at a height of 4,000 feet at the extreme northern end of Valtellina, Bormio is both a winter sports resort and a spa. Historically, its fortune was linked to those of the Visconti and Sforza families; today, traces of its noble past are still evident.

60 top left Any view of the Cima della Tosa is breathtaking. The mountain, seen here tinged with pink against the evening sky, has been smoothed from the effects of wind and rain.

60 bottom left The Brenta range next to the Dolomites is seen in this bird's-eye view. This is a favorite destination for courageous climbers who love venturing into its heights and glaciers.

60 top right The play of light and shadow on the Crozzon di Brenta emphasizes its natural beauty. The horizontal layers typical of the Dolomites and the Brenta range are clearly seen although, strictly speaking, the Brenta is not part of the Dolomite chain.

60 bottom right Cima della Tosa takes its name from its resemblance to a shaved head. It stands 10,335 feet high at the southern tip of the Brenta range.

61 The warm light of sunset plays on the jagged surfaces of the Brenta range. Situated west of the River Adige, it anticipates the shapes and colors of the Dolomite mountains farther east.

62-63 The tenuous colors of the evening light are projected onto the Torri del Vaiolet in the Catinaccio range. The three peaks that form the chain are named after the climbers who first scaled them, Delago, Stabeler and Winkler.

62 bottom left The Catinaccio range rises immediately west of the Marmolada group and appears to be a rocky bastion closed to exploration.

62 bottom right The Catinaccio is also known as the Rosengarten, or garden of roses, from a local legend in which King Laurino lived in a magnificent palace on top of the mountain; the palace was covered in roses which threw their reflection throughout the valley.

63 top The landscape of the Pale di San Martino is unique and the environment so precious that the National Park of Panaveggio-Pale di San Martino has been created to protect it. The Pale plateau is a sort of rocky desert at an altitude of over 4,500 feet.

63 center Sunset weakens the glare of the snow and gives the Cimon delle Pale an unreal air. Molded by the constant action of the glaciers, wind and rain, the pinnacles of Pale di San Marino have taken on extraordinary shapes.

63 bottom The rocks of the Piz Boé lit up by the evening light separate the intense blue of the sky from the brilliant white of the snow.

64-65 The Sella range is bounded by Val Gardena to the north and Val di Fassa to the south. It seems to be a set of natural amphitheaters created by glaciers. The summit of the massif is a long plateau that contrasts strongly with the surrounding peaks.

66 top left The Dolomites are a range of mountains that have been shaped by the weather into pinnacles, towers and massive walls of rock riven by clefts and channels. The snowline lies at roughly 9,000 feet.

66 top right The majestic Marmolada, the "Queen of the Dolomites," stretches upward to the heavens. Situated in the heart of the Dolomites, 10,964 feet high, it has a rather large glacier that in 1935 hosted the first giant slalom in the history of downhill skiing.

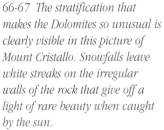

66-67 The stratification that makes the Dolomites so unusual is clearly visible in this picture of Mount Cristallo. Snowfalls leave white streaks on the irregular walls of the rock that give off a light of rare beauty when caught by the sun.

67 top left Piz Boé, 10,338 feet, is one of the most characteristic peaks that stand over the cylindrical mass of the Sella group. To the south, the massive rock walls slope down to Val di Fassa, on one side, and to Livinallongo, on the other, to create a splendid natural setting.

67 bottom left The Tofane triad, known as the "three sisters," is the pride of the Ampezzane Dolomites. The highest point is the Tofana di Rozes. The summit of this 10,580-foot high peak seems to be irregularly encircled by a group of rock pillars.

67 top right The Sassolungo (literally "long stone") is the symbol of Val Gardena. Seen from the valley road, it looks like a huge "stone."

67 bottom right The spectacular walls of the Sella range offer skiers and climbers excellent opportunities to test their abilities on challenges of all grades. An unbroken chain of lifts allows skiers to ski around the Sella without removing their skis from their feet.

68-69 *Some shepherds in Valle del Senales in Trentino-Alto Adige still practice a type of nomadic cattle breeding – transhumance – by transferring their flocks from Italian to Austrian pastures by crossing glaciers such as this one, the Similaun. The practice, however, has almost died out.*

68 bottom and 69 top Droving flocks is not a simple logistical exercise but rather a seasonal ceremony in which the whole family takes part.

Days of preparation are required in which the flock is brought together, the animals branded and their condition checked.

69 center The droving is long and tiring, constantly under the guidance of the shepherd who controls the movement of the animals, especially in the more difficult sections. The sheep have to deal with all types of terrain, including rock, snow and ice.

69 bottom The aid of the sheepdog during grazing and droving is absolutely necessary. On the snow-covered peaks, the dog carries out his tasks like a true professional and his understanding with the shepherd is perfect.

70 top The summit of Sass Pordoi seen from the Sella pass is shown covered in passing clouds. The 9,685 foot Sass Pordoi is one of the outer peaks in the Sella group which, in this part of the southern face, looks onto Pordoi pass.

70 center The brilliant colors of the dense Alpine conifers contrast with the pallor of the jagged Dolomite rocks, which stand out against a blue sky.

The wonderful divergence in colors and shapes is captured in this photograph taken from the Antermoia valley.

70 bottom The red, orange and ocher colors of sunset cover the Sasso delle Nove, in Val Badia, in a remarkable light. The play of light on the dolomitic rocks never fails to produce a breathtaking effect, particularly as evening draws on.

70-71 Wandering over the paths in the Dolomites, it is not unusual to come across settings that induce a moment of contemplation, like this one on Alpe di Susi with its marvellous view over the Sassolungo.

71 bottom left Mount Pelmo rises like a rocky dome in the area of Cadore at the eastern end of the Dolomites. Cadore, which was the theater of a bloody revolt during the Risorgimento (the

uprising of the Italian people against Austrian domination), winds along what is now the border between the regions of Veneto to the west and Friuli-Venezia Giulia to the east.

71 bottom right During the coldest time of the year when the evergreens stand out against the white background, the view of the majestic and solemn Sassolungo is a stirring sight as it points its wrinkled profile to the evening sky.

72 top left The bell-tower of the church in Ortisei, a holiday resort in Val Gardena, is topped by a peculiar spire commonly found all over Tyrol.

72 bottom left Val Badia is one of the valleys that cleave the Altoatesine Alps. There are corners here unspoilt by man and with centuries-old vegetation that are an oasis of peace.

72 right The church of St. Oswald was originally built in the 14th century and rebuilt a century later. It is the most interesting building in Sauris di Sotto, a small village in Friuli–Venezia Giulia. The top of the bell-tower is onion-shaped and rests on an octagonal drum.

72-73 The Sasso Nero against the background of the Castello di Tures. Originally built in the 12th century but altered many times since, this splendid bastion that dominates the Aurina valley seems to come from a fairytale.

73 bottom left The mansi *are typical of the eastern Alps. These buildings are linked to grazing and the word* mansi *is no more than a distortion of the medieval Latin word mansum.*

73 bottom right Under the brush-strokes of a thick snowfall, Lake washes against a part of the Tarvisio forest, a natural environment of extraordinary value.

74-75 and 75 bottom left The bright green of the conifers contrasts with the warm tints of the hay-fields. In Val Badia, as in all Alpine valleys, agriculture has always gone hand in hand with livestock farming.

74 bottom Val Gardena in Trentino-Alto Adige is where vegetation reigns unquestioned. All shades of green are present in a patchwork of extraordinary beauty.

75 bottom right At the access to the plateau of Alpe di Siusi, a small town has been transformed into a popular tourist destination: Castelrotto, whose church of St. Michael can be seen here, stands at an altitude of little more than 3,280 feet, surrounded by attractive scenery.

75 left Near Livinallongo, the white buildings scattered over the meadows stand out against the emerald slopes. With the approach of summer, the Alpine countryside bursts into all hues of green.

75 top right Cortina d'Ampezzo is without doubt the Alpine holiday resort par excellence. It is equipped with superb winter-sport facilities but is also popular in summer for its panoramic setting and because it is an excellent starting point for treks of all grades of difficulty.

76 top Villa Pallavicino is one of the magnificent residences to be admired at Stresa, the town on Lake Maggiore famous for luxury tourism. The building stands inside a private park beside the lake.

76 bottom The enchanting Borromeo Islands lie in Lake Maggiore. A small village stands on Isola dei Pescatori, in the foreground, over whose roofs can be seen the bell tower of the church of St. Victor. Palazzo Borromeo and its Italian style garden are situated on Isola Bella, seen here in the background. There is also a larger, third island, Isola Madre.

FRESHWATER REFLECTIONS AND DROPS OF LAND

76-77 Angera is a small Lombard village on the southern shore of Lake Maggiore. It owes its fame to its fort, which has a splendid view over the lake. The imposing construction was originally built for defense purposes but was later converted into a residence by the Borromeo family.

77 top left The village of Orta opens onto the lake of the same name. In front of the village lies the island of San Giulio with its austere church dedicated to the saint. The story goes that the saint himself actually started the construction of church.

77 top right The snow-topped mountains of Verbano act as a background for the patrician villas of Orta which lie next to the turquoise waters of the lake.

78 bottom right The village of Malcesine stands on the northeastern shore of Lake Garda. The tiny islet dell'Olivo lies just in front of the well-preserved center. Like many other local places, Malcesine has lived through turbulent periods, passing among the hands of the della Scala and Visconti families, and the Veronese and Austrian powers.

78-79 The Scaliger castle at Sirmione, spa town on Lake Garda, was built at the end of the 13th century for defense purposes. Its angular towers, with Guelph (swallowtail) or Ghibelline (square) crenellations, makes it particularly attractive. The castle, on the narrowest part of Sirmione peninsula, is almost entirely surrounded by water.

78 left Two boats bob in the port of Desenzano, a tourist town on Italy's largest body of freshwater, Lake Garda.

78 top right The unconventional genius of Gabriele d'Annunzio is well represented by his house-cum-mausoleum, the Vittoriale degli Italiani, that the poet built on Lake Garda and lived in from 1921 to his death. The open-air theater in the large garden is just one of the parts of the complex that d'Annunzio built to celebrate himself.

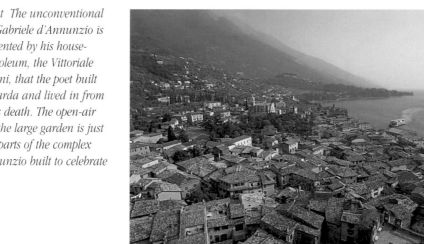

79 top *This is the minuscule harbor at Malcesine, on Lake Garda known as Benaco by the Romans. The village stands at the foot of Mount Baldo and was an integral part of the Scaliger defenses that wound along the lake shore.*

80-81 There are many wonderful villas surrounded by beautiful parks on the shores of Lake Como, also known as Lake Lario. One of the more appreciated decorative elements in such parks is the cypress tree. It is usually possible to reach these villas by boats which are moored by a waterside entrance.

81 top left Ossuccio is a small village on the shore of Lake Lario in front of Isola Comacina. The gracious Romanesque church of St. James stands just outside the pleasure-boat harbor.

81 bottom right Bellagio is the pearl of Lake Como and stands on the promontory formed between the two forks. This attractive situation has prompted the construction of many aristocrats' villas. Standing in the old center is the Romanesque St. James' church, restored at the start of the 20th century. The bell tower is seen against the background of Tremezzo on the other side of the lake.

81 bottom left The pretty holiday town of Iseo is situated on the southern shore of Lake Iseo. The lake, known by the Romans as Sebino, runs for 15 miles along the Brescia-Bergamo provincial border.

81 top right This is the view from Brunate hill in one of the southernmost points of Lake Como. The lake is in the shape of an upside-down "Y" with the western fork running down to the town of Como and the eastern fork to Lecco.

83 center *The solid-looking castle of Doria di Passerano in the province of Asti was eventually finished after a series of attempts between the 14th–16th centuries.*

83 bottom *A superb 14th-century castle stands at Pozzolo Formigaro in the province of Alessandria, once the dominion of the Marquis Del Bosco.*

84-85 *Long lines of vines run parallel across the rounded hills turning the land to all shades of red, yellow and green. La Morra, shown here, is one of the largest wine production zones in the area. Several delicious wines are produced here of which the best is Barolo.*

RICE FIELDS AND VINEYARDS

82 top left *Vicoforte stands among the gentle hills in the middle of a plateau at the feet of the Maritime Alps. The hilly countryside embraces the Vicoforte Sanctuary whose dome was designed by Francesco Gallo, the famous architect from Mondovì.*

82 top right *The hills of Monferrato, between the River Po and the Ligurian Apennines, seen in the early morning in a mixture of warm, almost autumnal, hues.*

82-83 *Wines from Monferrato such as Barbera, Grignolino and Freisa are known around the world. Vineyards alternating with cultivated fields and woodland near Ottiglio, where the church stands out among the houses of the town center.*

83 top *Near Magnano, on the Serra di Ivrea, the Romanesque church of St. Secondo stands in a beautiful frame of fields.*

86 top The River Sesia flows down from Mount Rosa on its way to the River Po. Its winding course marks the border between the provinces of Vercelli, to the west, and Novara, to the east. Its course often creates small sections of marshy land called lame *that are home to wetland birds. Some of the river's waters are diverted to flood the rice-fields in spring.*

86 center left In spring, the rice-fields are flooded and the countryside around Vercelli seems like a huge lagoon divided into sections by earth banks. Here and there, grangias (traditional and self-sufficient rural enclaves) and the occasional poplar tree stand out of the waters like a sort of mirage.

86 bottom left Casalrosso, a small farming center south of Vercelli, is reflected in the rice-fields below an unquiet sky. The first buds on the trees and the flooding of the fields indicate that the photograph was taken in late March or early April.

86 bottom right Pavia in Lombardy is identical to Vercelli in Piedmont as far as rice cultivation is concerned. Around Bereguardo, the many rice-fields turn bright green in late spring with the growth of the new plants.

86-87 The snowy peaks of Mount Rosa stand over the Vercelli plain, whose main crop is rice. Before the introduction of sophisticated machinery, cleaning weeds out of the rice was done by laborers. Today it is rare to see them; their work has been replaced by mechanical and far less evocative methods.

87 bottom The golden yellow of the ears shows that the rice is mature and ready for harvesting. This stage of the cycle takes place between August and October. The grains are separated from the remains of the plant and the skin, then treated and sold. Rice, originally from southeast Asia, is the main contributor to the economy of the Vercelli area.

88-89 The last rays of the sun to the west seem to set the flooded fields on fire. When the fields are flooded, the countryside around Vercelli is often surreal.

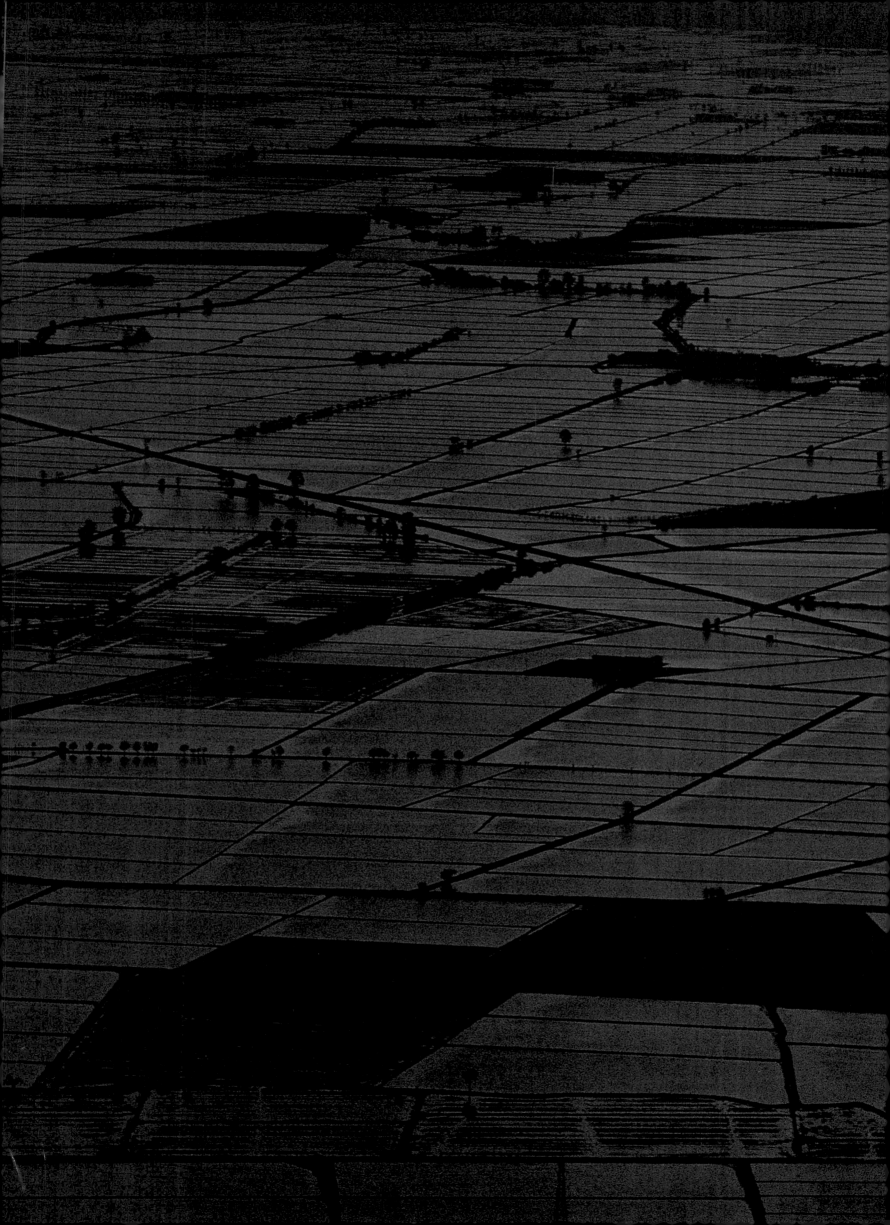

90 top The gently undulating land below Mount Dolada and Mount Cavallo in eastern Veneto form the hills of Marca Trevigiana.

90 bottom The Euganean Hills to the south of Padua are home to several famous resorts. One of them, Battaglia Terme, includes several stately villas surrounded by gardens and parks.

A LAND GENTLE BY NATURE

90-91 Bassano del Grappa is situated on the southern edge of the Sette Comuni plateau, a strategic position that has determined its fortunes over the course of history. The present attractive center is composed of the original medieval town and the Renaissance palaces surrounding it. Bassano also boasts a wooden bridge, Ponte Coperto, over the River Brenta. Following several alterations, its present design is probably the work of Andrea Palladio.

91 top left Little of the castle built by the barbarians in Conegliano Veneto can be seen in the recently altered version. The building is now the home of the Civic Museum.

91 top right It is not rare to find fields of sunflowers in the Trevigiano area, near Treviso. As the position of the flowers tells us, the photograph was taken from the south.

92 top and bottom left One of the many islands in the lagoon near Venice is Burano, originally a fishing village. The houses are brightly colored to distinguish the separate properties clearly. Like Venice, the island is crossed by canals suitable for small boats.

92 right Two islanders are engaged in mending their nets, still a fundamental chore for the inhabitants of Burano.

92-93 Seen from above, Burano is like a speck of land in the waters of the lagoon. The bell tower stands over the brightly painted houses while tiny harbors and open land line the edges of the island. In the distance, the island of Torcello can be seen.

93 top left Close to Burano, Torcello boasts some of the lagoon's most interesting buildings: primarily the cathedral of Santa Maria Assunta with its impressive bell tower visible miles away to those who arrive by ferry. The church was founded in 639 but underwent a series of

alterations in the 9th and 11th centuries. The simple façade denotes the division of the church into three naves. The huge windows along the sides of the church illuminate the interior with natural light.

93 top right The island of St. Francis in the Desert is the greenest in the lagoon. The name is derived from the belief that Francis stopped at the island on his return from the East. The religious buildings and brilliant coloring of the cypress trees give the island a particular attraction.

95 center Small fishing boats are moored near Scardovari in the Po delta. The water is stiller where the river meets the sea and is suitable for the cultivation of mussels.

95 bottom A fisherman patiently prepares his tools on the waters of Gorino.

WHERE THE PO
EMBRACES THE SEA

94 top Torre Abate is situated in the Po delta in the province of Ferrara. Marshland vegetation is just one of the various types found in the area.

94-95 The River Po winds its way through the patchwork of crops in the valley it gives its name to. The river terminates in a wide delta as it flows into the Adriatic sea. Continuous formation of sandy creeks pushes the delta roughly 76 yards farther into the salt water each year.

95 top An old fishing house seems to emerge from the waters of the Comacchio valley. This area in the province of Ferrara, south of the Po valley, has been largely drained over the last decades.

96 top The picture shows the sailing school of San Fedele in the well-known resort of Albenga, midway on the riviera between Genoa and the border with France.

96 center A narrow strip of sand separates the sea from the houses of Noli, a small tourist resort south of Savona.

96 bottom Noli boasts several small artistic treasures like the 13th-century municipal tower and the castle. A large 11th-century circular tower stands inside the walls of the latter.

A CLIFF CRESCENT-MOON
FILLED WITH THE SEA

96-97 Like many Ligurian towns and villages, Laigueglia, situated next to Alassio, used to be a trading town in the 12th and 13th centuries. Now, its mild climate and lovely position mean its main income is from summer visitors.

97 top left The breaking waves on the beach at Varigotti leave a rim of white foam. Although the beaches of Liguria are usually narrow and rarely sandy, this region has always been popular with visitors.

97 top right Varigotti seems to hide in the shelter of a rocky outcrop. The picture shows the multi-colored houses, the almost deserted beach and the coastal vegetation climbing among the rocks.

98 top San Fruttuoso is a minuscule Ligurian village on the slopes of Mount Portofino. It can only be reached by boat, then by climbing a mule track. The village is not only attractive for its position but also for a lovely monastery built by Prospero, Bishop of Tarragona, who fled to Italy after the arrival of the Arabs in Spain, bringing the ashes of the saint with him.

98 center left The extreme tip of Portofino promontory, coated in green mediterranean vegetation, stands out on the background of numberless inlets.

98 bottom left The old, pastel-colored houses of Portofino frame the square, a natural stage that slopes gently down to the harbor. The lovely, three-nave church of Portofino can be seen in the background.

98 bottom right Since the English consul, Montague Yeats Brown, bought Portofino fort in 1845, many members of the jet-set have followed him. There are many splendid villas hidden among the trees owned by artists, sportsmen, film stars, politicians and aristocrats.

98-99 The red, orange, yellow, and pink houses of Portofino with their green spots as shutters are a pretty backdrop to the boats swinging peacefully in the bay.

99 bottom The aerial photograph of Portofino bay shows one of Italy's most popular destinations for international jet-setters. The yachts belonging to the rich and successful float peacefully on the blue velvet of the sea.

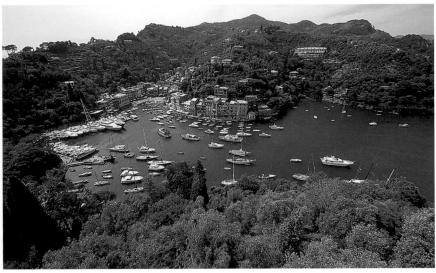

100-101 One of Italy's most exclusive resorts, Portofino is situated on a promontory that looks out to sea on one side and over the protected harbor on the other. The renovated houses that line the beach made up the original fishing village; then are perhaps better cared for than the large and expensive villas built on the promontory.

102-103 A ferry prepares to leave the port of Camogli north of Mount Portofino. Camogli became famous during the 19th-century for its commercial shipping fleet but the industry failed when technology progressed beyond the limited experience of the shipowners; today the local economy is based on tourism.

102 bottom left Hundreds of pleasure boats crowd the marina of Santa Margherita Ligure, one of the most chic resorts on the Ligurian coast. The old palazzi along the sea-front have been turned into elegant shops, restaurants and cafes.

102 bottom right Painted wooden boats are drawn up on the beach of Camogli safe from the breaking waves.

103 top The 16th-century castle of Rapallo rises out to sea, connected to land only by a small stone road from the port. The form's fortunes have always been linked to the rivalry between Pisa and Genoa to such an extent that, without adopting a position that would have limited its freedom, it made enemies of both cities and suffered retaliation from both.

103 center The island of Sestri Levante has been joined to the mainland by an embankment that also created a cosy little harbor. The sheltered beach, the climate and pretty views have made Sestri a popular seaside resort.

103 bottom The houses in the old quarter of Priaro around the harbor of Camogli are tinged with the colors of sunset.

104-105 Portovenere is a beautiful medieval town on a strip of land south of La Spezia. Of particular note are its city walls and the recently restored, 12th-century church of St. Lawrence.

104 bottom left Manarola is the most picturesque of the Cinque Terre, the five villages situated precariously on top of cliffs that drop sheer into the clear sea waters.

104 bottom right Vernazza is another of the Cinque Terre, situated between Monterosso al Mare, to the north, and Corniglia, to the south.

105 left Vineyards around Manarola have used the terrace system for hundreds of years. The grapes grown here are used to produce the Cinque Terre wines and the famous Sciacchetrs.

105 top right Riomaggiore is the administrative center of the Cinque Terre, the five fishing villages linked by that name.

105 bottom right The Cinque Terre are linked by a railway line dug out of the rock and seemingly suspended over the turquoise sea.

THE HEART OF ITALY, NATURALLY

107 top right Turrite Secca on the banks of the river Turrite is a village in the heart of Garfagnana, a lovely area of green slopes between the Apuan Alps and the Apennines.

108-109 The Tuscan Maremma is a fragile ecosystem protected by a nature reserve. Here one finds many species of trees lorded over by the sinuous trunks of the Corsican pine.

106 top Legnaro is an inland village in southern Liguria just beyond Monterosso. The bell tower of its small church stands out against Punta del Mesco.

106 center The Apuan Alps are part of the foothills of the Tuscan Apennine mountains. Their particular color is created by the marble content of their rock.

106 bottom The Abbey of St. Antimo, near Montalcino in the hills of Siena, was founded in the 9th century by the Benedictines but only the Romanesque church, renovated in the 12th century, remains.

106-107 The highly visible bell tower of Castelvittorio rises over the red roofs clear against the backdrop of hills.

107 top left Due to the clay content of the soil near Volterra, and the consequent landslides that the terrain is subject to, the hills here become very steep.

110 top Known world-wide for Brunello, a delicious wine made from a single type of grape, the Sangiovese, Montalcino stands on the slopes of the Orcia valley. The fortunes of Montalcino were always held in balance between the forces of Siena and the Medici family in Florence.

110 bottom One of the Medici's most splendid villas was built at Poggia a Caiano, a few miles from Florence. Giuliano da Sangallo was commissioned to build it by Lorenzo the Magnificent. The villa was enlarged and further decorated by Pope Leo X and renovated once more in the 19th-century.

110-111 Sorano, a few miles from the border between Lazio and the Tuscan province of Grosseto, still shows its medieval layout. The turrets in the warm colors of the local stone and the Ursinea Fortress look out over the lovely Lente valley.

111 bottom left The Castle of Four Towers was built in the 14th-15th centuries in the hills near Siena. The tall cypress trees that surround it are a typical feature of the highly appreciated Tuscan landscape.

111 bottom right The Tuscan countryside is sprinkled with villas built by the Medicis where the Florentine nobles liked to relax. One of them is the Villa La Peggio near Grassina which was bought by Francesco I de' Medici in 1569.

112 top Many people, foreigners too, have moved out of towns to live in old farmhouses in the Tuscan hills, where they are in closer contact with nature.

112 center The province of Siena is not just a land of vines and olive trees: the green fields that cover the gentle hills provide rich grazing for sheep.

*113 center and bottom
The farmhouses and the tracks that
connect them to the rest of the world
stand out clearly against the open
stretches of grass, the cultivated
fields and the cypresses of the
Tuscan hills.*

*112 bottom The low clouds seem
to touch the soft grassy blanket
that covers the rises and falls of
the valley and a group of cypress
trees carelessly casts its shadow to
the ground. This is Orcia valley,
one of the prettiest areas in
central Italy.*

*112-113 A white, beaten track,
like many in the Orcia valley,
winds through a meadow. On
either side, the cypress trees line
the track right up to the
farmhouse.*

*113 top There are many country
villas in the Tuscan hills like this
one in Radda in Chianti. In this
area, they are often surrounded
by long rows of vines which
produce the famous Chianti wine.*

114 top Capraia is an island of volcanic origin in the archipelago off the coast of Tuscany. Vegetation is sparse and the rocky coast is lined with grottoes and creeks.

114 bottom Portoferraio, preferred port of entry to the isle of Elba, lies on the north coast. The Tuscan island is the largest in the archipelago and the third biggest in Italy after Sicily and Sardinia. Elba depends almost entirely on tourists who go there to appreciate the wild Mediterranean maquis, a clean sea and a semi-tropical climate.

114-115 The tower of the Castle of St. George points up against the blue sky over Capraia. The Tuscan island, known by the Romans, is interesting for its geological formation: basalt, tufa and andesite combine to form this speck of land.

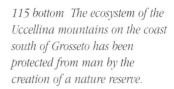

115 center The picture shows the port on Giglio island, also part of the Tuscan archipelago. Thick Mediterranean vegetation and a blue sea are the main features of this island that lies opposite the Argentario promontory.

115 bottom The ecosystem of the Uccellina mountains on the coast south of Grosseto has been protected from man by the creation of a nature reserve.

115 top The Argentario promontory extends into the Tyrrhenian Sea in the southernmost part of the province of Grosseto. This strange geographical feature combines the attraction of the mountain with that of the sea that laps against its jagged rocks.

116 top left Umbria is often defined as the green heart of Italy. The picture of the horses under an olive tree was taken near Ferentillo in Valnerina.

116 bottom left The ocher of an isolated farmhouse stands out against the green countryside of Umbria.

116 top right Trevi dominates the valley of Spoleto. In Roman times the town was called Trebiae.

116 bottom right The waters of the Marmore waterfall bounce from one surface to another in the luxuriant vegetation. The waterfall was created artificially during the 3rd century BC by bringing the waters of the Velino and Nera together to prevent flooding.

117 The harmony of the Umbrian countryside near Trevi is created by a group of elements: winding roads, parallel rows of silver-leafed olive trees and low, long farmhouses wrapped in the brilliant foliage of the surrounding trees.

118-119 The Sibilline mountains stretch along the border between Umbria and Marche. This area of the Apennines is particularly suitable for summer grazing. From May to September, all kinds of grazing animals live on the slopes of the Sibillines where they find plenty to eat throughout the summer.

118 bottom left Seen from afar, Spello appears like a brush-stroke over the verdant Umbrian countryside. The narrow lanes, Roman remains and Renaissance buildings of Hispellum, as it was known to the Romans, certainly merit a visit.

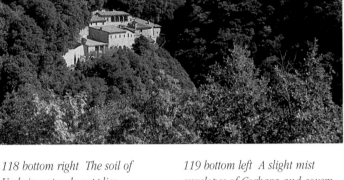

118 bottom right The soil of Umbria not only supplies typically Mediterranean fruit and vegetables but products with a foreign flavor—like tobacco in this plantation near Todi.

119 top left In the woods close to Assisi stands Eremo delle Carceri. This place was chosen by St. Francis and the members of his Order as ideal for meditation and prayer. Originally just a small church and caves, the site was later enlarged till it reached its present size.

119 bottom left A slight mist envelopes of Corbara and covers the artificial lake. The colors are attenuated by the morning dew giving the countryside a surreal atmosphere.

119 top right The area around Cereto di Spoleto, a village at the feet of the Umbrian Apennines, is one of the most attractive in the region for its exuberant flora.

119 bottom right Looking out from Spello over the surrounding countryside, the eye can wander at will over the unending meadows, woods, olive groves and solitary farmhouses.

120 top left Cocullo is a small village in the province of L'Aquila built over the remains of the Roman town of Coculum on the southern face of Mount Catini. The tower of its medieval castle dominates the houses from its position in the center of the village.

120 bottom left At an altitude of 4,100 feet, the village of Opi in the upper Sangro valley falls within the boundary of the National Park of Abruzzo.

120-121 The Corno Grande, here standing over an immense expanse of yellow flowers, is the highest peak of the Gran Sasso. The massif even has a small glacier, the Calderone, the most southerly in Europe. The Corno Grande is not just the highest summit in the Gran Sasso but the entire Apennine chain.

121 top The National Park of Abruzzo, opened in 1923, was the first of its kind in Italy. Besides the brown Marsicano bear, the park also protects the Abruzzo chamois and other species.

122-123 The village of Castelluccio, the highest in the Sibilline mountains, stands on the snowy slopes of Mount Vettore.

120 top right On the strip of Lazio that sticks out between Umbria and Abruzzo there is the Terminillo, a mountain standing 7,260 feet high popular with winter sports lovers.

120 bottom right The National Park of Abruzzo includes highlands such as Mount Marsicano which is snow-covered all year round.

124 top An attractive view of some buildings on Ventotene, one of the Pontian islands. The handrail of a stairway zigzags against the orange of the walls and green of the window shutters.

124 bottom Like the other islands in the Pontian archipelago situated off the Bay of Gaeta, Ponza is of volcanic origin. The soil consists of tufa and andesite and the jagged rocks fall sheer into the sea.

GREEN PROMONTORIES
AND SHINING BAYS

124-125 Cape Bianco (White Cape) is a small section of the coastline on the island of Ponza. Its white rocks drop vertically into the crystal-clear waters.

125 top left Ponza is the largest inhabited center on the island of the same name. The traditional agriculture and fishing are now supported by a flourishing tourist industry.

125 top right On the west coast of the island lies the Bay of Chiaia di Luna, where the luminescent white rock contrasts strongly against the dark sea.

126 top *The port of Gaeta is situated on the north side of the peninsula that extends into the Tyrrhenian Sea. The town has many beautiful monuments and buildings, both civil and religious. Its name is supposed to be derived from the Roman Caieta.*

126 center left *The isle of Capri seems to float on a blue velvet cloth. When seen from above, the island appears to be an extension of the Sorrento peninsula seen in the distance. Capri's unmistakable cliffs can be seen on the island's southeast coast.*

126 bottom left *The famous Blue Grotto is at the extreme north of Capri.*

126 bottom right *Piazza Umberto I, framed by the white houses with vaulted or terraced roofs, is the center of daily life on Capri.*

126-127 *At the foot of Mount Solaro in the highest part of Capri, the village of Anacapri is bathed by sunshine. This tourist resort, with its breathtaking views, can be reached by road or by cable-car.*

127 top *Sperlonga lies halfway between Terracina and Gaeta. Some of its medieval walls are still standing and, not far away, the remains of a Roman villa have been found—possibly the private residence of Emperor Tiberius.*

128-129 *Fishing has always been the traditional activity at Procida, the island in the Bay of Naples between Cape Miseno and Ischia. The nets are hung out in the sun and mended by hand.*

128 bottom *The harbor in the town of Ischia is situated in the most recently built quarter, Ischia Porto. The harbor is always busy and welcomes tourists wanting to take the waters in its spa or simply to enjoy the climate and beautiful sea of the largest island in the Bay of Naples.*

129 left Ischia castle stands on a tiny islet connected to the main island via a bridge. It is on the islet that Ischia's oldest and most interesting buildings are found. The original settlement, having expanded onto Ischia's shore, gave the quarter its name: Ischia Ponte (Ischia Bridge).

129 top right The pleasure boats that daily trip to and fro across the Bay of Naples are the "great-grandchildren" of the boats used by navigators of the past who had stopped off at Ischia since ancient times.

129 bottom right A fishing boat at rest in the tiny harbor at Procida, known as "La Corricella."

130-131 An extraordinary view of the Amalfi coast taken from the terrace at Villa Rufolo in Ravello. The luminous blue of the sky is reflected in the sea that gently laps the jagged rocks.

130 bottom The Amalfi coast is a breathtakingly beautiful section of the Tyrrhenian shoreline where traditional activities, such as fishing, have been progressively supported by tourism. Visitors first arrived in the area during "Grand Tour" era.

131 top left and center The majolica tiles and eastern shape of the dome and bell tower on the church at Praiano are similar to those on the Church of the Assumption in Positano. The white houses of Praiano on the Amalfi coast are surrounded by the colors and smells of the Mediterranean maquis.

131 bottom The clear terraced houses and the Church of the Assumption slope steeply down to Positano beach. The village, north of Cape Sottile, used to be only a fishing village but now it is one of the best-known tourist resorts on the Amalfi coast.

131 right The Amalfi coast's environmental and geographical features are unique. The sheer, white limestone outcrops, marked with brightly colored plants and flowers, make the shoreline most unusual.

132-133 The beach at Vieste, Gargano's largest town, is a huge expanse of sand that slips into the turquoise water. The medieval section of the town still exists around the castle built in that era.

132 top The Gargano promontory is surrounded by one of the loveliest seas on the Italian coast. The rocky spur on the "boot" of Italy extends west of Tavoliere della Capitanata.

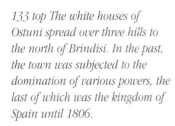

133 top The white houses of Ostuni spread over three hills to the north of Brindisi. In the past, the town was subjected to the domination of various powers, the last of which was the kingdom of Spain until 1806.

133 center left and bottom right The characteristic white houses of the old quarter of Monte Sant'Angelo are seen in two very different situations: the first is under the usual boiling southern sun; in the second, the roofs have been dusted with a sprinkling of snow.

133 bottom left The unmistakable white and gray cones of the trulli *are some of Italy's most celebrated constructions. Ancient dwellings originally from the Megalithic period, trulli are perhaps related distantly to the* nuraghe *of Sardinia. The small houses in Puglia are usually circular; they are topped by a false, dry dome (i.e., not using cement or other binding materials) which is either plastered or lined with strips of wood.*

134 left This unusual columnar basalt rock formation is found in the Gole dell'Alcantara, a river that enters the sea near Taormina in Sicily. The prisms of rock have been revealed by the erosive action of the water on lava.

134 top right The Madonie, limestone and dolomitic heights in northern Sicily, are covered with a thin layer of snow. The massif is not quite 6,561 feet in height and owes its name to the surrounding ancient fiefdom, Madonia.

A STONE'S THROW
FROM AFRICA

134 bottom right The rows of vines and grass fields near Alcamo in northwest Sicily cover the countryside like a chessboard.

135 Red-hot lava flows down the sides of Mount Etna. Symbol of Sicily, the mountain is both loved and feared. The volcano gradually emerged from the sea roughly 500,000 years ago.

136 top This spectacular aerial photograph clearly shows the two arms of land that extend from Taormina to the sea. They are Cape Taormina, left, and Cape Sant'Andrea, right.

136 center left Fishing boats are drawn up on the beach at Cefalu' on the north coast of Sicily. Traditionally a town that earned its living from the sea, it is now a popular holiday resort.

136 bottom left Fishing boats wait their turn in the harbor at Favignana on the largest of the Egadi islands. The island lies off Trapani and gets its name from the Favonian wind which favors tuna fishing.

136 bottom right Santa Tecla, near Acireale, is a picturesque village made from stones of lava. In the distance, majestic, snow-covered Etna dominates the countryside.

136-137 Cape Bianco on the Sicilian coast: the transparency of the sea, the whiteness of the limestone rocks and the wide sandy beach make this a small paradise.

137 bottom The ancient Greek city of Tindari and the salt lakes, formed by the action of the sea on sand, create an unreal landscape.

138-139 A Bronze-Age village has been discovered on Cape Milazzese on Panarea in the Eolian islands. This site archaelogical is particularly attractive as it is almost surrounded by the sea.

138 bottom The immaculate houses of Panarea contrast with the thick vegetation and unusually leaden sky. The island lies halfway between Lipari and Stromboli and is a paradise for snorkelers and divers.

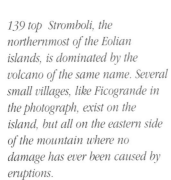

*139 top Stromboli, the
northernmost of the Eolian
islands, is dominated by the
volcano of the same name. Several
small villages, like Ficogrande in
the photograph, exist on the
island, but all on the eastern side
of the mountain where no
damage has ever been caused by
eruptions.*

*139 center and bottom
The unspoiled coast of Panarea is
lined with bays and coves. Bare
rocks are ranged along the shore
in a precise aesthetic order, like a
shower of small meteorites fallen
from space.*

140 left Lampedusa is the closest island to Africa in the Pelagian chain. It lies over 125 miles from Sicily but is very near to Tunisia.

141 top Cala Pozzolana is a beautiful sheltered cove on the island of Linosa. The northernmost island in the Pelagian chain, Linosa is of volcanic origin and almost completely uninhabited.

141 bottom Lampedusa was abandoned for a long time but repopulated in the second half of the 19th century. Today its port is filled with dozens of yachts year round.

142-143 Salina is the second largest of the Eolian islands for population and size. Its luxuriant vegetation makes an attractive contrast with the cobalt blue of the sea. Its mountain, Mount Fossa delle Felci, stands 3,126 feet high.

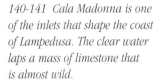

140-141 Cala Madonna is one of the inlets that shape the coast of Lampedusa. The clear water laps a mass of limestone that is almost wild.

140 bottom Isola dei Conigli, near to the southern coast of Lampedusa, is a marvel of white beaches and clear blue water. It is one of the loveliest places in all southern Europe.

144 top The Giara di Gesturi is a wild plateau in the heart of Sardinia that is home to a number of animals extinct elsewhere, for example, the small Sardinian horse with its long mane, which still lives wild here.

144 center The collection of rainwater in a region where rain is scarce has always been a problem. Lake Cedrino in Barbagia is an example of how the Sardinians have attempted to take advantage of torrent water for irrigation purposes without harming the environment.

WILD LAND, ENCHANTING SEA

144 bottom The huge Pula plain to the south of Cagliari is an example of the amazing variety of landscapes that Sardinia has to offer. The visitor will be surprised at the riot of color and Mediterranean vegetation in the meadows to be found inland on an island seemingly so barren.

144-145 Lula in Sardinia is surrounded by bare and wild mountainous countryside. The ridges are part of Mount Turuddu and the limestone rocks of Mount Albo. The verdant and lovely landscape might almost belong to the Dolomites.

145 top left The unusual morphology of the Marmilla in central-southern Sardinia is shown in the picture. The remains of a 12th-century castle on a pyramidal hill dominate the flat land roundabout.

145 top right Castelsardo takes its name from an ancient fort originally called Castel Genovese and built by the Doria family in 1102. When the Spaniards from Aragon governed the island, its name was changed to Castel Aragon but in 1769 the castle received its current name from the Savoyard regime.

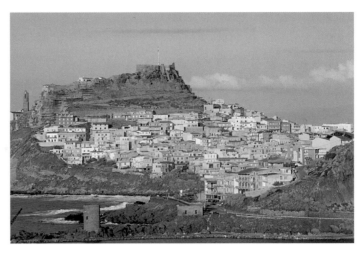

146-147 *The sandy beaches to the north of Palau on the Emerald Coast are protected by dunes that burst into color in spring. The roots of the flowers and plants that grow there are essential to hold the sand in place.*

146 bottom *The Costa Smeralda (Emerald Coast) and Sardinia's northern side in general boast beaches with pure coral sand and clear water the equal of any tropical island.*

*147 top and center right
The Gallura coastline is jagged,
riven with inlets and often fronted
by islands. Lookout towers are
often to be found on the mainland,*
*like that of Longosardo near Santa
Teresa. Santa Reparata Bay, like
those of Porto Quadro, Marmorata
or Conca Verde, offers views over
a sea of enchanting beauty.*

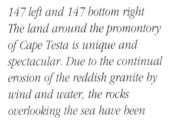

*147 left and 147 bottom right
The land around the promontory
of Cape Testa is unique and
spectacular. Due to the continual
erosion of the reddish granite by
wind and water, the rocks
overlooking the sea have been*
*carved into the strangest shapes.
The granite caves opened by
the Romans in this area can still
be seen; they left large square
blocks of granite that have now
been smoothed over the
centuries.*

148 bottom left Porto Pino in Sulcis takes its name from the large pinewood that used to surround the bay, one of the largest in the region. The 24 acres that have survived the ravages of men and time represent one of the last natural pinewoods in Europe. Large dunes of the whitest sand separate the vegetation from the sea along the coastline.

148 top right In Iglesiente, the morphological features of the land, the wind and the tiny grains of sand plucked from the sea have created an African landscape. Huge dunes are in continuous movement along the edges and sometimes invade the vegetation.

148 top left Unusual rocky formations fall into the sea at Nebida Bay in Iglesiente. The "Sugarloaf," a large limestone crag, can be seen in the center of the photograph.

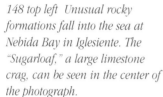

148 bottom right A colony of pink flamingos has nested on Molentargius cove, just outside Cagliari, over the last few years. This is an important but not unusual event in Sardinia, which is on the routes of many migrating birds.

148-149 Cala Viola is a splendid sandy beach bounded by exuberant vegetation in the inlet between the capes of Argentera and Caccia. The name comes from the wine-colored land, the Sardinian verrocano, a mixture of ancient rocky sediments.

149 bottom The Bay of Chia, in the center of the southern coast, is a palette of colors with the green of the uplands, the white of the rocks and the green-tinted blue of the water. The lookout tower, a not unusual sight in Sardinia, dominates the marvelous countryside.

150 top The Maddalena Archipelago in the north of Sardinia offers countryside of great beauty: pinnacles of granite and twisted rock alternate with lovely sandy bays that face onto a transparent, turquoise sea.

150 center and bottom The Maddalena Archipelago is formed by numerous tiny islets and seven large islands. Those lying further out to sea are Budelli, Razzoli and Santa Maria; those close to the mainland are Santo Stefano, Caprera, Maddalena and Spargi. The islands are connected to Gallura by sea whereas Caprera (see photograph) and Maddalena are connected by a bridge running between them.

150-151 Maddalena is the largest of the islands in the archipelago. Today it is appreciated for its natural beauty but once it was important for its strategic position. Maddalena belonged to the Pisan forces during the 13th century and became a military base under the Savoy family from the 18th century.

151 bottom left Rare strips of Corsican pines line the seashore in Iglesiente. The blues and greens separated by a strip of white rock seem to reach out to one another in vain.

151 top right Capo Coda di Cavallo (Horsetail Cape) is a promontory south of Aranci bay that points toward mainland Italy. It is an area of wild beauty with thick flora that almost reaches down to the shore and smoothly sculpted rocks that are reflected in the water.

151 bottom right Sardinia's history of continual invasions justifies the almost ever-present lookout towers around the more strategic sections of the coastline. No longer of any use, they now do no more than observe the passing of harmless pleasure boats.

152-153 These warm, clear waters – a dazzling turquoise – reveal the sea floor in one of the many coves on Isola della Maddalena, part of the Maddalena archipelago across from Palau and not far from the strait of Bocche di Bonifacio. The jagged coastline, used as shelter for centuries by fishermen and sailors, has now become the island's most important asset. Its harsh granitic terrain is ill-suited for agriculture, and this enchanting spot has thus become a favorite Italian and international tourist destination because of the beauty and variety of its shores.

154-155 The Ponte Vecchio is the oldest bridge in Florence. It has been rebuilt several times over the Arno at the point where the river is narrowest. Spared quite miraculously during World War II, it used to host the meat market; today its original appearance is derived from the small shops that line it on either side and from the passageway that passes over it. Built by Vasari to connect Palazzo Vecchio with Palazzo Pitti, is one of three bridges over the Arno in Florence; the other two are the Ponte Santa Trinità and the Ponte alla Carraia.

154 bottom The Tiber in the heart of old Rome passes around the Isola Tiberina which is supposed to have assumed the shape of the boat that brought Aesculapius, the god of medicine, to Rome. Downstream there stands a single arch of the Ponte Rotto, which is all that remains of a bridge rebuilt in the 16th century on the remains of the 2nd-century BC Ponte Emilio. The only ancient bridge still remaining is the Ponte Fabricio. An old hospital still stands on the Isola Tiberina.

One Country for
a thousand cities

"Our cities are the ancient centers of all communications of a large and populous province; all roads lead to them and all local markets depend on them, they are the heart to the system of the veins; they are the destinations of consumables and the origins of industries and capital; they are a point of intersection or rather a center of gravity which cannot be assigned to any other point at random." Carlo Cattaneo's 19th century analysis of the life and purpose of cities is as true today as it was then. Italy is the country with a greater variety and richness of historical town-centers in a relatively small space than any other: large and small, ancient or simply old, on the plains or in the mountains, built on lagoons, on rivers or by the sea.

The richness of Italy's urban centers, which includes diversity and quality of architecture and monuments, is a result of their history. The mainland has only been united during the Roman Empire (up until the 5th century AD) and from 1870 to the modern day. This means that for the greater part of its history it has been separated in different states. The quality of a "state" brings in its train the development of an autonomous society, its own political, military, social and economic events and therefore also artistic and architectural achievements. Each of these states had a capital with buildings representing civil, ecclesiastical and military power: the town-hall, the cathedral, the courts and offices of its guilds. During the age of the Seigniories, these states had their own courts with the richness of buildings that such a status demanded. The courts were used for government of the state and as a representation of the governing body's

power to its subjects and nearby states of which "magnificence" was a direct expression. At different periods, Turin, Genoa, Milan, Padua, Siena, Arezzo, Mantua, Venice, Ravenna, Parma, Modena, Lucca, Florence, Rome, Naples and Palermo have all been capitals, depending on the cycle of historical events. Their urban layout and architecture are direct evidence of their moments of splendor and consequent decadence.

155 top Milan's Duomo (Cathedral) seen from above is a majestic sight. Construction was started in 1386 by Gian Galeazzo Visconti but dragged on for the whole of the 15th and 16th centuries.

155 bottom The River Arno passes through the length of Pisa. The streets on either side of the river, here pictured from the Clock Tower, are lined with sober and discreet buildings that are lit up on every balcony on the day of the city's patron saint, St. Rainier.

156 top The Temple of Neptune and the Basilica of Paestum in Campania are located in one of the most interesting archeological sites of Italy. The Temple of Neptune was built in the mid-5th century BC in pure Doric style; the trabeation and the pediments are almost completely intact and the interior is divided into three naves. The Basilica stands on the Via Sacra and was originally dedicated to Hera (Juno); it dates from the middle of the 6th century BC and contains a peristyle of 50 Doric columns.

156 center The Temple of Segesta was built by the Dorians in 430 BC. Like the Theater it is well-preserved. It stands alone in a wide open landscape surrounded by a deep valley. It is bounded by a peristyle of 36 columns in gold-tinged limestone.

156 bottom The Temple of Concordia, in the Valley of the Temples in Agrigento, was built between 450-440 BC. It is the most impressive and majestic Doric temple in Sicily.

The history of town settlements in Italy began with the Etruscans, a people of uncertain provenance. During the 10th century BC they occupied what is now Tuscany. They then moved north of the Apennines toward Rimini, in one direction, and Mantua, in another. To the south they reached the river Sele in Campania where they founded the towns of Capua and Nola. The Latin historian Varrone noted that their town streets were based on a north-south and eastwest grid pattern. They were composed of three parts: the first one, called *arce*, which stood apart on a hill where it was used for defense and as a sanctuary; the second was the residential area and the third was the necropolis or burial ground for the dead. The necropolis is the only part to have survived intact until today. Traces of Etruscan towns still exist near Marzabotto in Emilia, at Fondi, Anagni, Segni, Ferentino, Teano and Alatri in Lazio, and at Santa Maria Capua Vetere in Campania, but they were soon replaced by Roman and medieval settlements. A strong Greek colonization started during the 8th century BC along the southern coasts and in Sicily which were included in the name *Magna Graecia*. The Greeks built ports and landing-places for their trade along the coasts of the Tyrrhenian and Ionian seas: Crotone, Locri, Sibari, Poseidonia, Naples, Cuma and, in Sicily, Naxos, Gela, Agrigento and Syracuse. Once liberated from the hold of the mother-country, these settlements became independent *polis*, city-states which transformed themselves into economic and military powers. But destruction and the sacking of these towns over the centuries have erased the cities themselves and left only the ruins of temples like at Agrigento, Paestum, Segesta and Selinunte the like of which are not found even in Greece.

156-157 The Theater of Segesta was built by the Greeks. It is in the shape of a semi-circle, 68 yards in diameter, on a rocky slope. The steps descend toward the Bay of Castellammare.

157 bottom The island of Sardinia has many sites of great historical value: for example, the ruins of the Punic city of Tharros (left) on a panoramic rise near Oristano, and the remains of the Roman theater of Nora (right), situated near Capo di Pula.

The mainland of Italy underwent new changes with the birth of the power of Rome. The Romans undertook an enormous project of territorial planning across the peninsular in which they established new cities and Romanized existing Greek and Etruscan ones. They organized a rational road system and a capillary division of the land. For the first time in history (and for the only time up until the modern era), the territory was dealt with as a whole and towns, road systems and rationalisation of the countryside were built up and developed together. Rome itself was the least typical of Roman cities because it grew in sections and was based on a unique hill situation. New Roman cities were built according to exact rules: on the flat, in a square boundary, with a grid of streets whose principal axes (called the *cardus* and *decumanus*) crossed at right angles in the center. Initially they were small

158 left Ancient Ostia occupies a large archeological area (top) around the decumanus maximus, *the main Roman road in the town. The 2nd-century BC Capitolium (center) was the largest temple in the town. The 4th-century BC house of Amore and Psyche (bottom) has preserved its mosaic floors and multicolored marbles.*

158 right The ancient Roman road, Via Appia, was begun in 312 BC; today it is like an open-air museum lined with the remains of villas and burial monuments from the imperial and republican eras.

in size: Florence covered an area measuring only 20 acres originally (300 yards by 300 yards), Lucca 50 acres, Aosta 100 and Turin 130. The pre-Roman town of Pompeii was a little larger covering 186 acres and held 25,000 people. All buildings, which could reach a maximum height of 65 feet, were inserted in the grid pattern of streets. It was these, and only these, that determined the structure of the town because the lie of the land had no effect on growth. At Verona, for example, which is situated on the inside of a bend in the river

Adige, the layout of the original Roman city was not affected by the presence of the river at all. During the long period of rule, the Romans created satellite power centers like the port of Ostia, the Villa Adriana at Tivoli and towns along the Lazio coast and in Campania. Pompeii and Herculanum were the best known Roman cities and today allow us to examine Roman life directly even if their town planning was Greek and not Roman. The eruption of Vesuvius in 79 AD buried them both in a time capsule.

158-159 and 159 bottom Villa Adriana in Tivoli in the hills around Rome was built during the reign of Emperor Hadrian (AD 76-138). The villa was practically finished in 134 but Hadrian, sick and in mourning for the death of his favorite lover Antinous, died four years later. Although the emperors that succeeded him continued to visit Tivoli, the villa was soon abandoned and fell into ruin. Between the 15th and 19th centuries, it was robbed of its art treasures which went to public and private collections. It was only since in 1870 that excavations were undertaken which brought the entire complex to light. The most impressive construction is the circular Maritime Theater (lower picture) formed by a portico and a central building separated by a canal. Moving south, the remains of a large nymphaeum can be seen and massive columns that belonged to a complex consisting of three semicircular rooms around a courtyard.

160 left The Roman town of Herculaneum, traditionally founded by Hercules himself, was buried together with Pompeii by the eruption of Vesuvius in 79 AD. The city was a fishing port but also inhabited by craftsmen and a patrician class that, for its beauty and its position on the gulf of Naples, had chosen it as a place to relax in. It was divided into five districts by three principal roads (decumanus) and had a variety of house types. The torrent of mud that covered the city filled every recess, so preserving the objects made of wood, such as the roof structures, beams, stairs, doors and partitions that were burnt at Pompeii. The entire city was lost and a great part of the population that attempted to escape. Ancient frescoes and marbles works and mosaic can still be seen in the houses in Herculanum today.

In a Roman city, the forum was one of the focal points but buildings like the amphitheater or circus, used for entertainment of the people, had their own importance. These were placed on the edge of the residential area near the walls, like in Pompeii and Aosta, but sometimes outside the walls completely, like at Capua, Verona and Spoleto. Always located outside were the hippodromes (horse-racing tracks). These attracted people from around the local countryside so arrival and departure of the public was made easier. The Romans gave Italy a magnificent network of roads that reached every part of the peninsular and which today are still followed. Roads irradiated from Rome like the spokes from a wheelhub: these were the Flaminia, the Cassia, the Salaria and the Appia; a large X formed by the Postumia and the Emilia crossed the Po Valley. The countryside was "centuried," i.e., divided by a grid of small roads, each block of land measuring 767 yards (perhaps 800 paces) by 767 yards. These were assigned to veteran soldiers transformed into farmers in

times of peace. The paths are still visible in the flat countryside of Emilia, Veneto (near Padua) and Lombardy (between Cremona and Pavia). The farming soldiers of 2000 years ago determined the paths of many of today's minor roads and of the network of canals that regulates the movement of irrigation water.

160 right and 161 The city of Pompeii was founded by the Oscian people in the 8th century BC but was influenced by the strong Greek colony at nearby Cuma during the 6th century BC. The town passed into the hands of the Samnites in the 5th century BC and underwent a period of prosperity until the 1st century BC. In 80 BC, Pompeii came under Roman control and became a well-known holiday town for rich Roman families who introduced new architectural and ornamental styles. At the time of the eruption of Vesuvius in AD 79,

Pompeii had 25,000 inhabitants but within two days the town had disappeared, covered by a blanket of ash up to 22 feet deep. Systematic and official excavations only started during the 18th century under the Bourbon king, Charles III. The discovery of the town had a great effect on the public throughout Europe. The Via dell'Abbondanza (top), the red Pompeian frescoes in the Villa dei Misteri (bottom) and the large Roman Forum with the statue of Apollo (on the right) are some of the most unusual monuments in the world.

Once the Roman empire crumbled in 476 AD, the Italian mainland was invaded by different tribes—the Lombards, Byzantines, Franks—who left clear evidence of their passing throughout the various regions, depending on the domination. In reply to these invaders, many of the old cities were abandoned by their inhabitants to live in safer locations which could be defended by walls. These new towns were often elliptical in shape with the houses built side by side to form a compact perimeter wall. There would then be one or two entrances and the town would have a tower in the center (from the 11th century on). Lucignano, Città della Pieve

and Monte San Savino are typical of this design.

New towns were built all over Italy during the Middle Ages. They were built everywhere, along rivers, on hills and on the plains based on varied designs. Often they would be adapted to fit the lie of the land meaning they might be cone-shaped, linear, stepped up the side of a hill or in a star shape. As towns increased in size and local communities became stronger, the system of using houses as a perimeter wall was no longer sufficient to defend the city so they invested in the largest and most expensive of public works and built proper town walls with towers at regular intervals. The local noble family lived in the castle which also acted as a refuge in times of war. The upper classes in some cities built houses with towers attached for personal defense: the

best example of this is at San Gimignano in Tuscany where each of the 14 towers represents the feudal origin of a noble family. In seafaring republics like Genoa and Venice, the rich merchants built the first private *palazzi*. These originally were built alongside other houses and distinguished by a particular architectural style or exterior decorations but, as they became larger, tended to occupy entire blocks.

Along the roads outside of the city walls, "suburbs" were established that were slowly integrated into the main city during subsequent expansions and surrounded by a second, exterior city wall. For the first time, buildings were constructed with porticoes which served as a covered extension for the various activities which took place on the ground floor: shops, workshops, stores etc. The porticoes in Bologna, Pavia, Treviso and

across the whole of the Po Valley were quickly copied elsewhere. Commercial buildings were the first to widen the porticoes to become galleries known as "loggias": today in Bologna there still exist the Loggia dei Mercanti (Merchants' Gallery) and the Loggia dei Banchi (Banks' Gallery) while Assisi and Terracina both have a Loggia del Grano (Wheat Gallery) and the oratory of Orsanmichele di Firenze was originally built as a commercial gallery. Each city had its own water source. A network of aqueducts was used to direct water to the public fountains which were often designed and produced by great artists or skilled craftsmen, for example, the Fontana Maggiore in Perugia, Fontana Grande in Viterbo and the Fontana Gaia, Fonte Branda and Fonte Nuova in Siena. Apart from serving a practical purpose, they also added

to the beauty of the city. Religious buildings played an important role in all towns, especially after the foundation of the two great religious orders, the Franciscans and the Dominicans. They were constructed for the first time inside the cities as opposed to the past when they were placed outside the walls. The church dedicated to the patron saint of each town had a particular importance resulting from the coupling of the building's religious offices to a function of civic representation. A town's main church might stand some distance from the cathedral but always in the center, perhaps in an elevated position, with an imposing flight of steps in front which emphasized the building's importance and its height, as for example at Siena, Todi, Arezzo, Amalfi and Salerno. Often the church was built slightly outside the residential area as in Ancona and Gubbio.

162 Construction of the austere Palazzo dei Priori in Perugia was started during the 13th century but the site was expanded over the following centuries. The façade overlooking the square includes a stately stairway up to the pulpit used for public addresses. Inside there are rooms painted with frescoes from the 16th century or lined with finely inlaid wood.

162-163 Monteriggioni is a medieval hamlet standing on a rise and enclosed by a wall. It was built in 1203 by the Sienese as an outpost against the Florentines and passed several times between the two. The walls, constructed in 1213-19 and strengthened in 1260-70, are nearly 600 yards long and have 14 four-sided towers, seven of which have been rebuilt in modern times. Dante referred to the walls in a canto of his Inferno.

163 top Trento cathedral was built during the 12th-13th centuries. This majestic building in Lombard Romanesque style was in the center of the square where the courthouse (Palazzo Pretorio), the tower of the Town Hall (Torre Civica) and the Cazuffi-Rella houses with 15th-century frescoes are situated. The city became famous for the Council of Trent held from 1545-1563 where the Church of Rome attempted to oppose Protestantism. After the Council had begun, the Counter-Reformation began bringing profound changes to Christianity.

163 center The town of Bergamo is split into two distinct sections: the lower, modern city and the upper, ancient town filled with beautiful monuments and buildings. Just behind the Colleoni Chapel stands the Contarini fountain with its imaginative sculptures.

163 bottom San Ruffino, the cathedral in Assisi, dates from the 12th century. Its Romanesque façade decorated with rose-windows is one of the most beautiful in Umbria. In this church, St. Francis, St. Clare, and Emperor Frederick II were baptized.

As the power of the town or city council grew, the cities constructed town-halls for the civil government of the city which also grew in size, like the one in Siena. These *palazzi* often looked out over a large square. The squares were designed to serve the same function as the "interior" of a house and became the place where the civil, religious and commercial life of the city took place. For this reason they were built away from the main streets to be protected from traffic. Piazza del Campo in Siena is typical of this new open space. It stands against the side of a hill along the top of which runs the city's main road so that the two are completely separate. The Campo slopes downward toward the Townhall on the lower side and appears to exist for public gatherings, whether political or for entertainment, just as happens when the Palio horserace takes place twice a year. Similarly in Piazza delle Erbe in Verona or the squares in the many cities along the Via Emilia such as Forlì and Reggio Emilia. The Piazza San Petronio in Bologna is not just far away from the Via Emilia, it is also off center with regard to the network of town roads. The square is considered the center of civil, commercial and religious life (the church of the city's patron saint, St. Petronius, stands in this square while Bologna cathedral, dedicated to St. Peter, is in nearby Via Indipendenza) and illustrates a second aspect that is typical of medieval squares: the fountain of Neptune is not placed in the center. The same is found in Venice where the monument to Colleoni in Piazza SS. Giovanni e Paolo stands beside the church. No criteria for shape or size exist that are common to medieval city centers throughout Italy which means that there is no one type of square. Squares have been created throughout the country to suit the geographical conditions so that, for example, where they cover a slope, steps have been incorporated which contribute to render the surrounding monuments more imposing as with the church in Todi and the public buildings in Pistoia. Some squares exist in the shape of an "L" like in Ferrara which separates the section faced by the cathedral from that of the Town-hall. Another model is that of San Gimignano where the three squares,

"Cisterna," "del Duomo" and "delle Erbe," follow one another distinguished by the different religious or civil buildings that face onto them. Around the beginning of the 14th century, civic administrations started to embellish and improve their cities by laying out new streets, widening squares and city walls. The walls were often much longer than necessary to allow space inside for the creation of new quarters. Some cities were created from scratch for strategical purposes. Cittadella and Castelfranco Veneto were built one in front of the other to defend the Paduan and Treviso territories respectively. Pietrasanta and Camaiore were built by the administrations of Lucca to guard the boundary with Pisa; Figline Valdarno and San Giovanni Valdarno were created as outposts of the Florentine republic to defend against Arezzo. The City Council of Bologna prepared a general defense plan with the foundation of Castel San Pietro, Castelfranco Emilia and San Giorgio di Piano at the extreme southeast, northwest and northeast of the territory over which they held jurisdiction. In 1256 the town of Manfredonia was built from nothing on the orders of King Manfredi to accommodate the inhabitants of Siponto which had been destroyed by an earthquake. The layout of the cities was often in symbolic shapes. The extension and development of medieval cities throughout Italy had a profound influence on successive centuries which was not equalled until the 19th century.

164 top Piazza delle Erbe in Verona is a market-place today but it was originally a Roman forum. In the middle of the square the Market column, the 16th-century Capitello or Tribuna, the fountain of Madonna Verona topped by St. Mark's column (1532) with its winged lion all stand in line.

164 bottom left Construction of the Franciscan church of Santa Croce was begun in 1294 and was completed in the second half of the 14th century. The façade and bell-tower, however, were erected 500 years later. The church looks onto one of the city's oldest squares.

164 bottom right The Umbrian city of Perugia has managed to retain its Medieval and Renaissance appearance. The main monuments from the era of city-states center on Piazza 4 Novembre: the Palazzo dei Priori, the Fontana Maggiore and the cathedral.

164-165 The heart of Bologna beats in piazzas Maggiore, Nettuno, and Porta Ravegnana which are surrounded by the city's important buildings. Piazza Maggiore is Bologna's nerve center; besides being the result of a major medieval urban design, it has been the seat of city government and religious and cultural institutions since its inception. City Hall, the palazzo of the Podestà and the church of St. Petronius all face onto it.

165 bottom The Gothic Loggia del Lionelli in Udine is the old City Hall. It takes its name from the architect who built it in 1457.

When the Renaissance was in full swing in the 15th century, the concept of designing the "ideal city" came into existence. It was often an intellectual exercise carried out by humanist architects on the commissions of Popes like Nicholas V, Paul III and Sixtus V, and of enlightened noblemen like Borso and Ercole d'Este and the dukes of Gonzaga. They all called in the best architects of their time to embellish, adapt and extend the capitals of their states and often, though sometimes only partially, achieved remarkable results. Perhaps the most interesting example of transformation was that of Piazza Campidoglio in Rome by Michelangelo. The artist knew how to create a masterpiece from a limited space with very different elements. He drew his idea from the obliqueness of the two existing buildings; by adding a third symmetrical building, he formed a five-sided space looking toward the palazzo in the background.

The political and social orders underwent notable change at the end of the 16th century. Many local administrations lost their autonomy and were sucked up into a single state. Florence and Siena absorbed Pistoia, Prato, San Gimignano, Massa Marittima, Arezzo and Pisa. To the north, the whole of Veneto was ruled by the Republic of Venice which stretched as far as Brescia and Bergamo in Lombardy. Within this new political setting, a new class of merchants and bankers was formed which partly joined and partly replaced the old class of noble feudal families. To show their new power, they built expensive *palazzi* that vied for importance with public buildings, for example the Pitti Palace in Florence. The introduction of gunpowder brought a transformation to the fortifications: towers disappeared and the walls were built thicker, lower and with the outside surface sloping to deflect cannonballs or other projectiles. The fortifications were also fitted with bastions and lunettes for more advanced techniques of defense.

During the 17th and 18th centuries, the Baroque and Neo-classical architectural styles left a firm imprint on cities throughout Italy.

The layout of the cities did not change much but the church started to adopt a more important role in the context of urban life. It became a more active religious center (this was the period of the Counter Reformation) to which cultural and social functions were added, including aid to the poor.

Large churches were built with convents, monasteries, hospitals or

educational institutes beside them in one architectural style. The façade of the church was the focal point for an onlooker so that it became almost the wall around the square. The single family, multi-storied house from medieval times that was present throughout the Renaissance disappeared from towns.

It was replaced by rented houses that could accommodate several families.

The large and very grand noblemen's houses remained which existed almost like little courts with their servants. These buildings had large entrances to allow carriages to pass and magnificent courtyards visible from the outside. Their staircases became another opportunity for architectural fancy. Fine examples of such houses are the *palazzi* in Naples in front of the royal palace.

Rome and Turin were the two cities that underwent most urban transformation during the 17th and 18th centuries. Rome became Italy's true capital with constructions by the greatest artists of the time. The most significant example was the redesign of St. Peter's square, the future urban model imitated by many architects in the centuries that followed. Gianlorenzo Bernini was commissioned by Pope Alexander VII, the last pope to dedicate his energies to the renewal and enrichment of the city, to redesign the square and render it

esthetical, functional and spiritual. Bernini had to include existing features, in particular the obelisk raised by Domenico Fontana on the orders of Pope Sixtus V and the fountain placed off-center by Maderno. Bernini succeeded magnificently and moreover created a square that was suited to processions and gatherings of large numbers of the faithful who crowded in to be present at blessings of the Pope from the gallery of the basilica and from the window of the papal chambers. During the 17th century, Piazza del Popolo and all the streets around it as far as Piazza Colonna also underwent transformation. On the other end, Turin tripled its size in the course of a single century. The city expanded according to a precise system of streets, Via Dora Grossa, Via Po and Via Roma, which all led into Piazza Castello so that this became the most representative part of the city center. All the large buildings along the main streets had beautiful porticoes which widened the streets to accommodate more shops and workshops.

At the beginning of the 18th century, a large construction project was undertaken in Sicily to create new or replace existing towns and villages that had been destroyed by the earthquake in 1693 in the southwest of the island. More than 50 urban centers had been ruined and 60,000 people killed. Reconstruction started immediately. Some cities, like Catania, were rebuilt on the same site but according to modern criteria; others, like Noto, Avola and Grammichele, were moved some miles away. The reconstruction of Catania was the work of architect Gian Battista Vaccarini. He designed the layout of streets and principal buildings to give the city a unified appearance. Different criteria were used in the reconstruction of Noto whose center was moved 11 miles away from the ruined town. Noto was rebuilt on the basis of the design by Angelo Italia and other local architects. The town was spread over the slopes of a hill along four parallel roads running lengthways. Three squares open onto the main road, the largest of which is the true town center. For both Avola and Grammichele, the basis of the designs was a center with radiating spokes. In the center of Avola there is a rectangular square from which four streets depart. As they continue, they widen into four other squares. In Grammichele, the central square matches the hexagonal shape of the city perimeter.

168 top St. Peter's Square is the unquestioned masterpiece of Gianlorenzo Bernini, the man who dominated artistic life in Rome in the 17th century. The colonnade that encloses the square in two long semicircles, 230 yards long in total, was constructed between 1656-67. The portico required 284 Doric columns and 88 pillars and was topped by a flat-tiled roof.

168 bottom Piazza Navona in Rome is built over Diocletian's stadium, occupying its exact area. In the center stands the Fountain of Rivers, a Baroque masterpiece by Bernini completed in 1651; the statues represent four rivers, symbols of the four corners of the world. The square is enclosed by palazzi and churches, one of which is Sant'Agnese in Agone by Borromini. It has a Baroque façade and a layout based on a Greek cross. The nearby 17th-century Palazzo Pamphili is especially beautiful.

168-169 Piazza San Carlo is at the center of Turin. Its square perimeter is lined with Baroque palazzi and a monument to Emmanuel Philibert (of Savoy) stands in the center.

169 bottom left The Sicilian town of Noto was completely destroyed in 1693 but rebuilt 6 miles from its original position.

169 bottom right The elegant Sicilian port of Catania stands with Mount Etna behind. Its rectilinear streets enhance Baroque monuments.

170 top The Royal Palace at Caserta was considered the Versailles of the Kingdom of Naples. In 1752 the Bourbon king, Charles III, ordered architect Luigi Vanvitelli (original name Van Wittel) to construct this massive palace. Vanvitelli was the most important architect during the period of late Baroque and Neo-classical architectural styles. The grandiose, rectangular building measures 272 x 207 yards and is five floors high. Its imposing façade has 250 windows and is fronted by columns.

170 bottom and 170-171 The Royal Palace at Caserta is justly considered Vanvitelli's masterpiece. The palace is surrounded by a park designed by Luigi Vanvitelli and his son Carlo. A series of fountains and pools with statues leads from the palace to the waterfall, 256 feet high. An example of the statues is that of "Diana and Atteon" (bottom) by Vanvitelli. An English garden was created to the right of the water-fall for Maria Carolina of Austria, a later queen of Naples.

Meanwhile, as the countryside became safer and more easily negotiable, large country villas belonging to noble families began to spring up, particularly in Lombardy, Veneto, Tuscany and Lazio. Whole villages would depend on these villas if they did not actually form a village in themselves. Special attention began to be paid to the inclusion of natural greenery in cities, until then largely ignored. Many parks and gardens in modern Italian cities were designed during the 18th century. In Parma and Modena, the principal aristocratic family in each ceded the gardens attached to their residences to the city council so that they could be enjoyed by the populace. In Florence several farming properties belonging to the Grand Duke just outside of the city walls were transformed into public parks; this is why some parks are known by the name "cascina" (farmhouse). In Milan, orchards and gardens belonging to monasteries and convents were confiscated to become state property for use by the public while in other cities unused military land was taken over, for example, the Lizza gardens in Siena which occupied the bulwarks and the Medici fort of Santa Barbara.

Inspired by Versailles, Charles III of Naples and Sicily commissioned Luigi Vanvitelli to design his new palace at Caserta. Progress was extremely slow, not beginning until 1753. Unfortunately, construction was not completed by 1759 when Charles abdicated to become King of Spain. He left the crown to his son Ferdinand IV who did not continue his father's project to its very end, that of making Caserta his capital.

171 bottom Vanvitelli was born in Naples in 1700. He worked in Rome, Marche and southern Italy. His greatest efforts were put into the Palace where he attempted to combine grandeur with harmony of proportions. The interiors are also based on this same principle. The entrance hall is an example; it gives access to the courtyards, the magnificent royal staircase (to the left) and the Sala di Marte (to the right) sumptuously decorated and furnished in Imperial style.

172-173 and 173 top Villa Pisani at Stra (also called Villa Nazionale) was designed by Girolamo Frigimelica for Alvise and Almorò Pisani. Work started in 1720 and took twenty years. The rectangular design with two internal courtyards is rather severe but the park, the stables, the "casa dei freschi" on the hill, the open-air theater and the tower in the park walls are more decorative. The rooms are decorated with high-quality frescoes like that by Gianbattista Tiepolo (top right photograph) entitled La Gloria.

172 bottom left The Rotonda near Vicenza is a celebrated work by Palladio. The square-based building is topped by a cupola. A colonnaded pediment opens on each side.

172 bottom right The Palladian Villa Foscari, known as the Malcontenta, stands on a bend in the river Brenta. The name comes from a Venetian noblewoman of the Foscari family who was rather displeased at being relegated from the city to this villa.

173 center Villa Giovannelli, in the unmistakable style of Palladio, stands at Noventa on the river Brenta.

173 bottom Villa Elmo at Montecchia was commissioned circa 1568 by Gabriele Capodilista from Dario Varotari, the Venetian architect and painter. Capodilista had been awarded the estate of Montecchia and wanted to create a house worthy of a nobleman. The villa's principal feature is that it was designed by the same person who created the pictorial decorations. Consequently, the building is an example of harmony between architecture and decoration.

174 top left The traditional images of Naples (the view of the bay at the foot of the Posillipo hill or the Vomero or lanes with children playing in front of the slums) are a world away from that of the modern and tall buildings in the business area, yet these two sides of the city exist just a few hundred yards from one another. The old quarter of Porta Capuana and that of the new offices are both close to the central station.

174 bottom left The glass and steel north tower of Skidmore, Owings of Merrill, named "Matitone" by the Genoese, rises shining out of the skyline of the Ligurian capital.

During the 19th century only small towns were created but, in imitation of Napoleonic France, large urban reorganisations took place. In Milan the Foro Bonaparte was opened which, when connected with the triumphal arch at the start of Corso Sempione, was the road which led to France. For this to be realized, the area around the Castle had to be transformed. The ramparts around Castello Sforzesco were demolished (as happened in many places in Italy in the euphoria of the Napoleonic occupation) which until 1801 had been a true Renaissance citadel. The resulting material was used to build the Arena to be used for sporting events which was inaugurated in 1807 in Napoleon's presence.

Following the earthquake of 1783, the reconstruction of Messina took place. The reconstruction of the palace overlooking the sea was based on the design by Minutolo and included a Neo-classical arcade formed by colossal semi-columns. The entire construction was the pride of the town's inhabitants until 1908 when the next earthquake destroyed the new palace completely.

The Industrial Revolution reached Italy from England and had a profound effect on the cities, especially those in the north where factories and new houses sprang up to accommodate the workers. In the 20th century, the Fascists drained many of the marshes in Lazio where they founded a number of new cities, many of which were designed by Marcello Piacentini, to populate those areas; for example, Sabaudia, Latina and Aprilia. Other towns were created in Sardinia for agricultural and mining purposes, all of which reflected the rationalist urban concepts of the 1920s and 30s.

At the end of World War II, Italy had lost 5% of its housing and suffered huge damage to its artistic heritage. Reconstruction was not organized and suffered accordingly; city centers were assaulted by speculators and suburbs were thrown up in a disorganized manner to create dormitory areas. When the economic boom came in the 1960s, the history of Italian cities coincided with that of the new tourist resorts at the seaside, by the lakes

and in the mountains. Nearly all of these were created without thought to the character that had permeated Italian city planning for centuries. Today, for better or worse, Italian cities reflect those two thousand years of life. They are "natural centers," according to the definition of Carlo Cattaneo, from which man "cannot easily separate," because "they are the work of centuries and of remotest events … whose causes are older than memory." The history of Italian cities is in fact the history of the Italians.

174 top right The Foro Bonaparte was designed in 1802 by town planner Giovanni Antolini in honor of Napoleon and should have surrounded all of Castello Sforzesco but the project which also included the Arena and the Arco was never finished.

174 bottom right Milan has undergone more development in this century than any other Italian city. During the years of the

economic boom, the Pirelli skyscraper, inaugurated in 1959, became the new symbol of the city.

175 Milan's Castello Sforzesco has experienced many episodes of construction, destruction, development and restoration in its centuries of history. The version seen today is the reconstruction undertaken at the end of the 19th century by architect Luca Beltrami.

176 top Piazza del Popolo is an oval closed by the twin churches of Santa Maria di Montesanto and Santa Maria dei Miracoli and by the Pincio Gardens. The square is a meeting place for Romans; the Flaminio obelisk stands in the center.

176 center The Vittoriale is the monument erected to King Victor Emmanuel II of Italy at the turn of the 20th century. It stands in Piazza Venezia in Rome. The tomb of the Unknown Soldier rests inside.

176 bottom Trinità dei Monti is the name that combines a square, a flight of steps and a church. With Piazza di Spagna and the elegant Via Condotti below, the area is one of the most "recherché" corners of Rome.

ROME:

THE ETERNAL CITY

176-177 Tradition has it that the Eternal City, Rome, was first settled here, on Palatine Hill and in the area occupied by the Forum, between the end of the 9th and start of the 7th century BC.

177 top left The Tomb of Augustus is a circular construction 98 yards in diameter on which work was begun in 27 BC. Once it lost its original function as an imperial tomb, it was transformed into a pit for building materials, a hanging garden, an amphitheater and an auditorium.

177 top right Construction of the Baths of Caracalla began in AD 212. The baths remained operative until the invasion of the Goths in 537. At the center of the baths is a large section measuring 240 x 125 yards surrounded by fenced grassy areas.

178-179 In AD 69, Vespasian started construction of the Flavian Amphitheater, one of Rome's most famous symbols, known as the Colosseum. The outermost of the four masonry rings that comprised it supported the wooden beams to which the velarium was fixed. This awning protected people from rain and sun.

180 center left Construction of the Pantheon was started in AD 27 as a place of worship, first for the gods of the republican and imperial Romans, later for Christians; but despite continuous alterations it has survived until the modern day. It is based on the layout of the ancient *thòlos*, a circular building typical of Aegean civilisation. The dome of the Pantheon is 141 feet across, exactly the distance of its height from the ground, which gives it a spherical and harmonious proportion emphasized by the light that enters from the oculus in the top. The outer colonnade has disappeared from the original construction and a grander entrance has been "invented" in its place.

180 bottom left Next to Trajan's Forum stand the Trajan Markets, separated from the Palatine Hill by the road, the Via dei Fori Imperiali. The markets were a large commercial area in the 2nd century AD which housed more than 150 shops and offices.

180 right The statue of the Prima Porta is the most famous of the more than 80 erected in honor of Octavian (Augustus), the founder, of imperial Rome.

180-181 The Temple of Castor and Pollux was named for the twin sons of the god Jove. Its alternative name is the Temple of the Dioscurii and is one of Rome's most ancient monuments. It was originally constructed in 484 BC but subsequently rebuilt several times.

180 top left This ancient stone face, known as the Mouth of Truth, is under the portico of Santa Maria in Cosmedin. It is said that the Mouth will cut off the hand of a liar if he should dare place it within.

181 bottom left Constantine's Arch was inaugurated in AD 315 to celebrate the victory of Constantine over Maxentius. It has splendid bas-reliefs taken from previous monuments. The arch stands in the Colosseum Square.

181 bottom right The Via dei Fori Imperiali, the road that passes through the Forum area and runs as far as the Colosseum, was built by the Fascists as a stage for military parades.

PIVS. VII. PONT. MAX.
QVOD. ABSOLVENDVM. SVPERERAT
ADDITO. CRATERE. EXCITATO. SALIENTE
SYMPLEGMA. CONSVMMAVIT
A. D. MDCCCXVIII. PONTIF. XIX.

182-183 The Quirinale is the seat of the President of the Republic of Italy and takes its name from the hill it was built on. The façade is a typical late Renaissance design by the architect Fontana.

182 bottom The so-called "chick" is in fact a baby elephant that supports the small Egyptian obelisk in Piazza della Minerva. Splendid Baroque palazzi provide a wonderful backdrop to the unusual monument.

183 top right Marcus Aurelius' column has a spiral frieze that recounts the emperor's military victories. It stands in Piazza Colonna and is surrounded by Palazzo Ferraioli, Palazzo Colonna and Palazzo Chigi, seat of the Prime Minister.

183 bottom right The imposing pyramid of Caius Cestius is joined to the Aurelian Wall. Built in the Egyptian style, which was fashionable after the conquests there, it is 118 high and has a base width of 98 feet per side. It was built as a tomb for the praetor, Caius Cestius Epulone.

183 top left Isola Tiberina, the island in the river Tiber, has been home to a hospital since ancient times and is also land that has been consecrated to Aesculapius, god of medicine. Roman tradition tells that the island was inhabited by the snake sacred to Aesculapius; after Aesculapius fell out of the boat bringing him to Rome, the Romans shaped the island like a boat.

183 bottom left The Barcaccia is the name given to the fountain in the center of Piazza di Spagna. It was commissioned by Pope Urban VIII in 1629 from Pietro Bernini, father of Gianlorenzo Bernini. It is in the shape of a boat that seems to float in a tank placed lower than the level of the square.

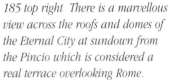

185 top right There is a marvellous view across the roofs and domes of the Eternal City at sundown from the Pincio which is considered a real terrace overlooking Rome.

185 bottom right Via Sistina is the road that connects Piazza Barberini with Trinità dei Monti. The Sistine Theater and Baroque church of SS. Ildefonso and Tommaso da Villanova.

186-187 All Rome's greatest artists during the first half of the 1700's worked on the Trevi Fountain. The magnificent work covers the whole of one side of Palazzo Poli.

184 top left The Fontana dei Fiumi (Fountain of Rivers) in Piazza Navona is one of Gianlorenzo Bernini's masterpieces. Built in 1651, the fountain represents the personifications of the rivers Ganges, Danube, Plata and (shown in the picture) Nile. The head of the Nile is veiled because at that time its source was still unknown.

184 top right Campo de' Fiori today hosts the fruit and vegetable market but at one time it was a site for games, races and even executions. The most famous person to die there was the philosopher Giordano Bruno, burnt alive in 1600 after an eight-year trial. A statue to him stands in the center of the square.

184-185 The Spanish Steps join Piazza di Spagna with the church of Trinità dei Monti. It is a favorite setting for fashion shows and a meeting place for Romans and tourists.

185 left The shape of Piazza Navona recalls the shape of Diocletian's sports stadium over which it was built. The name Navona is thought to have derived from the ancient word agoni meaning struggle (i.e., sporting competition); this probably developed into n'agone (therefore nagone) and then to the actual Navona.

188 top The Passion of Christ is represented along the Sant'Angelo bridge, which leads to the castle of the same name. The statues of the angels that hold up the symbols of the Passion were designed by Bernini but sculpted by his pupils.

188 bottom The church of St. Mary in Trastevere has very ancient origins and is built in the square of the same name; it was the first church in Rome to be dedicated to the cult of the Virgin. The beautiful façade is decorated with mosaics from the 12th-13th centuries which depict Mary seated on a throne surrounded by ten saints.

188-189 Castel Sant'Angelo is one of the capital's most famous monuments. Erected between AD 130 and 140 as the tomb for Hadrian, it was turned into a fortress, then a prison and then a papal residence. The massive cylindrical building today is enclosed inside a square wall and houses the National Museum of Castel Sant'Angelo.

189 top The solemn interior of the Basilica of St. John Lateran has a layout in the form of a Latin cross and five naves. Its current appearance was the work of Borromini who was commissioned by Pope Clement XI to restore it for the Jubilee of 1650.

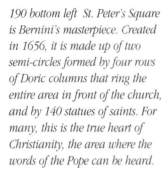

190-191 *The construction of Via della Conciliazione was a work of great symbolic value but is debatable from a town-planning point of view. Built between 1936–50, it required the demolition of old districts of Santo Spirito and Sant'Angelo. The road stretches from the River Tiber to St. Peter's Square.*

190 bottom left *St. Peter's Square is Bernini's masterpiece. Created in 1656, it is made up of two semi-circles formed by four rows of Doric columns that ring the entire area in front of the church, and by 140 statues of saints. For many, this is the true heart of Christianity, the area where the words of the Pope can be heard.*

190 bottom right *The Swiss Guard has been the armed force of the Vatican for over 500 years. The corps consists of 100 men whose purpose is to protect the life of the Pope.*

191 left *Five bronze doors give access to the interior of St. Peter's. The canopy over the papal altar, designed by Bernini, stands in the majestic Baroque nave directly below Michelangelo's dome.*

191 top right *The Church of St. Peter dominates the aerial view of the city: it covers 5.5 acres, is 239 yards long, 125 yards wide at the façade and the basic structure is 154 feet high.*

191 bottom right *The dome over St. Peter's was designed by Michelangelo. The vault is divided into 16 segments and is in two layers. The dome is 139 feet in diameter and has a total height of 449 feet.*

192-193 *The Sistine Chapel takes its name from Pope Sixtus IV who had it built between 1475-81. The rectangular chapel measures 131 x 46 feet and is 69 feet high. The walls and barrel vaults are decorated with frescoes by Botticelli, Ghirlandaio, Pinturicchio and Signorelli but what has made the chapel a* masterpiece known all over the world is the work by Michelangelo who was commissioned by Pope Julius II to add to the work. The artist worked on the ceiling (see photograph) from 1508-12 and on the wall behind the altar (The Last Judgment *is over 2100 square feet), which he finished in 1541.*

193 bottom *The theme of the Sistine Chapel ceiling is taken from the Book of Genesis. Michelangelo divided the central part of the ceiling in nine scenes and surrounded them with decorative motifs and trompe l'oeil with the so-called* ignudi *that support the false stuccowork in order to give depth to the massive fresco. Around the nine episodes taken from the Book of Genesis,* Michelangelo positioned seven gigantic prophets and five sybils. The nine incidents portrayed are (from the great altar): The Separation of Light and Darkness, The Creation of the Stars, The Separation of Water and Earth, The Creation of Adam, The Creation of Eve, The Original Sin and Banishment from Paradise (right), The Sacrifice of Noah, The Flood *and* Noah's Drunkenness.

193

194-195 The Raphael rooms (Stanze) are a series of unquestioned masterpieces in the Vatican Museums. The rooms were already sumptuous in 1505 when Pope Julius II engaged Raphael to enrich them further. Raphael and the members of his school worked on the four rectangular rooms with cross vaults from 1508-17. The last of the rooms to be completed is shown in the picture and takes its name from the fresco The Burning of the Town.

195 top The Loggias of Raphael were also completed by his pupils using the designs and sketches of the Master. The vaults show episodes from the Old Testament and the Life of Jesus.

195 bottom The Heliodorus Room also takes its name from one of the frescoes painted by Raphael himself: The Expulsion of Heliodorus from the Temple. The cycle of works in this room were chosen by Pope Julius II himself.

194 bottom The Constantine Room is one of the famous Raphael rooms and was used for official receptions in the Vatican. It is decorated with frescoes showing important episodes in the life of Emperor Constantine—his Baptism,

The Battle of the Milvian Bridge, The Apparition of the Cross, and The Donation of Rome which were designed by Raphael but completed after his death by his pupils. Raphael Sanzio, born in Urbino, died in Rome in 1520, when only 37 years old.

197 top The relationship of Turin with the Alps is very close. Ever since it was a Roman city called Augusta Taurinorum, the city has been an important stopping-off point on the way to Gaul from the rest of Italy.

197 center Palazzo Carignano is a magnificent example of the best of Turin Baroque architecture. It dates from the 17th century and is linked with important historical episodes: it was here that the Kingdom of Italy was proclaimed and here that its first Parliament met.

197 bottom The foliage of the trees embraces Corso Victor Emmanuel II, one of the main streets that cross Turin east-west.

TURIN:
THE "LITTLE OLD LADY'S" DRAWING ROOM

196 top left Seen from the Gran Madre, over Victor Emmanuel I Bridge, Piazza Vittorio Veneto is a square bordered by Piedmontese Baroque buildings that seems to give access to the heart of the city and, more distantly, the Alps.

196 top right Porta Palatina, a section of the old Turin walls still in a good state of repair, dates from the 1st century AD. In the square dominated by the two crenellated towers, the statues of Julius Caesar and Octavian, two copies of the originals, still look over what remains of the Roman road.

196-197 At the foot of the Alps, Turin preserves obvious traces of what was the capital of Savoyard Italy: the elegance of the palazzi in the old center, the geometrical design of its street layout and the large and well-looked after parks. The grandiose 18th-century Mole Antonelliana, symbol of the city, overlooks the city skyline from its height of 551 feet.

198-199 The River Po crosses the city north-south passing through the center where Valentino Park and Piazza Vittorio Veneto are to be found. In this section (photograph of the Murazzi), the severe, elegant Piedmont-style palazzi are reflected in the river's not always clean waters.

198 bottom Turin's most beautiful and inaccessible villas stand on the hill east of the Gran Madre and the Valentino in large natural settings. This is the most exclusive area of the city, sought after by those who wish to escape the confusion and traffic of the city center.

199 top The Gran Madre (left) and Mount Capuccini, with the church of Santa Maria del Monte and the Capuchin monastery (right) face the Po near Victor Emmanuel I Bridge. This hill rises from the river to the villages of Pino Torinese and Pecetto. It is the greenest area of Turin and dotted with large, expensive houses. The National Museum of the Mountains of the Duke of Abruzzi is also situated here.

199 center Valentino Castle is a strong and forbidding fortification on the bank of the Po, built in 1630 by Carlo di Castellamonte who took 16th-century French castles as his model. The fortress is surrounded by the 130-acre Valentino Park, created in 1830 by the Savoy family on the east bank of the river.

199 bottom The Borgo and the Medieval Castle are an unusual set of buildings built in Valentino Park last century to reproduce medieval constructions of Piedmont and the Aosta valley on behalf of the Savoy family.

200 *Palazzo Madama stands in Piazza Castello, the heart of Turin. The body of the building is medieval and is built around the remains of a Roman gatehouse. From the 15th to 17th centuries, the royal family of Savoy used the castle as a residence. It was heavily remodelled in the 18th century with the creation of the present imposing façade (see photograph) designed by Felipe Juvarra, the great Spanish architect. Now the building is used to house the Civic Museum of Ancient Art.*

201 top left *San Lorenzo is the Baroque masterpiece of Guarino Guarini. Born in Modena in 1624, the architect learned his trade by studying the buildings of Borromini, then developed his own style of highly imaginative geometrical forms. San Lorenzo is the epitome of this style: inside, its central body features extensive stuccowork and the use of marble and gold-leaf decoration; the outside is gentle and harmonious with an attractive cupola.*

201 center left *Palazzo Reale was built in 1660 in the sober and elegant style it still displays. It faces onto Piazza Reale, an extension of Piazza Castello, while lovely park behind it has been turned into public gardens. Until 1865, the palazzo was a Savoyard residence; now, its right wing houses one of the best collections of arms in Europe for pieces made between the 16th and 19th centuries.*

201 bottom left *The spirit of the Baroque style pervades the sumptuous and elegant interior of Palazzo Reale. The Throne Room where the king held audience was for years the center of Savoyard power. The regality of the room is evident in the quality of the decorations: the inlaid wooden floors, the gilded stuccowork, the enormous chandeliers and the purple velvet drapes that cover the canopy.*

201 right *The reception rooms on the first floor of Palazzo Reale are open to the public. They are decorated in the styles of 17th to 19th centuries with magnificent tapestries, furniture and other furnishings of superb manufacture. Unfortunately, part of this splendid building was destroyed by a fire in 1997, but the damage is being repaired and sensitive and detailed restoration is being carried out.*

202 top left Piazza Ducale is the pride of Vigevano, an industrial town in the province of Pavia. The cathedral that faces onto it is 1000 years old but has a 17th-century façade.

202 top right Ivrea was originally a Roman town and a Savoyard fiefdom along the Dora Baltea and ancient Via Francigeno. Evidence of its importance in the past are the 10th-century cathedral and 13th-century castle.

AMONG RICE FIELDS AND ANCIENT CHARTERHOUSES

202-203 The Certosa (Charterhouse) was built on the wishes of Gian Galeazzo Visconti. It stands 5 miles from Pavia and was started in 1396. The complex includes a large and a small cloister. Inside there are paintings by Borgognone and his school, Perugino, Guercino, Morazzone, Macrino d'Alba and Luini. The transept of the church includes funeral monuments of Beatrice d'Este and Ludovico il Moro.

203 top The church of St. Andrew, built in 1219 in Vercelli, is one of Italy's best examples of Cistercian Gothic architecture. Two towers stand on either side of the church façade; the lunette illustrating The Martyrdom of St. Andrew by Antelami is a masterpiece. Inside, the three naves have ogival vaults.

203 bottom The symbol of Novara is the church of St. Gaudenzio with its large dome, nearly 400 feet high. It was designed by the architect Antonelli who also designed the Mole in Turin. The church is from the 16th century but the dome was added in 1888.

204 top The Arch of Peace stands at the beginning of the road that leads to Sempione Park. Topped by a bronze chariot, it was designed by Luigi Cagnola in celebration of the triumph of Napoleon.

204 bottom The Madonnina is a 17 foot high statue that stands on top of Milan Cathedral at a height of 350 feet. It is made of copper and coated with 300 grams of gold. It was placed on the highest pinnacle of the cathedral in 1774 when Milan was controlled by the Austrians. The original version, by Giuseppe Peregò, was made from wood and is kept in the Cathedral Museum.

MILAN:

THE CITY THAT NEVER SLEEPS

204-205 The cathedral is without doubt the building that symbolizes the city. It is decorated with 3159 statues and even more pinnacles, the highest of which is 354 feet high and supports the Madonnina. Gian Galeazzo Visconti encouraged construction of the cathedral which was begun in 1386 but its majestic façade was only completed in the 19th century by the architects, Amati and Zanoia.

205 top left The tall buildings and towers that rise up behind the cathedral testify to the close relationship between historical and artistic Milan and the world of business. In the distance, though not so close to the city, are the Alps.

205 top right The 19th-century façade of the cathedral is lit up with a warm glow toward the end of a winter's afternoon. In the foreground, in the center of the square, stands the monument to Victor Emmanuel II.

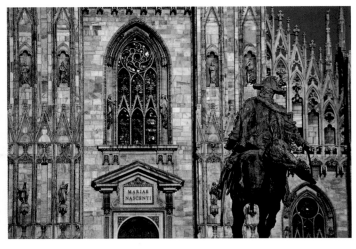

206 top left The Guastalla Gardens, Sempione Park and the area around the Sforzesco castle are the only open areas of the polluted and traffic-ridden city which, however, is required to provide quality of life for its inhabitants.

206 bottom left Villa Comunale faces onto Via Palestro. It was built in Neo-classical style by the Viennese architect Leopold Pollack, pupil of Piermarini. Pollack was very active professionally in Lombardy at the end of the 18th and start of the 19th centuries. Villa Comunale, also known as Palazzo Belgioioso, was partially damaged by a terrorist's bomb in 1993; today it houses to the Gallery of Modern Art.

206 top right Via Dante is one of Milan's main streets and connects two of the most important areas of the city: Piazza Cordusio and Castello Sforzesco (seen in the distance). The street is home to the Piccolo Teatro.

206 bottom right and 207 bottom left Milan is a middle-class city but filled with beautiful houses and elegant private courtyards enclosing hidden gardens. Typical treasures concealed in old Milan, they hide a few columns, a portico, an Art Nouveau gate and ivy climbing over the plasterwork.

206-207 The statue of Giuseppe Garibaldi on horseback surveys Largo Cairoli and its incessant traffic. In the distance stands Castello Sforzesco built in 1450 over the 14th-century Visconti fort. Actually, the only remains of the Visconti building are to be seen in the elegant features of the tower. The crenellated walls and large towers built by the Spaniards in the 16th-17th centuries are a reminder that the castle was practically impregnable for hundreds of years.

207 bottom right The Grande Disco by Arnaldo Pomodoro stands in Piazza Meda. It is one of the many works of art around the city, capital of modern culture and center of everything innovative in Italy.

208 top *The Galleria Vittorio Emanuele II was designed by Giuseppe Mengari between 1865-77. It is an elegant, 18th-century drawing-room that connects Piazza Duomo to Piazza della Scala. It is loved by both the Milanese and tourists and is a favorite place for a stroll, particularly in winter when the glass roof ensures shelter from the cold, misty air of the Po valley.*

208 center *The Galleria Vittorio Emanuele II, which is 218 yards long on its longer side, is shaped like a cross. In the center where the two arms meet, the floor is decorated with an enormous rose in colored inlaid marble. Every aspect of the Galleria is typical of 19th-century style: the architect, Mengoni, wanted it to be elegant and solemn, in keeping with its role as the lively center of the city.*

208 bottom *There cannot be a music enthusiast in the world who does not want to visit La Scala. The theater's name comes from that of an old church, Santa Maria alla Scala, which was built by Regina della Scala, wife of Bernabò Visconti. The church fell down in 1776 and the theater, with its luxurious interior and perfect acoustics, was raised from its ruins, in keeping with a plan by Piermarini.*

208-209 *The octagon where the two walkways of the Galleria Vittorio Emanuele intersect is illuminated by the light from the enormous glass dome above. Several of Milan's most famous and elegant restaurants and bars are under the glass roof of the Galleria, where the heart of Milan beats most strongly.*

209 top left *Milan's most beautiful luxury shops are located in an area bounded by Via Montenapoleone, Via della Spiga, Via Sant'Andrea and Via Santo Spirito. Here the visitor will find the shops of Armani, Ferré, Versace, Prado, Gucci, Krizia, Valentino and Trussadi, arbiters of fashion around the world.*

209 top right *Milan has made fashion into a huge industry and has always been the "city of tailors." It does not have a tradition of great aristocrats or noble families, rather, it is the city of workers which will happily reward successful entrepreneurs, artists, editors or stylists, whoever they may be.*

210 top Santa Maria delle Grazie was built in the mid-15th century in a Lombard-Gothic style by architect Guiniforte Solari. During his career, spent mostly in Lombardy, Solari was also responsible for the construction of the interior of the Certosa of Pavia. The lantern on the church roof and the Renaissance platform inside were later modified by Bramante.

210 bottom From Piazza della Vetra, can be seen the perimeter, early Christian towers and the drum and cupola of the church of San Lorenzo Maggiore, rebuilt at the end of the 16th century. On the front of the church some of ancient Milan's most impressive remains have been preserved: several Attic-Corinthian columns rebuilt to form a four-sided portico, and the statue of Emperor Constantine.

211 The Basilica of St. Ambrose and the Duomo are Milan's two most important churches. St. Ambrose's church was originally built in 386 during the life of Ambrose, the patron saint of Milan. Between the 7th-9th centuries it was altered several times until it took on its present form, that of a solid and beautiful Romanesque church.

212 center and bottom left Fairs, local festivals and antiques markets are some of the occasions on which the Navigli become the center of Milanese life again. This quarter of the city is called Porta Ticinese; it grew up around the dockyard and is filled with lanes and tiny shops.

212 top left and right After the Cerchia ring canal was covered, the Navigli canals lost the role they had played for centuries. At the end of the 20th century, what remains of the Navigli is making a comeback. The Darsena, Naviglio Grande and Naviglio Pavese canals have their origin in Piazza 24th May, traditionally a site of markets and gatherings. At one time this area was the haunt of low life but today has become a center of night life: pubs, music bars, restaurants, etc. The inhabitants of the large blocks of flats have accepted that the new influx is the price they have to pay for bringing this area back to life. The old inns and shops have been restored and reopened and the slow waters of the Navigli have begun to reflect Milanese life once more.

213 Milan is also a city of water and has made use of redirected water courses since classical times. Originally they were used as a means of defense: an ancient dyke fed by the Seveso, Nirone and Mussa streams ringed the Roman walls but now is part of a drainage system. A second dyke, dug and fortified in 1156 and called the Inner Dyke, corresponded to what today is called the "Cerchia dei Navigli." In fact, the Cerchia was almost completely covered for reasons of hygiene and "decorum" in the 1930s. The first navigable canal was the Naviglio Grande which was dug to facilitate transport of materials for construction of the cathedral. The special flat-bottomed boats carried marble and lumber for centuries. The Naviglio della Martesana, which terminated at Brera, was dug in 1457. The Naviglio Pavese which connects Milan to Pavia was the last to be completed. Notably, the Naviglio Paderno was designed by Leonardo da Vinci.

214 left Dedicated to St. Alexander, Bergamo cathedral was first built during the Longobard era but rebuilt several times during the 13th-17th centuries. The cathedral is laid out on the plan of a Latin cross with a single large nave. Inside there are paintings by Tiepolo, Previtali and Moroni. The greenish dome of the cathedral and the dome of the Colleoni Chapel are the two symbols of the upper city; Piazza Duomo, in the center, is surrounded by Bergamo's most important monuments.

214 top right Seen from a hill above upper Bergamo, the Lombard city looks like a succession of houses and hills. At the top left of the picture, the domes of the cathedral and the Colleoni Chapel and the Torre del Gombito can be seen. Ancient Bergamo (the upper city) is completely walled; the lower, modern city is the result of the industrial boom the city has enjoyed since World War II.

BERGAMO AND BRESCIA:
CLASSICAL PASTS, MODERN PRESENTS

214 bottom right Piazza della Loggia is the "drawing room" onto which Brescia's most famous buildings face: the Monte di Pietà (15th century) and the Clocktower. The square was the scene of a terrorist bomb in 1974 whose victims are remembered by a memorial stone. The square is named after the Loggia, the City Hall, which was built between the end of the 15th and mid-16th centuries.

215 Built between 1472-76 as a monument to the famous troop commander, Bartolomeo Colleoni, the Colleoni Chapel is probably Bergamo's most important building. Built in typical Renaissance style in the upper city by architect Giovanni Antonio Amadeo, the Chapel has a dynamic façade with colored marble, fretwork and rich ornamentation. Inside, frescoes by Tiepolo decorate the wall lunettes.

217 top The picture shows a
detail of the face on the
Clocktower in Piazza delle Erbe
built in 1473 by Luca Fancelli.

217 top The picture shows a
detail of the face on the
Clocktower in Piazza delle Erbe
built in 1473 by Luca Fancelli.

217 center Palazzo Te was built
on a single-story, square design
in 1525 by Giulio Romano for
Federico II Gonzaga. Today it
houses the Palazzo Te Civic
Museum. The unusual name
comes from the locality in which
the palazzo was built: Teijto, later
shortened as "Te."

MANTUA:

THE CITY OF THE GONZAGA FAMILY

216 top left The old city center of
Mantua is seen here from the so-
called "Smaller Lake" created by
a bend in the River Mincio as it
passes around the city. The
cathedral and St. George's Castle
are recognisable among the
ancient palazzi.

216 top right The medieval
buildings that line Piazza delle
Erbe include the 13th-century
Palazzo della Ragione, the 14th-
century Clocktower, the
Renaissance Rotonda di San
Lorenzo and the church of St.
Andrew.

216-217 and 217 bottom The
Sala dei Giganti in the Palazzo Te
was decorated by Giuliano
Romano and his school in the first
half of the 16th century. The vault
fresco of Olympus depicts Jove's
revenge on the rebel giants.

218 top The National Museum of Ravenna is housed in the cloisters of the ancient monastery of St. Vitale. It holds an interesting collection of Roman, early Christian, Gothic and Byzantine pieces. The early Christian church of St. Vitale dates from the 6th century; the interior of the octagonal body of the building is decorated with a mosaic cycle in Byzantine style from the 6th century.

218 center The church of St. Apollinaris in Classe stands three miles from Ravenna where its port, Classe, once existed. It was built with three naves and a wide atrium (now lost) by Giuliano Argentario in the 6th century. The huge cylindrical bell-tower was built at a later date.

RAVENNA:
A BYZANTINE ATMOSPHERE

218 bottom Important Byzantine sarcophagi stand along the side naves of St. Apollinaris in Classe, separated from the central nave by elegant marble columns. Splendid 6th and 7th century mosaics decorate the apsidal bowl-shaped vault and the triumphal arch.

218-219 The treasures of the monastery of St. Vitale are the fretwork of the capitals, the marble and, above all, the mosaic cycle which shows emperors, bishops and their courts. Empress Theodora can be seen with her entourage in the photograph.

219 top left 14th-century buildings and the 18th-century Palazzo dell'Orologio line the large and long Piazza del Popolo, one of the centers of life in Ravenna.

219 top right The Tomb of Galla Placidia was built in the 5th century to hold the remains of the empress. The inside is decorated with mosaics of great beauty.

221 center The uncommonly green dome topped by a red lantern belongs to the cathedral of Trent. The 18th century Fountain of Neptune at the bottom stands in the center of the square, overlooked by elegant but austere medieval buildings.

221 bottom Miramare Castle is a 15th-century stronghold built over previous medieval forts. It offers a splendid view over the city of Trieste.

THE NORTHEAST:

LAND OF ART AND WORK

220 top left Piazza dei Signori is the civil and artistic center of Vicenza. It contains some of the city's most important monuments, such as the Palladian Basilica, the Loggia del Capitano and the medieval Torre di Piazza.

220 top right The elegant Gothic-Venetian Palazzo del Comune and the harmonious Portico of St. John, over which stands the 15th century Clocktower, close the magnificent Piazza della Libertà in the center of Udine.

220-221 The imposing building on the north side of Piazza delle Erbe in Padua is the Palazzo della Ragione. It was built in the 12th century but was enlarged and enriched at the start of the 14th century.

221 top The Cappella degli Scrovegni is perhaps Padua's most important building. It was built in the 14th century and contains the cycle of 38 frescoes by Giotto telling the stories of Mary and Christ, which help teach the Christian faith.

222-223 When the lights of the
bridges and the city are reflected
in the waters of the Adige at dusk,
Verona returns to the time of
Romeo and Juliet. In fact, Verona
is a bustling commercial city of
300,000 inhabitants and rich
and lively enough to have earned
itself the role of "crossroads of the
northeast." The region as a whole
has an industrial productivity
rate equal to Japan's.

222 bottom The Scaliger bridge
is a sort of extension of the
Castelvecchio, a magnificent
example of medieval fortification
built by Cangrande della Scala
on the banks of the Adige and
incorporating ancient buildings
probably of Roman origin.
The bridge has three crenellated
arches – like the fort – in the
Ghibelline style; it connects
Castelvecchio to Piazza Arsenale
in Borgo Trento. The fortress today
houses the Civic Art Museum with
a valuable collection of paintings
from the Venetian school.

223 top left Piazza Bra is the heart of Veronese life. The square is dominated by the Roman Arena, one of the symbols of the city, and includes the Liston (a favorite promenade of the Veronese). The busy, old center of Verona is triangular in shape, bounded by a bend in the Adige on two sides and by the Via Roma, Via degli Alpini and Via Pallone on the other.

223 bottom left Stage scenery has altered the interior of the Arena: a production of "Carmen" is being staged, one of the most popular operas for the thousands of opera lovers who flock here every summer.

VERONA:
TRANQUIL BEAUTY

223 top right The 1st-century Roman amphitheater is one of the three largest buildings of its sort to reach us almost intact; the other two are the Colosseum in Rome and the amphitheater of Capua. At the time of its construction, its 44 tiers were able to seat 25,000 spectators.

223 bottom right Palazzo Giusti on the far side of Ponte Nuovo is famous for its Italian-style gardens, terraces, lookout point, avenues lined with cypress trees, and interesting layout. The design of the flowerbeds and the statues give the gardens a classical spirit. There is a beautiful view over Verona from the upper terrace.

224 top left Venice is the most incredible city in the world. Daughter of the waters, mistress of the seas, it seems to be in unstable balance on its narrow strip of land surrounded by water. Yet, despite its precarious situation, Venice manages to preserve a sort of immutability by means of its unique atmosphere, its extraordinary historic and artistic palazzi and other monuments.

224 bottom left The dome of St. Mark's is seen in front of the roofs of the old houses in Campo San Lorenzo and Campo San Zanipolo. Seen from the bell tower in St. Mark's Square, Venice is an austere city, rich and severe as befitted the Serenissima.

VENICE:

THE CITY OF THE DOGES

224 top right The Punta della Dogana da Mar (the Customs offices), seen here with the church della Salute, separates the mouth of the Grand Canal from the Giudecca canal. It was in this place, that looks like the bow of a ship, that goods arriving by sea used to be unloaded and their cargoes charged duty.

224 bottom right The Grand Canal and the Rialto Bridge are two points of attraction for the tourists who besiege Venice all year round.

225 The long, narrow shape of the island of Giudecca gave it its original name of Spinalonga (long spine). Once the island had orchards, vineyards and palazzi. In more recent times, the growth of industry has meant it has been built over with public housing. The drop-shaped island of San Giorgio Maggiore can be seen at the top of the picture, in the center.

226-227 The story goes that the body of St. Mark was brought to Venice in 828 by Rustico da Torcello and Buono Tribuno da Malamocco, two merchants who had stolen the body from Alexandria, Egypt. The remains were brought to the Doge's Chapel. Construction of St. Mark's church started soon after but it retained the status of Doge's Chapel until 1807 when it was upgraded to the Cathedral of Venice.

226 bottom left The winged lion is the personification of the patron saint of Venice: aggressive, proud and armed with a sword, the Golden Lion in St. Mark's Square was a just representation of the power and grandeur of the Serenissima.

226 bottom right The Tetrarchs, better known as the Moors, are part of the cell that holds the Treasure of St. Mark. Probably a Syrian work of the 4th century, it shows the

tetrarchs and emperors Diocletian and Maximian together with Galerius and Constantius in an embrace that symbolized the unity of the Roman empire.

227 top Two magnificent marble ambos flank the iconostases placed along the transept of Saint Mark's Basilica, composed of three sections. A late-14th-century silver crucifix by Marco Benato hangs over the central section, followed by the coeval statues of Our Lady of

Sorrows, St. John the Baptist, and the Apostles, located on the sides. Around the podium of the structure, a series of small windows open onto the crypt.

227 bottom With its "naturalistic" and careful geometric design, a Gothic rose window dating back to the 14th to 15th centuries contrasts pleasantly with the Byzantine splendor and the gold decoration of the transept of the St. Mark's Basilica.

228-229 The interior of St. Mark's is a treasure of mosaics. In the Dome of the Pentecost (left), the Holy Spirit in the form of a dove descends on the Apostles with tongues of fire. Between the two domes moments from the life of Christ alternate with holy episodes. The Ascension of Christ observed by the Twelve Apostles, two archangels and the Madonna is illustrated in the dome to the right.

230 bottom right *Every part of the Ducal Palace seems designed to astonish. An example is the so-called Golden Stairway, initially designed by Sansovino but finished by Scarpagnino in 1559. It was given this name for the richness of its ornamentation in white and gilded stuccowork.*

231 top left *The Senate Room, which was popularly known as the Room of the Pregadi, was the seat of a formal body of 60 members elected by the Greater Council from among the noblemen who had distinguished themselves in public duties.*

231 bottom left *The Room of the Greater Council was the place the Venetian nobles used to make laws and to celebrate more solemn events. The impressive ceiling is covered with gold while the far wall is covered with Tintoretto's enormous fresco of Paradise.*

230-231 and 230 bottom left *The Ducal Palace was the seat of government of the Serenissima (Republic of Venice) and so had to truly represent the power and glory of the city. It was the residence of the Doge but also the seat of the Republic's principal magistratures, and the Public Archive. In some manner, it also performed the functions of the law-courts.*

231 top right *The sculpture depicting the "Drunkenness of Noah," by Lombard masters of the 14th-15th centuries, stands on the corner of the Ducal Palace facing the Paglia bridge.*

231 bottom right *Splendid marble reliefs – or, as in this example, proper sculptures – decorate the front and side façades of the Ducal Palace. A recurring theme is the Lion of St. Mark brandishing his sword or resting a paw on the open book "Pax tibi Marce Evangelista meus" (Peace be unto you, Mark, my apostle).*

232-233 The Rialto Bridge reflects the pale evening light over the Grand Canal, the main thoroughfare for gondolas, ferries and motorboats. The first version of the bridge was made in 1175 from wood and rested on boats. After the bridge was destroyed by fire, between 1588-91 architect Antonio da Ponte constructed the stone bridge based on a single arch 91 feet wide and 24 feet high.

232 bottom Ca' d'Oro is the pearl of Gothic Venetian architecture. Its name recalls the gilding which once covered the decorations and marblework. It was designed by the Lombard, Matteo Roverti, and the Venetians, Giovanni and Bartolomeo Bon. Now it is the home of the Giorgio Franchetti Gallery.

233 top The Benedictine buildings of San Giorgio Maggiore are colored by the reddish glow of sunset. The Palladian church, the bell tower, the monastery and their works in marble are the jewel on the "Island of Cypress Trees."

233 center The blue and white striped moorings rise from the Grand Canal like trees in a submerged forest. In the background, the splendid palazzi facing onto the canal draw the attention toward the Rialto Bridge.

233 bottom The success of tourism in Venice is based on the city's setting in the lagoon, but this same water continually invades the city and is the cause of the widespread belief that it is in constant danger. The city's attraction also derives from the hundreds of islands it is founded on, the approximately 500 canals that criss-cross it, and the more than 400 bridges that connect the islands.

234 top and bottom Gondolas are the unique and magical boats that characterize Venice as much as its canals and bridges. Elegant and festive or rustic and workmanlike, they slip through the water like enchanted black swans under the power of the elegant strokes of the gondolier. The details (in this case the decorations in wrought iron and the waterproofed canvas covering of the prow) illustrate the care and love endowed in their manufacture and use.

234-235 The Grand Canal winds through the city, dividing it into two parts. The colored "column" or "palazzo" moorings that line the canal to berth the gondolas are often decorated with a frieze or coat of arms. They also indicate the boundary of the water belonging to the palazzo outside which they stand.

235 top Some gondolas wrapped in their waxed covers are moored on the Riva degli Schiavoni after a day's work. The church of Santa Maria della Salute and Punta della Dogana can be seen in the background.

235 center Gondolas are still the best way to explore Venice from its canals. The curves and beauty of this unique means of transport are emphasized by the six-toothed iron symbol on the prow, known as the "comb," one tooth for each district of the city.

235 bottom Traditional carpentry tools for making boats and gondolas still exist at San Trovaso. The choice of materials is at least as crucial as the design and the construction itself. For a good quality gondola, eight different types of wood are required: deal, larch, cherry, walnut, elm, oak, lime and mahogany. The shape is decided by the maestro who refers to centuries-old designs. They are usually painted black.

236-237 *A soft orange light emphasizes the late-Renaissance forms of the church of Santa Maria della Salute. It was built as an act of thanksgiving after the plague of 1630 in one of the most attractive places in the city, in front of the dock at St. Mark's. Baldassare Longhena was the architect responsible for the unusual octagonal layout of the church.*

238-239 The lamps glow in the dark and slightly misty air that enfolds St. Mark's Square. It is dusk: Venice's "drawing room" is readying itself for another elegant evening and the bars begin to welcome their customers of all ages and provenance. This glimpse of the Serenissima from San Giorgio Maggiore is of disquieting beauty.

238 bottom A freezing winter's morning: the low sun reflects coldly in the Grand Canal as it peeps from behind Santa Maria della Salute but the plying of the gondolas, full of tourists, never ceases. A sprinkling of snow on the roofs and domes accentuates the dreamy atmosphere.

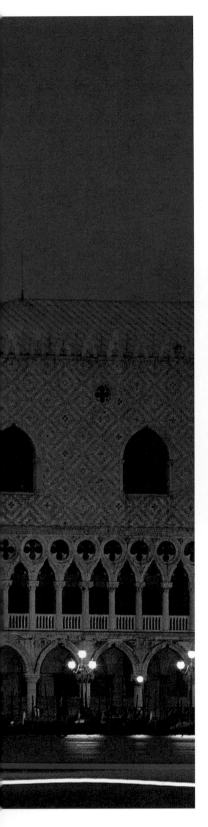

239 top left Riva degli Schiavoni is the natural extension of St. Mark's Square to the east. This wonderful promenade over the many bridges offers superb views over San Giorgio Maggiore (see photograph) and glimpses of Venice's history; for example, the Bridge of Sighs that connects the Ducal Palace to the Prisons.

239 bottom left The Caffè Florian is probably the oldest of the bars in St. Mark's Square. The luxurious interior, the vaguely middle-European atmosphere, the elegance of the furnishings and the style of the staff have always made it one of the city's most exclusive haunts.

239 top right The evening shadows fall over the Clocktower and the Moors, the figures that ring the hours. The tower was built around 1496, probably to the design of Renaissance architect Mauro Coducci who was also responsible for the façade of the church of St. Zachary and the two palazzi, Zorzi and Correr. The Clocktower has an enamelled and gilded face that indicates the time, the phases of the moon, and the movement of the sun.

239 bottom right With its sophisticated Renaissance architecture and colored marble façade looking onto the Grand Canal, Ca' Dario is a splendid building. Its fame, however, is sinisterly linked to a curse that seems to have weighed on its owners, often condemned to a violent death.

241 top During the Fascist era, architect Marcello Piacentini and other famous town-planners worked to give Genoa the air of the maritime capital that the Mussolini government wished it to be. The influence of the reorganization of that time is still felt in Piazza Vittoria and the district that fronts the railway station at Brignole, where old residential areas were replaced by wide roads, squares and monuments.

241 bottom The lighthouse that shines out to sea in front of the port of Genoa is called simply "La Lanterna" by the Genoese. It is 380 feet high, can be seen from 33 miles away, and has been taken up as the symbol of the city.

LIGURIA:

PORTS OF ART AND COMMERCE

240 top left The sea-facing façade of Palazzo San Giorgio is the first glimpse of Genoa for incoming sailors. The frescoes in the building were painted by Raimondo Sirotti on 17th-century designs by Tavarone. The fresco of St. George killing the dragon underlines the religious and sea-going affinity between Genoa and England.

240 top right Via XX Settembre, designed in 1892, is one of Genoa's most important streets. Today it is a parade of elegant shops, cinemas, restaurants and bars; it is always busy and full of traffic.

240-241 The soul of the city of Genoa is its port. Historically, the city's fortunes have depended entirely on its maritime traffic. The port is huge, among the best equipped in Europe, and has for the last few years been undergoing restoration work aimed at recovering buildings in disuse. In general, the port is an area that risked remaining detached from the rest of the city.

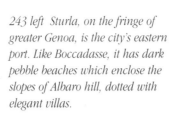

243 left Sturla, on the fringe of greater Genoa, is the city's eastern port. Like Boccadasse, it has dark pebble beaches which enclose the slopes of Albaro hill, dotted with elegant villas.

243 top right The line of houses facing the sea and the small, stony beaches are all that there is at Boccadasse, one of Genoa's outlets to the sea. Yet the village is besieged by city residents every weekend and on late summer afternoons.

243 bottom right Porto Maurizio is one of two villages that merged to form Imperia; the other is Oneglia, now an industrial and commercial center. The former is the old center of the city, its medieval buildings stand on a narrow promontory, called locally the Paraxo.

242-243 The long arterial street, Corso Italia, is lined with sea-bathing facilities. At the end of the Corso stands the village of Boccadasse.

242 bottom left The entire city of Savona is built around its port which was first its pride and later its hope for centuries. Fishing and sail boats today line the old port .

242 bottom right The wharves of La Spezia were considered by Napoleon to be part of "the loveliest port in the world." The city is now Italy's largest military port.

245 top Built at the request of Maria Louise, estranged wife of Napoleon, the Teatro Regio is one of Parma's most important buildings. Parma is a rich Emilian city for which opera is almost a religion.

245 center Famous for a Charterhouse that never existed except in Stendhal's novel, Parma has a wealth of architectural and art treasures including the unfinished Palazzo della Pilotta and the Baptistery.

245 bottom The church of St. John the Baptist was built in Parma in the 15-16th centuries. It has frescoes by Correggio, wooden choirstalls and, in the Benedictine monastery next door, a beautiful library in the Sala Capitolare.

BOLOGNA:
IN THE HEART OF EMILIA

244 top left Bologna is the capital of wealthy and industrious Emilia Romagna which is also rich in artistic and architectural treasures. Bononia was founded as an Ibero-Ligurian settlement; it was called Felsina by the Etruscans and Bolonia by the Romans. It experienced a period of prosperity between the 12th and 15th centuries when the University was established. The historical center and the city towers, symbol of the city, are reminders of that flourishing past.

244 top right Asinelli Tower, seen here from Piazza Maggiore, stands at one end of Via Rizzoli. The tower was built during the 12th century for military purposes.

244-245 Palazzi of great beauty face onto Piazza Maggiore (called Piazza Grande by the Bolognese). Two of them are the City Hall, altered in the 15-16th centuries, and the Gothic cathedral of St. Petronius.

246-247 Lucca is a city with a profusion of art treasures within its walls. It used to be the seat of the Marquis of Tuscany; it was an independent city and maintained its political pre-eminence in Tuscany until the 19th century. It retains few traces of its Roman past but the unmistakable appearance of Piazza del Mercato built over the 2nd-century amphitheater illustrates how much of that era has characterized the modern layout of the city.

246 top St. Michael in Foro is a church in the Pisan-Luccan style from the 12th century with a façade that was added during the 14th century. Its appearance is similar to other Tuscan churches of the same period: tall, slender arcades topped by several rows of small loggias running from the center outward to the bell tower. The triple-nave interior contains magnificent works by Luca della Robbia and Filippino Lippi.

247 bottom St. Frediano is a beautiful church in Lucca built around the mid-12th century over an early-Christian basilica of which some remains can be seen inside. The sober façade, uplifted in the 1200s and fitted with a massive crenellated bell tower, is enlivened by a mosaic of the "Ascension of Christ" attributed to the pupils of the Berlinghieri. Despite undergoing heavy restoration in the last century, it still retains the expressive power and colors typical of the Lucca school in that period. The interior is also worthy of a visit: in particular, the 12th-century holy-water stoup and the Trenta Chapel with works by Jacopo della Quercia.

LUCCA:

THE WALLED CITY

247 top Overlooked by a lovely lunette portraying the Annunciation (in background of photo), the font of the church of San Frediano represents one of the most valuable 12th-century sculptural works in Lucca. The sculptor was Robertus Magister, who came up with the concept of a large external pool composed of six parts joined by metal tenons, decorated with illustrations of the prophets and episodes from the life of Moses. Inside, a smaller basin on a pedestal is decorated with portrayals of the Apostles and by an "almanac" with the months and their related farming tasks.

249 top The statue of Cosimo I de' Medici stands over Piazza dei Cavalieri (Square of the Knights), the heart of Pisa rebuilt and ennobled by Vasari in the 16th century. Details of the friezes on Palazzo dei Cavalieri can be seen in the background: this too was rebuilt by Vasari and today is the seat of the University.

249 bottom In Piazza dei Cavalieri, at the base of the statue of Cosimo I, sculpted in the late 14th century by Pietro Francavilla, this beautiful but time-worn fountain is the work of the same master. The French sculptor was actually named Pierre Francheville and worked in Italy as of 1574. Toward the end of his career and life, he was recalled to France by King Henry IV, who became a great admirer of his renowned Orpheus, today displayed at the Louvre.

PISA:

MIDWAY BETWEEN ART AND UNIVERSITY

248 top left Tinged by the sunset, the palazzi along the banks of the River Arno at Pisa reflect orange. Famous for its stupendous Campo dei Miracoli, Pisa also has many other sites of rare beauty.

248 top right and 248-249 Campo dei Miracoli is the international symbol of Pisa, city of art and tourism like few others in Italy. This is not just a square where glorious examples of Romanesque architecture are grouped, it is an absolute and perfect set of buildings, even to the contrast of the green of the grass against the white of the marble, in which the imperfection of the Leaning Tower is set. The group of buildings in Campo dei Miracoli (baptistery, cathedral, tower and cemetery) was built over a period between the 11th and 13th centuries as a monument to God and a testament to the wealth the city had accumulated from shipping.

250 top The church of Santa Croce was begun on the design of Arnolfo di Cambio in 1294 but its façade (designed to complement the original style) was only completed in the 19th century. It is decidedly inferior to the other jewels of Florence. The church plays a unique role in the city and is the Florentine Pantheon where Alfieri, Machiavelli, Michelangelo, Vasari, Rossini and Ugo Foscolo are buried.

250 bottom The detail in the picture shows the beauty of the thin columns and fretwork of the arches in Giotto's bell tower, one of the marvels of Florence. The Tuscan artist only worked on the tower for three years before his death in 1337.

FLORENCE:
THE HEART OF THE RENAISSANCE

250-251 Piazza San Giovanni, better known as Piazza Duomo, is one of two crossroads in Florence: the other is Piazza della Signoria. The buildings it contains (cathedral, bell tower and baptistery) make it a smaller version of the Campo dei Miracoli in Pisa though no less valid artistically. Giotto's bell tower and Brunelleschi's dome dominate the city when seen from any point of view.

251 top left Piazzale Michelangelo on the road to San Miniato al Monte gives a magnificent view of Florence from south of the Arno. The square has a monument to the artist and is a favorite stop for visitors wanting to photograph the city.

251 top right Ponte Vecchio crosses the Arno near Palazzo Pitti and connects the Boboli Gardens with Piazza della Signoria. It is lined on both sides by craft shops and goldsmiths.

252 top left Santa Maria del Fiore is a masterpiece of Italian Gothic architecture. Work began on the site of the previous cathedral in 1296 based on the designs of Arnolfo di Cambio. When the architect died, others were employed on the project, including Giotto and Brunelleschi. The façade was rebuilt in the 19th century but several doors are the originals from the 14th century, for example, those of the bell tower.

252 bottom left Palazzo Medici-Riccardi, of which we see a glimpse of the courtyard, was built during the Renaissance by Michelozzo. It used to be the residence of Lorenzo the Magnificent and today houses the offices of the Prefecture.

252 top right Santa Maria del Fiore, the Baptistery and Giotto's bell tower form an architectural set that is famous around the world. Together, the monuments combine the best of western architecture between the 11th and 14th centuries. The greatest artists of the age worked on them, including Arnolfo di Cambio, Brunelleschi, Giotto and Ghiberti.

252 bottom right Santa Croce is a Franciscan basilica founded in 1228 and remodelled several times since. The entire structural basis and majestic interior of the original Gothic temple, praised by author Ugo Foscolo in his Sepolcri, still remain.

253 Palazzo Vecchio, started in 1299, was in the 19th century the seat of the government and the Chamber of Deputies for the Kingdom of Italy. It is now home to Florence City Council.

254 top right The original version of Michelangelo's David stands in the Galleria dell'Accademia but an identical copy is still shown in Piazza della Signoria next to the entrance to Palazzo Vecchio. The statue is an important work in the tormented career of an artist equally able to produce sculptural, pictorial and architectural masterpieces and who was the real precursor of the Baroque period.

254 bottom right The church of Santa Maria Novella is the first work of art seen by visitors arriving in Florence by train. It was begun in the mid-12th century and is a marvelously harmonious example of Italian Gothic architecture. The arches that adorn the façade were designed by Leon Battista Alberti, one of the masters of the Renaissance. Geometrical designs and floral decorations merge into a gentle classical motif.

254 left Among the superb monuments that adorn Piazza della Signoria, is the famous "Biancone" (fountain of Neptune's Chariot), a late 16th-century work by Bartolomeo Ammannati. This artist and architect also collaborated on the expansion of Pitti Palace.

254-255 Florence was founded on the banks of the River Arno and developed into a trove of artistic treasures. Cities like Florence are capable of producing, what is called the "Stendhal Syndrome," i.e., fainting induced in some people when confronted by the beauty and perfection of outstanding artistic creations.

255 bottom The Boboli Gardens created at the request of Eleonora, wife of Cosimo I. They are Florence's most important park. Their layout reflects late-Renaissance style with grottoes, avenues, fountains, large grassy areas and shaped hedges. The highest terraces of the gardens provide marvelous views over the city.

257 Siena's cathedral is lined with white and black marble, a flash of Gothic architecture in the center of a medieval, brick city. The artistically grandiose temple (shown by the beauty of the Romanesque bell tower (above) and the exuberant façade (below) was to become the transept of an immense church if the plans of the 14th century City Council had gone ahead. Unfortunately, events in the life of the city and the geological situation brought the project to a halt but the importance of the arcades of the unfinished building, now occupied by the Museum of the Metropolitan Opera, is clear to see.

SIENA:

A PEARL AMONG THE HILLS

256 top left The Palazzo Pubblico, built between 1288 and 1342, is one of Siena's most original and elegant examples of non-religious Gothic architecture. It features three brick sections with Guelph crenellations. It stands in the shadow of the Torre del Mangia, designed toward the mid-14th century by Minuccio and Francesco di Rinaldo.

256 top right Siena's cathedral was the fruit of the work of many artists from the mid-13th century. The interior and exterior have in common patterns in two-colored marble and enormous decorative richness.

256-257 Piazza del Campo is a reddish shell reached through a maze of alleys. It has a natural slope. It is the center of Siena and the site of the twice yearly Palio horse-race, a tradition at the heart of what it means to be Sienese.

258 top *The rich trading town of San Gimignano developed on the Via Francigena, the most important route during the Middle Ages. The richest families built houses with towers, for defensive reasons and for status—the higher the tower, the greater the status of the family. During its richest period, San Gimignano had 65 towers but today only 8 remain. The photograph shows Piazza della Cisterna where the inhabitants have drawn drinking water for over 800 years.*

SAN GIMIGNANO:
CITY OF THE TOWERS

258 bottom *A cycle of frescoes by Barna da Siena, Stories from the New Testament, decorates the right-hand nave of the Collegiata, San Gimignano's 12th-century cathedral. The church was also decorated by other artists such as Taddeo di Bartolo, Benozzo Gozzoli, Bartolo di Fredi and Domenico Ghirlandaio.*

258-259 *The view of San Gimignano from the hills of Val d'Elsa. The towers, like early skyscrapers, are evidence of the wealth the medieval town accumulated trading local products: Vernaccia wine, saffron, and decorated leather products.*

259 top *The History of St. Fina is a cycle of late 15th-century frescoes by Domenico Ghirlandiao in San Gimignano cathedral (Death on the left, Burial on the right). The frescoes, like the architecture by Giuliano and Benedetto da Maiano, are artistic jewels.*

260 left Despite its severity and lack of ornamentation, the cathedral of Arezzo is unquestionably majestic. The steps lead to a standard three-nave interior decorated with frescoes and large windows. The left-hand nave has a famous fresco Mary Magdalene, by Piero della Francesca, painted in the 16th century.

260 top right The ruins of the Cistercian Abbey of St. Galgano stand in the countryside between Siena and Arezzo. It was founded by a nobleman who retired here as a hermit but by the early 15th century the building had already begun to fall down, leaving the naves open to the sky.

AREZZO:
IN THE LAND OF GOLD

260 bottom right Piazza Grande in Arezzo, like Piazza del Campo in Siena, has a natural slope. It is surrounded by the city's most important buildings: the Palazzo del Tribunale, Palazzo della Fraternita' dei Laici and the Palazzo delle Logge, this last designed by Giorgio Vasari.

261 The 13th-century church of St. Francis looks over the square of the same name in the old walled city of Arezzo. The church is to all intents an art museum: it contains Piero della Francesca's extraordinary cycle of frescoes, The Story of the True Cross, which gathers all the themes and forms of Renaissance painting into one work.

UMBRIA AND MARCHE:
THE GREEN HEART OF ITALY

263 bottom left Situated on the edge of a large green hollow, Gubbio unites the natural beauty of its district with artistic masterpieces and monuments from the Middle Ages. Via dei Consoli and Via Baldassini are the ancient roads that pass through the town and are the sites of the most important buildings: the church of St. John the Baptist, the Consuls' Palace (respectively in the picture), the Ducal Palace and the church of St. Francis.

263 top right Urbino is joint provincial capital with Pesaro and a jewel that lies in the hills of Marche. The old center is ringed by ancient walls and is an incomparable treasure of Renaissance architecture.

263 bottom right Construction of the Ducal Palace in Urbino was started in 1444 by Maso di Bartolomeo and then transformed many times. Inside there is a "Courtyard of Honor" which is considered the highest expression of civil Renaissance architecture.

264-265 Filippo Lippi painted the magnificent Coronation of the Virgin Mary in the apse of the cathedral of Spoleto, his birthplace, around 1460, at the end of his career as a painter. The fresco, which was completed by his son Filippino, is part of a cycle of the Life of the Virgin Mary, including the Nativity, the Annunciation, the Death of the Virgin, and of course, the Coronation. The artist was buried in the right transept of the church.

262 Standing on a hill over a wide Umbrian valley, Spoleto has maintained its appearance of an important medieval town (it used to be the capital of a Longobard duchy before being passed to the Catholic Church). Its cathedral was built at the end of the 12th century and partially retouched in the 17th. Its severe Romanesque façade is original while the bell tower dates from the 16th century.

263 top left Todi has also managed to maintain its noble medieval appearance. Piazza del Popolo was built over the original Roman forum and is one of Italy's most beautiful squares. Facing onto it are the Priors' Palace, the People's Palace, the Captain's Palace and, from the top of a symbolic flight of steps, the Gothic cathedral, begun in the 11th century and completed between the 12th and 16th centuries.

ORVIETO:

THE CITY THAT STANDS ON TUFA

266 The history of the city of Orvieto, built on a steep hill of tufa, goes back to before the Classical era. It was inhabited long before the Etruscans took it over, then passed to the Romans and then flourished during the Middle Ages with the name of Urbs Vetus. Its medieval wealth is still apparent in the artistic heritage of the two squares, Piazza Duomo and Piazza del Popolo.

267 Orvieto cathedral was built between 1290-1330 following the most classical dictates of Italian Gothic architecture. Its façade, designed by Maitani and finished in the 16th century, is heavily decorated with sculptures and mosaics. Pinnacles, loggias, columns and delicate marble filigree render the cathedral visually interesting and confer on it a sense of lightness. The interior and the museum hold masterpieces by Simone Martini, Signorelli and Andrea Pisano.

268 top Perugia was originally a Neolithic settlement. It then became an independent city-state and is now a rich, industrial city. Yet it retains traces of its past in the layout of the town and in its principal buildings. Perugia's artistic heritage is mainly to be seen in the Oratory of St. Bernadino, the city's most important Renaissance building, a 15th-century masterpiece by Agostino di Duccio.

PERUGIA, ASSISI AND NORCIA:
ON THE TRAIL OF ST. FRANCIS

268 center The Basilica of St. Francis of Assisi is one of the Christian world's most famous churches. It was probably designed by Brother Elia, spiritual son of St. Francis and second in command of the Order. The church was begun in 1228 and consecrated in 1253.

268 bottom The statue of St. Benedict, born in Norcia, seems to protect the square named after him. In the background stands the cathedral built in 1560.

268-269 Assisi is a city of remarkable cultural, environmental and artistic resources; it is also a place of pilgrimage for followers of the Christian faith.

269 top Meetings of Perugia City Council used to take place in the Sala delle Udienze in the Collegio dei Cambi (left) and the Sala dei Notari in the Palazzo dei Priori (right). The first was decorated by Perugino in the late 15th century; the second by Roman masters who were already working on the Basilica of St. Francis of Assisi.

270-271 *The Basilica of St. Francis contains two churches, the Lower and the Upper, decorated with frescoes by Giotto and Cimabue. The lower of the two seems like a church in a crypt and acts as a foundation for the upper one. They have low ceilings, wide cross vaults and stupendous 14th-century decorations. The vault is embellished with allegories of the three virtues – Poverty, Chastity and Obedience – and the fresco of* The Triumph of St. Francis *by Giotto and his school.*

270 bottom *The center of the single nave in the Lower Church of St. Francis of Assisi is magnificent yet not heavy with decoration. Contributors to its wall-frescoes were Andrea da Bologna, the so-called Maestro of St. Francis, Giotto, Cimabue and Pietro Lorenzetti.*

271 top right *The left transept of the Lower Church of St. Francis has frescoes by Pietro Lorenzetti:* The Crucifixion *(photograph),* Madonna with Child *and SS. Francis and John,* The Descent from the Cross *and* The Deposition in the Sepulcher. *Clearly influenced by Giotto and his school, Lorenzetti was one of the masters of 14th-century Italian painting.*

271 bottom right *Pietro Lorenzetti painted this* Entrance to Jerusalem *during the 1320s. The new and important role of scenic elements is evident, in particular the details of the Gothic architecture that symbolizes Jerusalem. The fresco is part of the cycle that decorates the left transept of the Lower Church.*

271 left *The Chapel of St. Martin in the Lower Church was entirely decorated by Simone Martini, one of the precursors of international Gothic style. The fresco,* St. Mary Magdalene and St. Catherine of Alexandria, *was painted in 1317 along with the icons of other saints and wall paintings at the entrance to the chapel. Also present in the chapel is the cycle,* The History of St. Martin.

272 top left The cycle of frescoes by Giotto in the nave of the Upper Church of St. Francis of Assisi was begun in 1296. The subject (The Life of St. Francis) and the magnificence of their execution make them an absolute masterpiece of pre-Renaissance Italian painting. The lack of symbolism and the straightforwardness of the scenes reflect the social changes of the times: a class of craftsmen and merchants had been created which required spiritual education but linked to the objects of everyday existence. Indeed it is the commonplace that is the main element throughout all 28 episodes in the life of the saint (whose Order was at the height of its influence at the time): Francis is shown as a contemporary of Giotto – solid and dignified – and not at all the poor ingenuous soul he is traditionally portrayed to be.

272 bottom left Like other well-known episodes in the cycle of St. Francis, including Preaching to the Birds and Miracle of the Spring, this Gift of a Cloak to a Poor Man is characterized by a high degree of realism for the era in which it was painted. St. Francis is shown in a faithful reproduction of the environment Giotto lived in, shown by the architecture of the town in the background. There is little room here for symbolism or mysticism; all is related directly to the reality of the late 13th century.

272 right The splendid cross vault of the Upper Church contains superb geometrical and floral decorations that frame the frescoes. They exemplify the magnificence with which the Basilica of St. Francis of Assisi was ornamented. The frescoes of the four Doctors of the Church – St. Jerome, St. Augustine, St. Gregory and St. Ambrose – are attributed to Giotto as a young man and are believed to have been painted in about 1293.

272-273 The Upper Church of St. Francis of Assisi was built around the mid-13th century, the buildings of the religious complex were inaugurated two years before the death of the saint in 1226. As soon as the work was begun, the city became the heart of the Franciscan order. The friary contains two churches, one on top of the other. The Lower Church contains the tomb of St. Francis and therefore soon became a popular place of pilgrimage as well as being a place of sanctuary. The Upper Church was built using the lower one as a foundation; one of its purposes was its use for preaching (a crucial role of the Franciscan doctrine based on poverty and continual contact with the poorer members of society) and liturgical activities in general. The two churches each have a single nave, supported by long cylindrical beams and flying buttresses. The beautiful cross vaults and apse of the Upper Church (see photograph) are decorated with frescoes by Cimabue, now partially damaged. Besides taking many lives, the 1997 earthquake wrought incalculable artistic and historical harm which will require long and painstaking restoration.

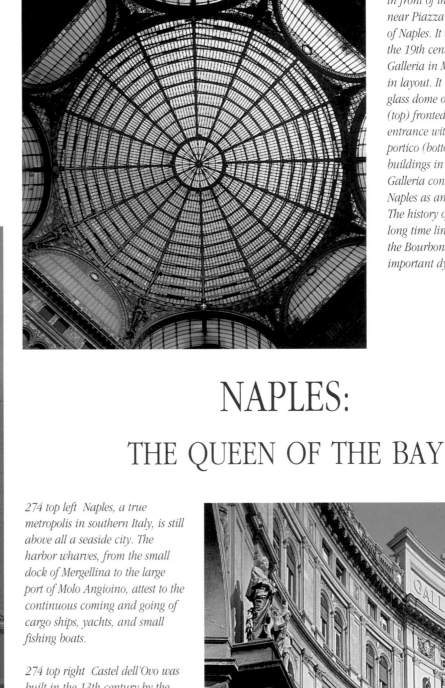

275 *The Galleria Umberto I stands in front of the Teatro San Carlo near Piazza Plebiscito, the center of Naples. It was built at the end of the 19th century and resembles the Galleria in Milan aesthetically and in layout. It is covered by an airy glass dome on an octagonal base (top) fronted by an enormous entrance with colonnade and portico (bottom). Like many other buildings in the old center, the Galleria contributes to the status of Naples as an international city. The history of Naples was for a long time linked to the fortunes of the Bourbons, one of Europe's most important dynasties.*

NAPLES:
THE QUEEN OF THE BAY

274 top left Naples, a true metropolis in southern Italy, is still above all a seaside city. The harbor wharves, from the small dock of Mergellina to the large port of Molo Angioino, attest to the continuous coming and going of cargo ships, yachts, and small fishing boats.

274 top right Castel dell'Ovo was built in the 13th century by the port of Santa Lucia. It is one of Naples' most famous buildings and a natural end to the promenade along the sea-front.

274-275 Mergellina at the foot of Posillipo at sunset. The sea-front of Via Caracciolo rings the bay; in the distance, Castel dell'Ovo is hidden in the evening mist.

BARI, BRINDISI AND LECCE:
IN THE HEART OF BAROQUE PUGLIA

277 top left *277 top left The port of Bari stretches between the old city and the Trade Fair area. The port is equipped for high volumes of international commercial shipping and also pleasure boats.*

277 top right The importance of Bari's past can be seen in the old city, laid out during the Middle Ages. The clear division between the old and new cities was the result of expansion during the Napoleonic era.

276 top The cathedral in Brindisi is an 18th-century restoration of the previous 12th-century Romanesque church. It stands in Piazza Duomo in the heart of the city with the Loggia Balsamo, Portico dei Cavalieri and Palazzo Vescovile. The old city is surrounded on three sides by the sea and was the center of an important port area during the Roman era.

276 bottom Santa Croce is Lecce's fullest example of Baroque architecture. It was built in the 16–17th centuries with a splendid façade filled with decorations of all kinds in which the contributions of the different sculptors commissioned during the various phases of work can be recognized.

276-277 Regional capital of Puglia and modern and dynamic city, Bari is the third largest city in southern Italy and sees itself as a bridge between the east and west of the Adriatic. The old city (see photograph) is wedged in the sea between the port and the modern city.

278 top left Palermo is the second largest city in southern Italy. Despite dramatic growth after World War II, the Sicilian capital has managed to maintain the heritage of its historic and artistic glory. It had been inhabited even before it became a Punic city called Ziz but then passed into the hands, in turn, of the Romans, the Byzantines, the Saracens and the Normans. Clear evidence has been left of the city's centuries-long domination by the Spanish.

278 center left The church of St. John of the Hermits stands in Via dei Benedettini. It is one of Palermo's most celebrated buildings. It was built on the wishes of Roger II in 1142 during Norman rule and shows clear eastern influences in the red domes and cloister.

278 bottom left The fountain in Piazza Pretoria was built for Don Pedro de Toledo and was bought by the Senate of Palermo in 1578, then erected in the square.

SICILY:
FROM MAGNA GRECIA TO THE THIRD MILLENNIUM

278 top right Palermo is a city of culture that has never stopped growing and which offers the visitor many surprises. For example, a bronze quadriga by local sculptor Mario Rutelli looks out from the top of the Politeama Garibaldi, built in the second half of the 19th century by architect Damiani Almeyda; some of the rich ornamentation of the façade is visible on the frieze.

278 bottom right The masterpiece of Norman architecture, Monreale's Cathedral, was built between 1172-89 on the edge of the city.

279 The 17th-century sanctuary of St. Rosalia stands on the slopes of Mt. Pellegrino with its slender towers pointing to the Sicilian sky.

280-281 Mt. Etna dominates
the city of Catania. In the
photograph, it overlooks a
building in late 19th-century style
that stands in the Bellini Garden.
The garden is the city's most
important park and is home to
animals and centuries-old trees.
It used to house a couple of
elephants which were so loved by
the residents that an elephant was
chosen as a symbol for the city.

280 bottom Mt. Etna seems to
peep over the port of Catania.
The port has been one of the two
engines that have brought wealth
to the city, one of the most
industrious and active in Sicily.
The other is the ancient
university.

281 top The stately city of Syracuse came into being in ancient times, originally founded by Corinthian settlers. It experienced alternating periods of turbulence and prosperity up until the year 1000 when it fell under Norman domination but, like the rest of Sicily, it was conquered by the kingdom of Aragon during the 14th century. The cycle of invasions and dominations however did not destroy the great Greek and Roman monuments which have turned the area into an important archeological site.

281 center The small town of Piazza Armerina on the slopes of the Erei mountains is a holiday resort and archeological site of major importance. The center is dominated by the 17th-century cathedral built over the remains of a 15th-century church. Not far from the town, the marvellous floor mosaics of Villa Romana del Casale can be seen, considered an extraordinary document of Roman art and customs.

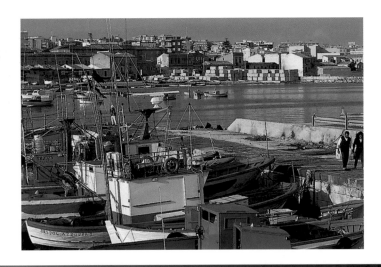

281 bottom At nearly 3,280 feet altitude, Enna is the highest provincial capital in Europe. It has attractive views over the Dittaino valley and inland Sicily. Originally a Byzantine stronghold, Enna flourished briefly during the Middle Ages and under Aragonese domination. Its most important buildings, the Lombard Castle and the cathedral, date from that period.

282 left Cefalù owes its name to the rock that stands over it, which from certain points of view resembles a head. The town was founded during the Greek era and did well under the Normans who left it a solemn monument— the cathedral. Built on the wishes of Roger II, it is one of Sicily's most beautiful buildings and dominates the skyline of the town.

282-283 The Baroque palazzi illuminated at dawn stand over the dark roofs of Ibla. This town was completely destroyed by the 1693 earthquake and rebuilt according to the taste then in vogue. Today it is almost a part of the city of Ragusa, built on the hill behind, and the two are connected by a series of bridges and steps.

283 bottom Erice stands on a rise of 2,600 feet near Trapani. It is internationally known for its Majorana Science Center. It looks like an intact medieval town with houses in the Arab-Spanish style, each with a patio. Among its monuments stands the Castle of Venus, so named because it was built over an ancient sanctuary of Venus.

284 top The Church of the Holy Trinity in Saccargia, south of Sassari, was founded in 1116. It is considered a masterpiece of Sardinian Romanesque architecture. It was given to the Camaldolese monks by Costantino di Torres who had it built in "Tuscan" style by Pisan stonemasons at the end of the 12th century. The placename means "the Friesian cow" in honor of a cow that was supposed to have knelt in front of an invisible spirit in this area.

284 center The Bastion of St. Rémy is one of the scenes decorating the castle in Cagliari built in Neo-classical style at the end of the 19th century.

SARDINIA:

THE TREAUSURES OF THE PROUD ISLAND

284 bottom Piazza d'Italia and Piazza Duomo are the two centers of life in Sassari. The Provincial Council has its offices in Palazzo Provinciale in Piazza d'Italia.

284-285 The capital, Cagliari, is Sardinia's most important city. The original settlements were colonised by the Phoenicians and Carthaginians. Its history is made up of a cycle of invasions and dominations but it experienced a period of particular splendor under the kingdom of Aragon and the Spanish. The city's most important buildings, grouped in the acropolis, all date from those eras.

285 top Alghero owes its name to the abundance of seaweed around its foundations ("alguer" is the Catalan word for seaweed). It is a beautiful city on the north-western coast of Sardinia. Founded in the 12th century, it has an exceptional church, St. Michael, (right) with a dome covered in colored majolica tiles.

Festivals, traditions and folklore of an ancient people

286 left *The largest and healthiest cows are the winners in the "Battle of the Queens" that takes place on the third Sunday of October in Valle d'Aosta. The award is contested at the final at Croix Noir among successful contestants from the knock-out stages, all of whom must be in calf. The most impressive cows confront one another and the ones that take a step backward are eliminated. The final winner is covered with garlands of flowers and paraded.*

Songs sung during harvest time and those sung on the festival of the patron saint; the ceremonies that signal the end of the farming year or the start of spring; the competitions and contests between rival quarters of a city; parades, processions during Carnival and Holy Week, exorcisms, spells and counter-spells. To subsume these topics and all the others in which a people manifests its collective spirit and culture in one collective noun, W.J. Thoms, the English antiquarian, coined the term "folklore" in 1846.

In Italy, this word takes on even greater meaning than in other countries for geographical, social and historical reasons. Its position in the center of the Mediterranean and its connection to the heart of Europe have made it a land open to all surrounding peoples and civilisations. The richness and variety of its scenery, its historical capacity to produce culture, its having been the cradle of Christianity and Latinism but also, in large measure and for many hundreds of years, a country of peasant subsistence, have give the peoples that lived here an unusual capacity to assimilate different mentalities, experiences and cultural expressions, to fuse them with their own, adapt them to their own spirit and to express them in authentic and original ways in its own folklore.

Today Italy is one of the major industrial powers in the world, but its farming roots are still very much evident and influential. The ancient ceremonies can still be seen in the repetition of the thousand celebrations each year, though not perhaps understood very deeply, that so charmed travelers to Italy in the 19th century such as Goethe.

286 top right and 287 *The traditional costumes of the valley of Gressoney are brightly colored and embroidered. The stiff head-covering for women ends with ribbons sewn with gold thread.*

286 bottom right *Carnival in the mountains, such as the one in the valley of Gran San Bernardo, is based on unchanged customs dating back to ancient times.*

288-289 *The contest is the culminating moment of the Sartiglia in Oristano. It begins with the dressing of the rider by priestesses who then lift him onto his horse to ensure his feet do not touch the ground. He then blesses the crowd with a bunch of violets and periwinkles while the crowd in turn showers him with corn and flowers.*

288 top left and 289 top
All the riders in costume in the procession during the Sartiglia wear female masks and men's clothing. The cumponidori *however is androgynous and wears both women's and men's clothing. After the contest, in which the riders have to skewer a ring in a star with their swords or lances, the procession moves off to an area where the town wall once stood and where two*

towers remain. Here they undertake a series of daring acrobatic feats in what was once the moat. A group of three or four horses gallop side by side while the riders—either two to a horse or standing on the horse's back— perform acrobatics to the sound of trumpets and roll of drums. These equestrian tricks were believed in the past to strengthen the walls by creating a magic circle around them.

Spring representing the awakening of nature and the season of love is the spirit of many ancient popular and traditional ceremonies while marriage services which reflect rustic fertility rites often are part of many public festivals. Several of these, for example the *Sartiglia* of Oristano in Sardinia, repeat interesting ancient initiation rites. The *Sartiglia* is held on the last Sunday and Tuesday of Carnival. The festival begins with a long parade in brightly colored medieval costume in ancient Spanish or Sardinian styles. Then a sort of jousting competition takes place where the riders have to run their sword or a lance through a star-shaped ring hanging from a cord while at the gallop. Unlike other forms of Carnival which are generally comical or satirical, the *Sartiglia* is calm, almost solemn. Masks are used purely to indicate theatrical or ritual characters and the most important moment of the ceremony is the strictly ceremonial investiture of the *componidori* (the principal rider whose task it is to skewer the star first) but the whole procedure maintains complex and allegorical meanings. The young man is taken to a setting decked out with branches, leaves and flowers and is prepared by a group of women known as *massaieddas* under the guidance of a senior woman known as *sa massaia manna*. The young man is made to sit on a seat placed on a table and, from that moment on, may not touch the ground with his feet. He is dressed by the younger women with a white shirt decorated with colored ribbons over his own costume. His face is made up like a woman's, a wedding veil is placed over his head and, on top of

that, a black top hat. He is then carried onto his horse and given a bunch of violets and periwinkles to hold; the bunch of flowers is known as *sa pippia de maiu* (young girl of May) and is a symbol of male and female together. The *componidori* then blesses the crowd as he is showered in grain and flowers. Finally, he is ready to ride to the jousting ring with the other riders whose faces are also made up like women's but who wear men's costumes. The result of the jousting tournament is taken as an omen for the new farming year while the outcomes of other cavalcades have no significance and are considered simply tests of skill. When this phase of the festival is finished, the procession moves on to another site for exhibitions of expertise and daring. Groups of three or four riders gallop side by side while riders acrobatically move from one mount to another to the accompaniment of trumpets and the roll of drums. Italian folklore has many examples of worship of the solstices which have remained at the root of Christian festivals in December. December 25th, the birth of Christ, also used to be a Roman festival. Magical rites, divination and Christian religion are mixed in representations that celebrate the nativity and which, in some places, involve processions of hundreds of people with sheep, horses, oxen and pigs to the place of the birth.

288 bottom left, 288 bottom right, 289 bottom The modern version of the Sartiglia dates from the Spanish domination of Sardinia and its name probably comes from the Castilian word sortija *meaning ring (what the riders have to catch on their lances while at the gallop). The last Monday of Carnival the celebration, called Sartiglietta, is reserved for children who present the adult version in every detail.*

The festival that more than any other
fuses pagan rites, Christian spirituality,
magic, exorcism, history, legend, playfulness
and death is Carnival. The roots of Carnival
go back to the Roman *lupercali,* rituals that
took place in mid-February in which the
luperci, young men consecrated to the god
Pan, ran nude holding the skins of sacrificed
goats that they used to lash sterile women.
This was a propitiatory ceremony to
celebrate the end of a period of sterility
(winter) and the onset of fertility (spring).

This pagan rite did not disappear with the advent of Christianity but was transformed and became part of the new religious and cultural context. During Carnival, ugly puppets and masks are paraded (representing winter) which get battered, damaged and are ultimately destroyed; alternatively, symbolic characters (scapegoats for the excesses that take place during Carnival celebrations or during the year) are burned.

For the hundreds of years between

medieval times and the 18th century, Carnival represented the negation of constituted order and the principles that governed social behavior; it was "the world turned upside-down" in which there were no prohibitions and where the exchange of roles between the governed and the governors was permitted. At one time in Rome, Carnival was celebrated by a carriage of mad people touring the city with the keys to the asylum in their hands. In many places, mask wearers were allowed to enter houses without identifying themselves; another custom was to sprinkle flour and soot over passers-by (today that mixture has happily become confetti). Modern day Carnival is celebrated throughout the towns and villages of Italy with different festivals and ceremonies. The most well-known are those of Venice and Viareggio. Carnival in Venice brings great crowds in masks and fancy dress into the lanes, campiellos and squares for an entire week. Dressing up has always been central to Carnival in this city. Venetians, whether courtesans, beggars, debtors, ruffians, rich or poor, have always loved putting on their masks to escape identification even outside Carnival time. This habit became so common and was considered so dangerous that a law was passed in 1268 prohibiting the use of masks at any other than the Carnival period. The festival still follows the ancient ritual with the flight of the dove in St. Mark's to open proceedings, then the parade of boats on the Grand Canal on the Saturday before Easter and the burning of Pantaloon (a character representing miserliness) on Shrove Tuesday in St. Mark's Square.

The Carnival in Viareggio is the most spectacular in Italy where 16 floats process through the town inspired by Italian and international politics; this follows the Carnival tradition of making fun of those in power. Besides these there is a group of fifteen or so similarly masked revellers and others in varying costumes. The first Carnival celebration took place in Viareggio in 1873 when the place was a large naval town. The procession was made up of decorated carts and small allegorical constructions, later came carts dedicated to the triumph of progress and universal peace and, finally, the mood turned to political satire. The first parades wound along Via Regia which stretched inland from the sea but in 1921 the route was changed to the seafront. During that period the locals learned to use papier-mâché which was of great effect in producing unusual effects. A profession was born, that of the *carristi* (cart-decorators), at which they are still masters.

291 right The Carnival in Viareggio was started in 1873 as a public masquerade. Now it has the largest parade of floats in Italy on which the locals work the whole year round. When the floats parade down the sea-front, it is a marvelous sight: some are 65 feet high and 33 wide. The symbolic figure of Viareggio's Carnival, is King Burlamacco, as fat as Falstaff and just as cheerful, leads the procession, often accompanied by an actress or television star in costume. Other events that take place during Carnival are feasts in the different quarters of the town, gastronomic fairs, theatrical and puppet shows, exhibitions, sports competitions, concerts and open-air dancing.

292 top and 293 bottom right The first palio in Siena, dedicated to the Madonna of Provenzano, takes place on July 2nd. The second, dedicated to the Madonna of the Assumption, is held on August 16th. The Madonna is the patron of the city, which has been known as the civitas Virginis *(City of the Virgin) since 2 September 1260 when Siena officially gave her its allegiance by deed. To experience the Palio in Siena to the full, the visitor must arrive in the city at least four days before the race and stay a few more afterward. This allows time to enjoy the preparations, the ceremonies (such as the blessing of the horse in the church in each city quarter), open air dinners for the whole district at enormous tables, and the dazzling procession in Piazza del Campo that accompanies the palio itself (the portrait of the Madonna) or* cencio *as it is called in Siena.*

292-293 and 293 left During the race the only thing that matters is winning. There are no rules at the Palio and it is not unusual for riders to be bribed by rival quarters. Only 10 riders of the 17 quarters can take part in the race and they are selected on a rotating basis. The 7 excluded the previous time race plus 3 chosen at random.

293 top right and center The ceremony at the beginning of the race is complex; it is directed by a starter who attempts to line the horses up. Once the 'off' is given and the tension rises even further, the jockeys have to circle the piazza three times. The race only lasts 80 seconds during which anything can happen—the jockeys might use their whips on the horses of their rivals to distract them and even on other jockeys! Blocking rivals or pushing them toward the barriers is quite legal and if a jockey falls, his horse can go on to win riderless.

The Italian August Bank Holiday (*ferragosto*) is rooted in Roman tradition. It is the modern version of the *feriae Augusti*, the celebrations for Augustus. In Italy it is traditional to celebrate this day with competitions, tests of skill, processions and parades of carts that carry gifts to the churches. The Palio between the quarters of the city of Siena is the most well-known example of *ferragosto* celebrations. It goes back to equestrian sports practiced by the Etruscans, which continued through the Middle Ages. Today the passion of the medieval tussles are still as frenzied as they have ever been and the ceremony involved in the presentation of the horses, the course trials in Piazza del Campo, the noisy dinners before and after the race and the processions in costume is no less diminished. Whoever wins (even a horse alone if the rider has been thrown) is presented with the portrait of the Madonna (palio), which is then carried into church for a thanksgiving *Te Deum*. The festival finishes in the victor's quarter with a feast.

294 left and bottom A splendid procession through the streets of Siena to the Piazza del Campo precedes the Palio. Fourteen groups take part in the procession with a total of 600 people on foot to the sound of drums and trumpets and to the sway of the banners. The costumes are perfect copies of original medieval dress. Each quarter bears its standards which, in the photographs from top to bottom, are of the following quarters: the Dragon, the Wolf, the Goose, and the Snail.

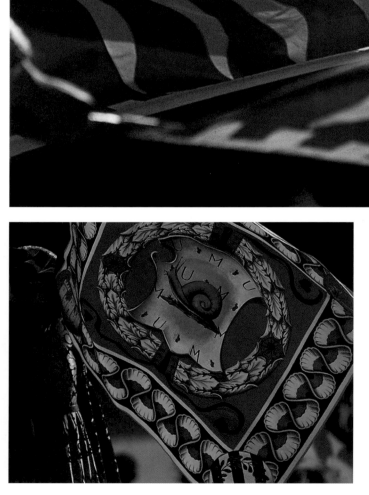

294-295 There are 17 quarters in Siena, symbolized here by flags. Life in each becomes especially animated during the period immediately prior to and after the Palio. Three days before the race the presentation of the horses and practice runs take place. On the eve of the race, the quarters taking part organize huge open-air dinners for all their members and their friends.

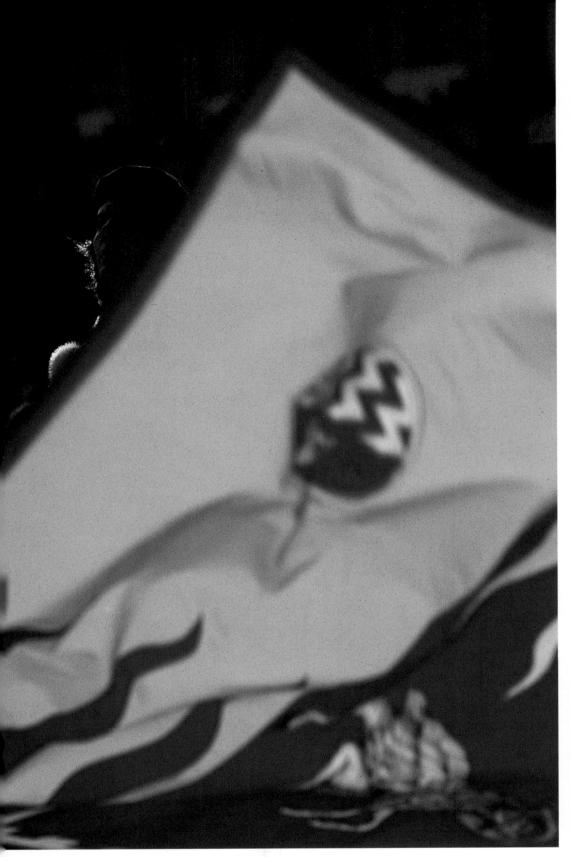

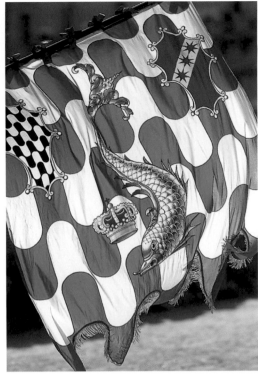

295 bottom left Each jockey wears the symbol of his quarter— in this case a turtle for the quarter of the same name. The horses taking part are treated with maximum care and attention before the race to ensure that they are not interfered with by rival quarters. The competitor is actually the horse and not the rider as a horse may win whether its jockey is still mounted or not.

295 right The Palio of Siena opens with a large historical procession preceded by flag-bearers like those of the Wave (top) or those of Valdimontone (bottom). They constantly practice their techniques, which are handed down from father to son. The reason for such dedication is that the higher the flag reaches, the more advantageous it is to the quarter, but if it should be dropped, bad luck ensues.

296-297 and 296 bottom The Palio at Asti is run on the third Sunday in September and ends a period of festivals started with the Douja d'Or at the beginning of September. The Douja d'Or is the presentation for production of the best wine. At the end of the second week of September, a festival of country cooking takes place with typical local dishes prepared in the piazza by 50 representatives of the Asti province and with parades of local groups in costume. This period is an orgy for lovers of good food and drink. Then come the "propitiatory" dinners in the 21 quarters and villages that participate in the Palio. When Sunday arrives, a historical procession with 1200 participants in medieval costume takes place. The procession is started by the winning quarter of the previous year's Palio and is followed by all the others. When they arrive in Piazza Alfieri, the Palio begins. First there are the elimination stages, then the final when the horses are ridden bareback.

The Palio in the city of Asti is run on the third Sunday of September. It is a very old festivity which goes back at least to 1275. On the first Saturday of May, the Mayor officially announces the race. Organisation of the event then starts, particularly of the historical procession. On the day of the race, the horses and riders are blessed, each wearing the colors of one of the 14 quarters in the city or of the municipalities round about. The procession starts in the afternoon which involves 300 horses and 1200 people. They wear costumes made from brocade and velvet copied from the miniatures in the 13th century "Codex Astensis" and from the frescoes in the churches. The entire city is in party mood. The colors of the quarter that won the previous year lead the procession. The parade includes the *carroccio*, a large

297 right It was only in 1967 that Asti Palio again took up the tradition that dates back to 1275. This consists of two separate parts: first, the offer of the Palio itself (a bright red sheet of cloth) to the church of San Secondo which takes place on the first Tuesday of May and marks the start of the celebrations in honor of the city's patron saint; and second, the race itself in September. The race is preceded by propitiatory ceremonies in the parish churches of the city and by a splendid procession in costume from Piazza Cattedrale through the streets of the center to the course. The procession consists of the Carroccio, 100 or so horses and 1200 people wearing the colors of their quarter. There are damsels, knights, pages, armour-bearers, drummers, standard-bearers, flag-bearers, grooms, the Captain of the Palio, officials and the prize-bearers. The race, as in Siena, has no rules—anything goes—the only thing is to win.

297 left The members of the procession wear splendid clothes made from brocade and velvet copied from miniatures in the 13th-century Codex Astensis and from frescoes in the churches. Utmost care is taken in the reproduction of these costumes: every little detail must be correct so as to make the event as representative as possible. The procession is not just a bit of folklore but celebrates some of Asti's proudest historical moments. The Palio at Asti, like that in Siena, attracts a large number of tourists.

farm cart pulled by pairs of oxen, on which the standard of the city is displayed, and a bell, the Martinella, is carried whose tones mark the marching rhythm of the warriors. The riders that take part in the race are often those who race in the Palio of Siena; they ride bareback and without spurs using only bridles, reins and knees to guide the horses. The race is made up of six knockout rounds and a final. The winning horses from each round compete in the final around a course of 460 yards in Piazza Alfieri.

298 bottom left and right
In November 1974, a group of Venetians, who already organized a regatta for six-oared boats, met on the island of Burano on the feast day of St. Martin to give life to a unique, noncompetitive rowing event for any type of boat provided it was powered by oars. The event has met with such success each year that now there are more than 3,000 participants from all over the world. The course starts at Bacino San Marco and passes by Burano, Mazzorbo, Madonna del Monte and San Giacomo in Paludo; it then enters Murano via the island's own Grand Canal and heads for Venice. It passes Cannaregio, works its way down the Grand Canal and ends at the Customs in front of St. Mark's.

298 top left and 299 The Venice Regatta, as it has been called since 1889, is held on the first Sunday of September (the name comes from the word remigata meaning a rowing race). The first regatta was held on the Grand Canal on 16 September 1274. Now it is Venice's great festival when the inhabitants hang cloths, tapestries and damasks out on the balconies and roof-terraces along the Canal to welcome the many unusual boats in the procession, among which are the Bucintoro and the Bissona. Today the Regatta culminates with the race of the two-oared gondolas although at one time galleys with twenty or fifty oars participated. On arrival at Ca' Foscari, the winners receive a multicolored banner and the last a booby prize of a suckling pig.

300 top On the second Sunday of May in Camogli, the "Padellata" (padella meaning pan) takes place, a large festival dedicated to fish. The festival has its origin with a vow made on a terrible night during World War II when a group of youths, who had gone out to sea to fish, entered an area planted with mines. Nevertheless they were able to return to land without damage and with their nets full. The local population were so grateful that they decided to offer their entire catch of a night and a day to St. Fortunato once a year.

300 bottom The festival of Corpus Domini is usually in June and is celebrated with processions. It is not unusual for whole streets to be decorated with carpets of flowers, the "Infiorate," herein Diano Marina. All of the road to be covered by the procession becomes a carpet of bright colors.

300-301 and 301 bottom left On the night before the feast, bonfires burn on the beach as the villagers wait for the boats to return to port. In the morning an enormous pan measuring more than 13 feet in diameter is brought to the port square. This is used to fry the two tons of newly caught fish which

are then offered to the spectators as a sign of prosperity. When the fish is offered, the saying is "San Fortunato, pesce regalato" (St. Fortunato, a fish offered) and it is believed that whoever eats this fish will have peace and prosperity all year. The festival closes with a procession and a fireworks display.

301 top right On the first Sunday in August, the same town of Camogli honors the Stella Maris (Star of the Sea) which corresponds to the Madonna, protectress of sailors and all those on the sea. The procession of boats decorated with holy markings makes its way from Camogli and Punta Chiappa where there is an image of the Madonna. In the darkness, the colored lights make an attractive sight as they are reflected in the water.

301 bottom right On the evening of 14 August in Lavagna, the festival of the Fieschi is held. A cake weighing 1.5 tons commemorates the marriage in 1230 of Count Opizzo Fieschi to Bianca de Bianchi, a noblewoman from Siena, when the event was celebrated by the donation of a huge cake to the local population. Today the festival ends with a procession in 13th-century costume with medieval music and dancing.

302 top, center and 302-303 The festival of St. Ephysus has been celebrated in Cagliari on May 1st each year since 1657. In that year the inhabitants of the city made a vow that they would honor the saint with an annual festival if he caused the plague to halt. The event is especially dear to the hearts of the inhabitants of the quarter of Stampace where the church dedicated to the saint stands. It was built over a prison in which, it is said, he was shut up before being put to death on the order of Diocletian. An effigy of the saint is clothed in formal dress—a white cloak lined with red damask, a blue ribbon on his shoulder, a sash decorated with votive offerings, jewels, necklaces and rings—and hoisted onto an old white coach painted with gold lacquer. He is then led down the streets by thousands of people in multicolored costumes from all parts of Sardinia accompanied by the notes of three-reed flutes. When the procession reaches the church in the nearby village of Giorgino, the saint's sumptuous clothes are changed for more common ones and his statue is placed on a farm cart. The following morning the procession goes to Nora where it remains the whole day. It then returns to Cagliari with the original clothes and in the painted carriage to end the celebrations on May 25th.

302 bottom and 303 top
Processions are a feature of the
Christian world and are
particularly popular in Sardinia
where old traditions are an integral
part of popular culture. The
procession commemorating the
crucifixion of Jesus takes place on
Good Friday in Alghero (top) and
Castelsardo (bottom) with the
participation of many local
religious houses.

303 center The Sardinian
Cavalcade takes place in Sassari on
the penultimate Sunday of May.

This is a large parade to
commemorate a victory by the
Sardinian and Pisan forces over
the Arabs in the year 1000. Groups
from across the island thread
through the streets of the city in
a dazzle of colorful costumes.
Roughly 3,000 people take part, all
in beautiful traditional costumes
from the various areas of Sardinia,
differing in their shape, materials,
ornaments and colors.
The principal characters are the
knights in costume with their
beribboned horses who take part
in the parade in the morning and

in the afternoon challenge each
other in races and daring tricks.
In the late afternoon, groups
meet in Piazza Italia to dance
and sing. The festival ends,
naturally, with banquets in
the evening.

303 bottom The Mamuthunes
are the main characters in the
Carnival at Mamoiada.
The origins of these figures are
very old and the dances that they
perform with their faces hidden
by wooden masks have a mixture
of archaic and pagan meanings.

304 bottom left, 304 right, 304-305 To celebrate John's day on 24 June, in Florence a type of football match is played in costume. The match is preceded by a parade from the cloister of Santa Maria Novella to Piazza Santa Croce. Mace-bearers, trumpeters, sergeants and the referee take part; behind them come heralds, flag-wavers, musicians and, finally, the drovers with the calf which will be offered to the winners. The four teams taking part wear various outfits and are each composed of 27 players. The goal is a stake covered with cloth and topped by a net. The ball can be pushed with the hands or feet and wrestling is allowed. When the ball passes the stake, the team wins a shot or a point.

304 top left On Easter Sunday in Florence, the "burning of the cart" takes place. It is taken around the city by the City Council's trumpeters to be burned in front of the cathedral during Easter Mass. The cart looks like a black pyramid decorated with ribbons, frills and flowers and has had this appearance since 1764. The event takes place to commemorate the participation of Pazzino de' Pazzi, from the rich family of Florentine merchants, on the first Crusade to the Holy Land.

305 bottom left The Regatta of the Marine Republics attracts thousands of visitors to Pisa every year. The regatta on the River Arno is actually a historical commemoration but tends to turn into a boat race due to the rivalry between the teams taking part. The event is noted for its rich costumes and the competitiveness between the youths of Pisa, Venice, Genoa and Amalfi.

305 bottom right The Luminaria of St. Rainier takes place at Pisa on 17 June. Rainier was a lay brother who spent time in the Holy Land as a hermit, then lived in Pisa in a monastery. When he died he was buried in the cathedral. On the evening before the saint's day, a procession takes place of his reliquaries accompanied by thousands of wax lamps enclosed in glass beakers which light up the façades of the palazzi along the Arno and are reflected in the river. The four quarters of the city— Sant'Antonio, Santa Maria, San Francesco, and San Martino— take part by racing rowing boats on the river. Each boat has eight oarsmen, a cox and a "climber"; he is called this because the winner has to attach his banner to the top of a pole 32 feet high and placed on a boat anchored in the middle of the river by climbing a hawser. The celebrations finish on the last Sunday of the month with the "bridge game": a hundred or so people divided in two teams in the middle of a bridge attempt to push a small cart to the opposing team's bank.

Religious processions are a feature of the whole of the Christian world. There are all sorts, from the most humble in small villages to the choreographed splendors in large cities or places with religious traditions. Routine processions are timed to take place on particular holy days while others are tied to particular circumstances and have to be authorized by the local bishop. Whatever type of procession it is, whether unpretentious or a large festive display, the same rules have to be obeyed: the cross must lead followed by members of the fraternity and clergy; the more important members of these stay close to the officiator who holds up the ostensory and walks in front of the holy image. Many such processions take place at Easter which is often celebrated with sacred representations that involve whole

villages.Beyond its religious significance, processions are a collective ceremony that represent an occasion for universal participation of members of a religious community and the public. Processions in ancient times were often linked to sacred ceremonies but in Rome there were also marriage and funerary processions. Two others were of great importance: the first was for the opening of the circus games when the parade started at the Campidoglio and ended at the Circus Maximus. It was led by a official on a cart and followed by youths, charioteers, athletes and priests bearing images of the gods. The second was the *pompa triumphalis* to celebrate the triumph of a victorious general who was borne on a cart to the temple of Jove Capitolinus, followed by officials, priests, officers and their followers from the defeated army, and by his own soldiers who jeered at the vanquished.

306-307 During the first ten days of June in Val Badia, the festival of the Holy Heart of Jesus is celebrated. Everyone dresses up in the local costume for the procession: the characteristic features of the costume of the musicians is the joppe, *a thick jacket of red or brown loden, and a green felt hat. Children wear crowns of flowers and married women a decorated apron and black lace head-covering. During the ceremony, the statues and traditional standards are carried on shoulders along paths and through fields around the village. Besides its centuries-old traditions preserved by the area's geographical isolation, Val Badia offers spectacular views. Colfosco, Corvara and La Villa, the main centers of the valley, are famous holiday resorts at the feet of the Dolomite mountains, in wide, green airy valleys of extraordinary beauty.*

308 left The Pasquali take place in Bormio on Easter Sunday. This is one of the most characteristic of popular traditions in Valtellina. The young people of the quarters of the town each choose an Easter theme around which to decorate an allegorical cart. The materials used are natural—moss, leaves, flowers and wood—with which they build a tabernacle dedicated to their chosen theme. The tabernacles are then placed on elaborate carrying boards. A lamb with a red ribbon around its neck is always present nestling in the moss. Each group takes a live lamb to church carried by a shepherd or placed in a decorated basket. The procession ends in the Piazza del Kuerc (which means "cover"), an area with porticoes where justice used to be administered. The Pasquali are blessed on the courtyard outside the nearby church.

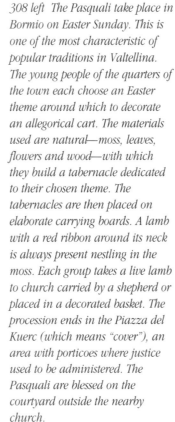

308 top right and 309 Every May the Procession of the Rosario Fiorito is held in Alagna in Valsesia. All the village's inhabitants wear traditional costume and follow a long path through meadows carrying the statue of the Madonna and the standards of the village.

308 center and bottom right The baptism ceremony in Fobello has maintained its ancient medieval rite in which nature and religion are mixed. Dressed in local costume, the godmother carries the baby in its cot over her head from the baby's home to the church. The covering over the cot bears the traditional message, "Nature smiles through her flowers, God through our children."

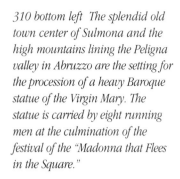

310 bottom left The splendid old town center of Sulmona and the high mountains lining the Peligna valley in Abruzzo are the setting for the procession of a heavy Baroque statue of the Virgin Mary. The statue is carried by eight running men at the culmination of the festival of the "Madonna that Flees in the Square."

310 right With the Tiro della Balestra that takes place on the last Sunday of May, the Corsa dei Ceri (Candle Race) is the main folkloric event in Gubbio. It is held in mid-May and is dedicated to St. Hubald, the patron saint of the city and of builders.

310 top left The two most important folklore celebrations in Gubbio are the "Tiro della Balestra," on the last Sunday of May, and the "Corsa dei Ceri" (Candle Race) dedicated to St. Hubald, that takes place in the middle of the month.

310-311 The Corsa dei Ceri takes place in Gubbio on 15 May and is dedicated to St. Hubald, patron saint of the city and of builders. The Ceri are three gigantic wooden constructions, 16 feet high and each weighing 900 lbs. They are made of two octagonal prisms topped by statues of St. Hubald, St. George and St. Anthony Abate. The Ceri are raised in the morning: each team leader jumps up on the stretcher that supports his Cero and pours a jugful of water over the attachment point,

the jug is then thrown into the air. The bits of the broken jug are collected by the crowd and kept as good luck tokens.

311 bottom left On the first day of May in Cocullo, the procession of the Serpari, dedicated to St. Dominic, takes place. Grass snakes placed on the statue of the saint curl around his head and clothes and, according to tradition, are miraculously tamed.

311 bottom right A rather special procession is held in Sulmona during Holy Week. Having learned of the resurrection of her son Jesus, the Madonna begins to run down the street, losing the black veil that covers her face. At the end of the ceremony, a flock of doves is let loose and the bells are rung.

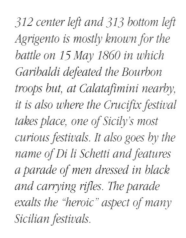

312 center left and 313 bottom left
Agrigento is mostly known for the battle on 15 May 1860 in which Garibaldi defeated the Bourbon troops but, at Calatafimini nearby, it is also where the Crucifix festival takes place, one of Sicily's most curious festivals. It also goes by the name of Di li Schetti and features a parade of men dressed in black and carrying rifles. The parade exalts the "heroic" aspect of many Sicilian festivals.

312 bottom left One of the most widespread forms of entertainment at a popular level is the puppet theater. The skills of the puppet masters make this a real art form. The shows, generally recounting heroic exploits, are held in theaters in front of loyal and enthusiastic audiences. The characters are nearly always taken from the paladins of France whose deeds are told in the Song of Roland.

312 top left At San Fratello in the province of Messina, the Abballu di li Giudei is held during Holy Week. Jews are represented in the procession wearing red muslin jackets and trousers with stripes of different colors, rough leather shoes and a pair of gaiters. Their heads are covered by a mask made of the same muslin with a long, shiny tongue hanging down, long eyebrows and an ugly mouth which give them a diabolical appearance.

312 center right At Adrano in the province of Catania, the Diavolata takes place at Easter. This is a representation, like the one at San Fratello, that has its origin in an antipathy toward the Jews who were thought responsible for the death of Christ. The show takes place on a stage divided into Heaven and Hell; five devils headed by Lucifer argue with Death, with the Soul (a young girl), and with an Angel (a young boy). In the end, it is the young boy that saves humanity by forcing the devils to say the words "Viva Maria" (Long live Mary).

312-313 Carnival in Sicily, like this one in Acireale and Mezzojuso, starts on the day of St. Anthony Abate, protector of animals and fire. From this day on, rituals are performed which attempt to distance the negative events of the farming year just ending which might threaten the imminent sprouting of the corn. The different forms of this Carnival are a hangover from the rites used to celebrate mythological gods connected with corn in ancient times.

313 bottom right and 314-315 The Passion and death of Christ are commemorated on the Thursday and Friday before Easter with processions and representations. In the past, dramatized sermons and other ceremonies were held. Today the processions, like this one in Enna on Good Friday, are serious and solemn with the presence of confradies, the local brotherhoods. The rhythm of the processions are marked by the sound of a large drum, the tabbala.

MASTERPIECES OF
Italian art

The Italians have made a stunning contribution to the history of Western Art. In the sculptures of antiquity they have transformed cold marble into living, breathing flesh. In the ornate and soaring churches of the Middle Ages they have turned mere earth and stone into a spiritual homage to religious faith. In the paintings of the subsequent centuries they have illustrated the sights and scenery of Italy and the passions of its people. Let these extraordinary photographs and insightful text serve as your guide through centuries of Italian architecture, sculpture, and painting.

TEXT BY
MARIA LAURA DELLA CROCE

317 Gianlorenzo Bernini, Rape of Prosperine, *detail, 1621-22, marble, Borghese Gallery, Rome.*

318-319 Michelangelo, Moses, *1515, San Pietro in Vincoli, Rome.*

A genius for portraiture

One of the most outstanding elements shared by the majority of the pictures in this chapter is the great importance the artists attached to accurate portrayal of the human form. In both their religious and secular portraits, these artists show a vast range of feelings and emotions.

In addition, the artists used various symbols and physical attributes to send particular philosophical, theological, and moral messages to the viewer. Each work of art's original audience was familiar with this "code." The way in which the subject of the portrait is dressed, his clothing, hair style, the way he holds himself, the way he occupies the space of the portrait . . . today, these clues give us information about the history and tradition of the society to which he belonged.

The eighteenth-century French writer Stendhal, writing in his history of Italian painting, pointed out that different painters would paint the same subject quite differently. For example, the Adoration of the Magi: Michelangelo, he said, would show strength and awe; Raphael would stress the purity of Mary and the child; while Leonardo da Vinci would emphasize the nobility of the kings. Leonardo da Vinci's somber colors would have a somewhat depressing effect; on the other hand, Correggio would paint an amazingly rich feast for the eyes.

Stendhal also suggested that the twenty or thirty great painters would all have used different means to achieve their goals. The colors chosen, the ways of applying them, the use of light and shade, and certain accessories would all be part of the work. He pointed out, almost ironically, that a woman does not wear the same hat when she is meeting her lover as she does when she is going to confession; similarly, each artist brings to the subject matter his own view of society and reflects the role he played in it.

For centuries, artists considered themselves to be no more than somewhat refined craftsmen. Through at least the first half of the fifteenth century, they were modest people living modest lives, with neither their background nor their education separating them from the ordinary craftsman. Andrea del Castagno was the son of a farmer, Paolo Uccello of a barber, Filippo Lippi of a butcher, and the Pollaiolo brothers were the sons of a poultry seller. Giorgio Vasari, the great biographer of Italian artists, reports that Filippo Lippi couldn't afford a pair of socks; Paolo Uccello, when he was old, not only had no possessions, but also could no longer work and had an ill wife.

Viewed in this light, the great masters were workmen, following orders from a buyer, or religious conventions, or political necessities. For centuries these artists were asked to represent Divine Glory or the power and prestige of the Empire, and they did so.

With Giotto, at the beginning of the fourteenth century, the position of the artist began to make a slow change. Artists began to exercise an influence on contemporary culture while also interpreting this culture.

The Gothic period saw similarly complex changes. As great cathedrals were built in the name of God, there was a simultaneous movement toward humanization in sculpture – an abandonment of the solemnity and static nature of previous centuries' artwork. Freedom, great diversity of movement, more expression, richness, and variety in detail all appear in this period.

321 Masaccio, The Crucifixion, 1426, Capodimonte Museum, Naples.

322 Donatello, David, c. 1430, bronze, Bargello Museum, Florence. The David, which Donatello sculpted for Cosimo de' Medici around 1430, is based on the classical concept of a natural size nude statue. Although referring back to Greek models, the sculptor nonetheless brought his own original interpretation to this work. This David has almost the air of a street urchin beneath his comic head covering. He combines a victorious figure with something of a painful and restless adolescent, revealed by his ambiguous smile.

A comparison of the many statues in the Or San Michele (commissioned by the guilds of craftsmen that led Florence's economic prosperity at the end of the fourteenth and beginning of the fifteenth centuries) shows this development clearly. For fifteen years, artists including Lorenzo Ghiberti, Nanni di Banco, and Donatello worked on this monument side by side, each bringing his own special talents to the work.

During the Renaissance, a man-centered view of the universe evolved. Artists moved to the forefront of civic life because they were the first to express fully the new aims which were becoming part of the cultural and political climate of Florence. The impact of the work of these artists was much stronger than any written manifesto could have been.

Stendhal pointed out that public demand for statues produced such artists as Donatello, Brunelleschi, Ghiberti, Filarete, Rossellino, Pollaiolo, and Verrocchio. They worked in a variety of materials, including marble, bronze, and silver, and their works were displayed throughout Florence. The artists' fellow citizens were greatly impressed, believing the works to equal the masterpieces of antiquity, although at that time no statues dating from the classical period had been found.

The discovery of perspective was formulated by Filippo Brunelleschi and discussed by Leon Battista Alberti in his "Trattato della Pittura" of 1436. Perspective is much more than just a skill and a technique for showing space. It is both a science and a relationship to reality which gives not only the artist but also the viewer access to a harmonious space with proportional relationships that faithfully reflect reality. Because the mechanical arts had both theoretical and scientific foundations, they gained new dignity and became part of the so-called liberal arts, thereby raising the prestige of the artists.

With the individualistic and practical development of the Florentine bourgeoisie, references to the classical world increased and a high regard for the individual and for creative activity developed. This led, albeit slowly, to a view of the artist as intellectual rather than as almost a manual laborer. Considering this, the tendency of artists to insert self-portraits into their paintings can be viewed as the artistic equivalent of the new autobiographical genre, first introduced by Lorenzo Ghiberti. Starting in the fifteenth century, the portrait developed its own autonomy, linked to the new importance of the individual. This was a major change from the Middle Ages, when portraits were almost always part of larger compositions.

This is especially true of the portrait bust, so characteristic of Roman times, which once again became extremely important. The fifteenth-century version was secular, and (like its Roman antecedents) reflected a desire to display the civic virtues of the person portrayed. The two major styles were vivid realism and idealization. For a long period idealization was to dominate; it became one of the most evident hallmarks of the new taste and of Renaissance culture.

During the sixteenth century, art reflected the contemporary view that self-control was the most desirable feature of a personality. Thus emotions, which in the fifteenth century had remained as relics of the late Gothic period, disappeared from art and portrait painting.

Mary without tears or gestures views her dead son, just as in pictures of her with the baby Jesus all plebeian emotion is repressed. Balance is, in everything, of major importance; order and discipline in art reflected the sobriety and restraint of sixteenth-century life. The ideal was a sublime regularity, calm, and stability, in life as in art.

The concept of beauty is dependent on the human ideal of the aristocracy, with beauty and physical strength as the expression of spiritual value. The sibyls and Madonnas of Michelangelo show a gigantic, confident, and proud humanity expressing tremendous energy. The human ideal, presented by Baldassarre Castiglione in his book discussing ideal behavior in courtly circles, had tremendous influence not only in Italy and other countries on the Continent but as far away as the English court. He expressed these ideals as being not only attainable but often, indeed, as already attained. It was this ideal that is taken here as an example. The courtly ideal itself has all the essential characteristics of the image of man which sixteenth-century art gives us. Castiglione demanded from the perfect man of the world versatility, balanced development of physical and intellectual gifts, ease in the use of arms and in society, experience of poetry and music, and familiarity with painting and science.

The beauty and nobility of sixteenth-century heroic figures reflect in their images this human and social ideal. This style, strongly influenced by antiquity and often referred to as neoclassicism, is exemplified by such artists as Raphael and Michelangelo. It is also reflected in the ease of the figures' movements as well as in their relaxed and calm poses.

It was perhaps inevitable that there was a reaction to the neoclassical period. Following Raphael, who died in 1520, a new style emerged which is now called Mannerism. Its proponents – Pontormo, Parmigianino, Bronzino, Beccafumi, Rosso Fiorentino and Tintoretto – broke with the simple regularity and harmony of classical art and replaced its universality with more subjective and emotional characteristics. This rejection of classical forms manifested itself in many different ways, including a new spiritualism, a new intellectualism which deliberately deformed reality (often in favor of the bizarre), and a newly refined taste which rendered everything in terms of subtlety, acuteness, and elegance. This view of life granted new and previously unheard-of importance to dreams, which take real connections and turn them into abstract relationships between objects; taken to an extreme, this focus on dreams verges on the Baroque. In fact, Mannerism and near-Baroque style meet in some of the works of Raphael and Michelangelo, in which passionate Baroque expressionism meets with the intellectualism of Manneristic art.

The true character of Baroque is to expand the limits of reality, intensifying it in a thousand different ways, each more surprising, triumphant, and joyful than the previous one. The fashion of painted ceilings – gigantic optical illusions which inspire a particular type of dizziness – is, perhaps, one of the most impressive examples. Monumental sculpture also developed more creatively, thanks to such skilled portraitists as Gianlorenzo Bernini, who was highly gifted in conveying his own religious feelings of ecstasy and mysticism to others.

Even his treatment of draperies was new, serving to accent the dynamic and dramatic effect of his work.

Painting is part of mankind's wish to "put the world on stage." To this end, it began to invent different trends and artistic schools, such as still life, landscape, and traditional domestic scenes. In the seventeenth century, each of these schools became isolated from the others, pushing artists to specialize in one or another of these genres: there were painters of flowers, ruins, musical instruments, battles, and so on. (The setting of scenes in a somewhat disjointed manner or from a diagonal viewpoint was also popularized at this time but it had less significance.)

For seventeenth-century critics, Caravaggio sheds great light on genre painting, particularly that of still lifes. He himself said that there was no difference between a painting of fruit and a painting of people. Caravaggio also brought to art a new and courageous way of painting light. The most important thing in his pictures is the presence of bodies, the solid and detailed reality of the object. His poetic originality lies in the way he used the maximum contrast of light and shadow; parts of his figures are drowned in darkness, from which a face, an arm, or a hand emerges in surprising relief. It has been said that Caravaggio's greatness lay in his ability to help us realize the dark side of the world and to surprise us with light and moving forms.

Sculptors also gave themselves over to this movement, learning from Bernini how to use a light whose source cannot be seen by the spectator. In contrast with the clear and diffused light of Renaissance artists, directional light seems transitory, giving spectators the feeling that the scene itself is transient. The light of Bernini is distinctly warm – and revolutionary.

But the cold and classic light of Antonio Canova shows a return to the basic beauty of early sixteenth-century classicism, inspired itself by classical antiquity. Canova's sculpture is the main Italian example of the rediscovery of classicism, which would become one of the bases of neoclassical art.

326-327 *Caravaggio,* Supper at Emmaus, *1606, canvas, Brera Art Gallery, Milan.*

Canova presents in his work the image of both an intellectual and sublime grace, in which cold light has both metaphysical and symbolic meaning. Such coldness was seen by hostile critics as overly artificial, affected, and impersonal. Even today there are critics who feel the marble sculptures of Canova are smooth and cold (and, incidentally, erotic). Canova, however, took seriously a suggestion made by the major theoretician of the period, Johann Joachim Winckelmann – a suggestion that a return to classicism was necessary, and that strong emotions should play a part in art.

Canova's terra-cotta models have an immediacy, spontaneity and vitality which is extremely vivid. They have been cited more than once as proof that there was more than one side to Canova, a man who so loved the classics that he had the works of ancient writers read to him while he worked. It is said that Canova never tired of polishing and cleaning his works, attempting to give the marble a softer appearance by staining the statues with soot after polishing them to a high gloss.

The great artists of this era were so gifted that at times they created images more real than reality itself. Even their biographies point out their distance from ordinary life. Anecdotes are told of Caravaggio's quarrelsome and scandal-prone nature, the bizarre behavior of

Pontormo, the fear that Michelangelo could inspire, da Vinci's dabblings in the occult, and Raphael's melancholy attacks. Little has changed in the modern world; even today opinion tends to recognize artists as extraordinary beings whose temperament and habits differ greatly from those of ordinary people. Artists are forgiven for many forms of extravagant behavior, for which other people would be condemned.

It should be noted that works of art have often been believed to have magical powers in and of themselves. During the Renaissance period, statues of bronze and wax were actually made for magical purposes. There is widespread belief that a strong connection exists between a painted or sculpted representation of a person and the person himself. This is the basis for one form of black magic, in which an image is damaged with the intent that the pain will be felt in the portrayed individual.

Of course, this belief is reciprocal – there is widespread belief that the damage that occurs to a person will be reflected in his portrait, as in Oscar Wilde's tale of Dorian Gray. Despite the continuing secularization of art, there is a human tendency to identify it with magic – and, in certain circles, to view the producer of these images as a magician. In Italy it is possible to identify with all of these many facets of art.

LIGHT AND DETAIL
IN GOTHIC PAINTING

330 Simone Martini, The
Annunciation, *1333, central part
of the multi-paneled work, panel,
Uffizi, Florence. This is the last
dated work made by the Sienese
painter Martini before he moved
to Avignon. In this painting, he
expresses his own idea of spiritual
beauty not only in the figures but
also in the objects, the fabrics, and
the flowers. His technique adds
elegance to the line and a veritable
glow to the images.*

331 Duccio da Buoninsegna,
Rucellai Madonna, *1285, Uffizi,
Florence.*

332-333 Duccio da Buoninsegna,
Maestà, *multi-paneled work, back
of the main panel, divided into
fourteen panels in two rows. Museo
dell'Opera del Duomo, Siena.*

334-335 Duccio da Buoninsegna,
Maestà, *detail.*

THE FASHIONABILITY
OF PORTRAIT BUSTS

336 left Andrea Verrochio, La Dama col Mazzolino, (Woman with a Nosegay), 1475-1480, marble, Bargello Museum, Florence. The Florentine artist Verrochio was originally a goldsmith. His training as a craftsman and his vast experience both in drawing and in the execution of chased work is evident in his delicate, smooth, graceful sculptures.

336 right Francesco Laurana, Bust of Battista Sforza, c. 1472, marble, Bargello Museum, Florence. Francesco Laurana was a Dalmatian artist who worked in both Sicily and Naples. In Naples he worked at the court of Alfonso of Aragon. For Federigo da Montefeltro,

Duke of Urbino, he produced this portrait bust of the Duke's wife, Battista Sforza, which shows an almost geometrical purity of form.

337 Verrocchio, La Dama col Mazzolino (Woman with a Nosegay), detail.

338 Benevenuto Cellini, Bust of Cosimo I, *detail, 1545-48, bronze, Bargello Museum, Florence. This is an idealized portrait, superbly produced by the most fashionable artist of the day for a great patron of the arts, the Prince and Lord of Florence. By this time Florence was the capital of a modern state.*

339 Antonio del Pollaiolo, Hercules and Antaeus, *c. 1475, bronze, Bargello Museum, Florence. Pollaiolo, like Verrocchio, was a goldsmith who also painted and sculpted. He preferred to model small bronzes rather than larger sculptures. In this work, light and shadow play against each other to animate the sculpture.*

DEVOTION IN THE WORK OF FRA ANGELICO; THE BATTLES OF PAOLO UCCELLO

340 Giovanni da Fiesole, known as Fra Angelico, Crucifixion and Saints, *after 1438, from the frescoes in St. Mark's Convent, Chapter House, Florence. A Dominican friar and member of the Order of Preachers, Fra Angelico was a strongly religious artist whose work provides an intense and fascinating insight into monastic life in the 15th century. His frescoes were painted in the cells and corridors of the San Marco monastery, which had been rebuilt at Cosimo de' Medici's expense. The frescoes were designed to provide the monks with subjects on which to meditate. Quite often a Dominican saint is included as an example and inspiration.*

341 top Fra Angelico,
Transfiguration of Christ, *cell 6
of the monastery dormitory*.

341 bottom Fra Angelico,
Adoration of the Magi, *cell 39*.

342-343 Fra Angelico,
Crucifixion, *detail*.

344-345 Paolo Uccello, Rout of San Romano, c. 1465, panel, Uffizi, Florence. This painting was commissioned by Cosimo de' Medici to commemorate the victory of the Florentines over Siena at San Romano in 1432. Although not actually historically correct, it was used by Paolo Uccello to show his own taste for the dramatic and perhaps a degree of skepticism. The event it depicted was soon forgotten, and the three panels which make up the scene were later often described simply as "jousts" or "tourneys."

THE WORK OF PIERO
DELLA FRANCESCA

346 Piero della Francesca,
Portrait of Battista Sforza,
c. 1465, Uffizi, Florence.

347 Piero della Francesca,
Portrait of Federigo da Montefeltro,
c. 1465, panel, Uffizi, Florence.

This pair of portraits of the Duke and Duchess of Urbino shows a strong taste for the meticulous detailing found in Flemish portraits. Piero della Francesca was an expert mathematician and the author of a basic treatise on perspective; here, he manages to paint the distant village in proportion with the irregularities of the Duke's very realistic profile, which includes curls, warts, and wrinkles.

349 *Piero della Francesca,*
The Dream of Constantine, *1452-
59, from the frescoes in the church
of San Francesco, Arezzo. The ray
of light which shines from the
angel and hits the cone-shaped
tent is one of the first nocturnal
views in the history of 15th-century
painting.*

350-351 *Piero della Francesca,
frescoes in the church of San
Francesco, Arezzo, detail of
the* Queen of Sheba.

THE ARRIVAL OF
LEONARDO DA VINCI

352-353 Leonardo da Vinci,
The Annunciation, *c. 1475,*
panel, Brera Art Gallery, Milan.

MATER DOLOROSA

354 Giovanni Bellini, Pietà, 1460, panel, Brera Art Gallery, Milan. This poignant Pietà by Giovanni Bellini reveals a sad intimacy, both in the juxtaposition of the faces of the Mother and Child and in the clasp of their hands against the dark light of the background. Giovanni Bellini, the son of Jacopo, was the brother of Gentile (official portraitist of the Doges and brother-in-law of Andrea Mantegna).

355 Christ Against the Column, 1480-1490, tempera on panel, Brera Art Gallery, Milan.

356-357 Giovanni Bellini, Pietà, detail.

THE DOMINANCE
OF LINE

358-359 *Sandro Botticelli,* The
Birth of Venus, *1482-84, panel,
Uffizi, Florence. Botticelli's art
has been described as delicate,
musical, dream-like, and
melancholy. He was only a few
years younger than Lorenzo
the Magnificent, and was perhaps
the artist most closely linked with
the Medici circle. His two famous
allegorical paintings – Primavera
and The Birth of Venus – were
painted for Lorenzo's cousin,
Lorenzo di Pierfrancesco,
and were placed in his villa
at Castello. Botticelli used
an undulating, clear-cut,
and exquisite line to explicate the
neo-platonic ideal of a spirit which
must be released from the material
world to achieve divinity. Beauty,
here symbolized by Venus, is the
principle governing the universe.*

360-361 *Sandro Botticelli,*
The Birth of Venus, *detail
of the goddess face.*

362-363 *Sandro Botticelli,*
Primavera, *detail with the*
Three Graces, Cupid, and Flora.
Flora almost seems to have
emerged from the poetry of

Poliziano, who wrote of her
honest figure, her modest dress
decorated with roses, flowers,
and grass, and the ringlets
accenting her forehead.

364-365 *Sandro Botticelli,*
Primavera, *1478, panel, Uffizi,*
Florence.

TELLING STORIES

366-367 Vittore Carpaccio,
The Arrival of the Ambassadors,
*1490-95, from the series of large
canvases showing* The Legend
of St. Ursula, *Academy, Venice.
The Venetian painter Carpaccio*

*placed miraculous stories in
an immediate, understandable
reality by paying careful
attention to detail in clothes,
furnishings, attitudes, and
fashions.*

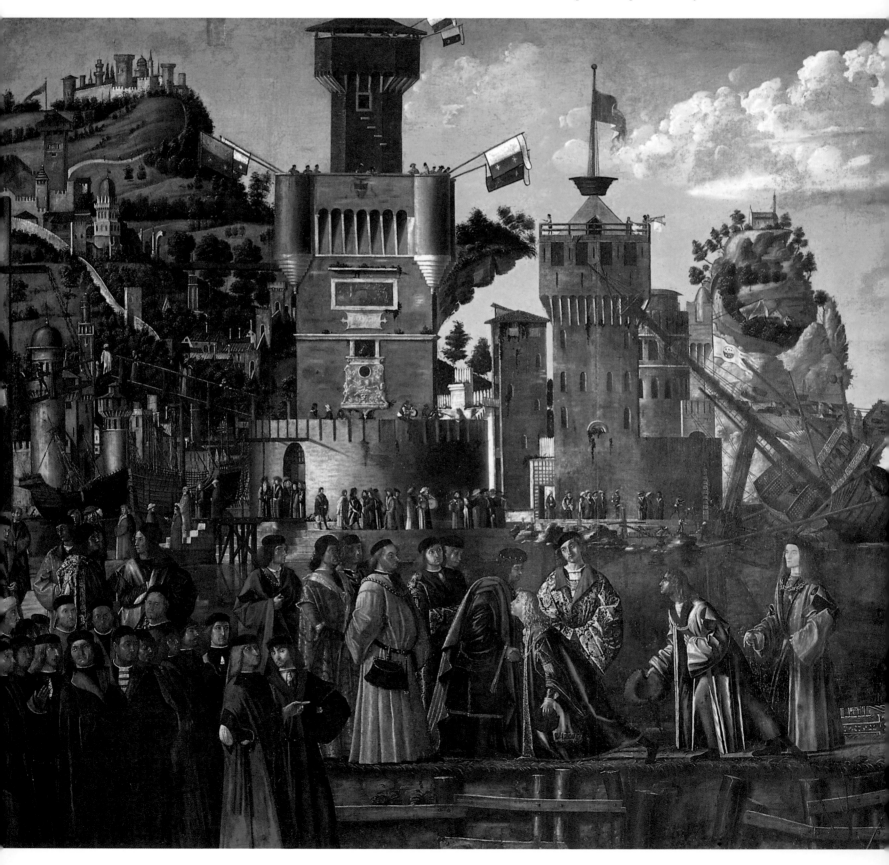

368-369 *Vittore Carpaccio, details from* The Legend of St. Ursula. *The Italian term* teleri *(literally, "textiles") is used to describe large canvases of linen or hemp mounted on frames and used for painting in Venice toward the end of the 15th century. The greater elasticity of the canvas made the paintings more resistant to humidity.*

Carpaccio (the official painter in Venice, along with Gentile Bellini) used this technique with great success. In this view of the city, he used bright colors, foreshortening of houses and palaces, and a crowd of personalities, all executed in minute detail. The splendid force of Vittore's color came to mark the Venetian school of painting.

VICTORIS CP

THE CITY
AS BACKDROP

STRENGTH AND EMOTION

374-375 Niccolò dell'Arca, Pietà, 1485, terra-cotta, Santa Maria della Vita, Bologna. Niccolò dell'Arca's work is considered to mark sculpture's transition into the sharp and dynamic work of the Ferrara school of painting. He came from Apulia but worked mainly in central Italy. Niccolò produced this Pietà with strong contrast, theatricality, and previously unseen dramatic strength. His frenzied, grieving Mary Magdalene acts, through her disheveled clothing, as a tribute to the popular medieval tradition of sacred representations.

376-377 Niccolò dell'Arca, Pietà, detail.

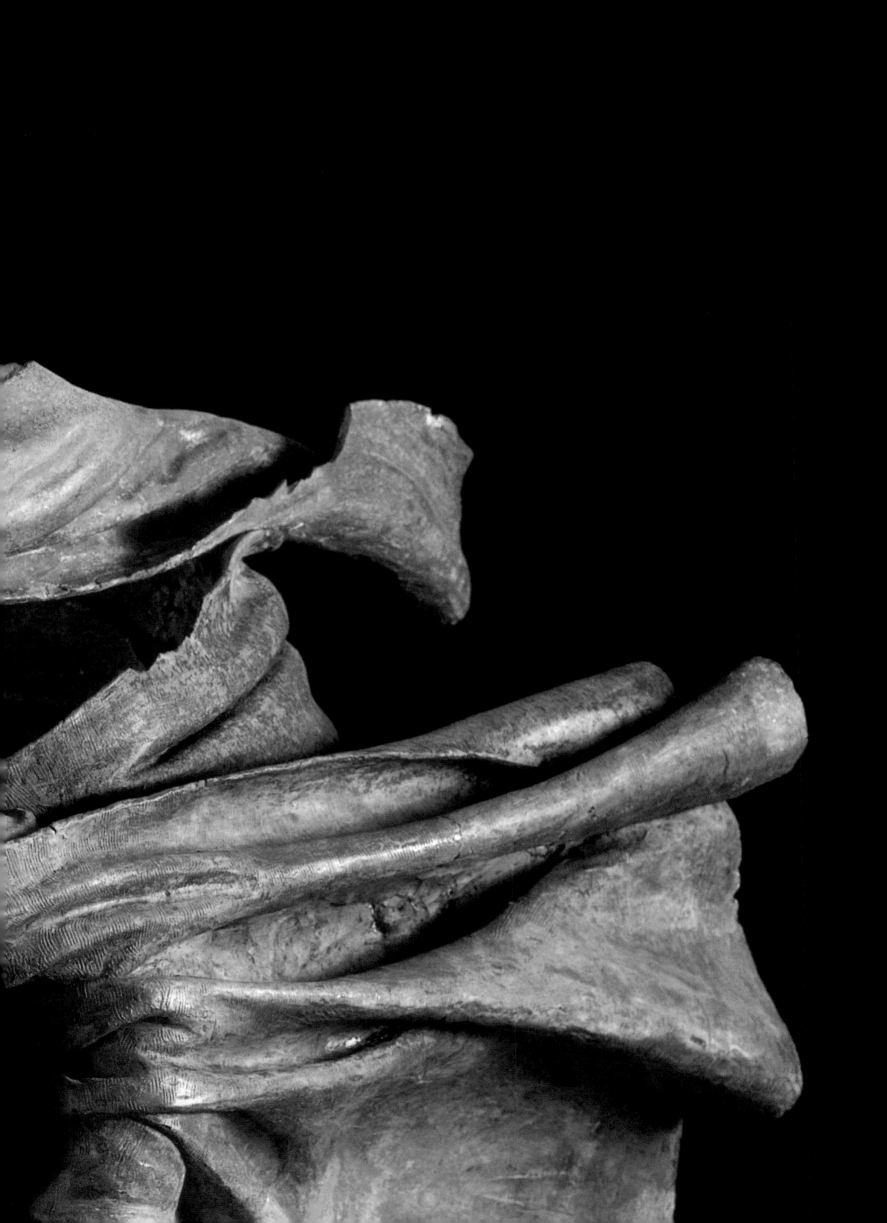

378-379 Jacopo della Quercia, Tomb of Ilaria del Caretto, *1406, marble, Cathedral of San Martino, Lucca. Here is an equally exciting sculpture formed in a* completely different way, showing tenderness and a vague melancholy. The figure of the young Ilaria has come to symbolize the humanist tomb.

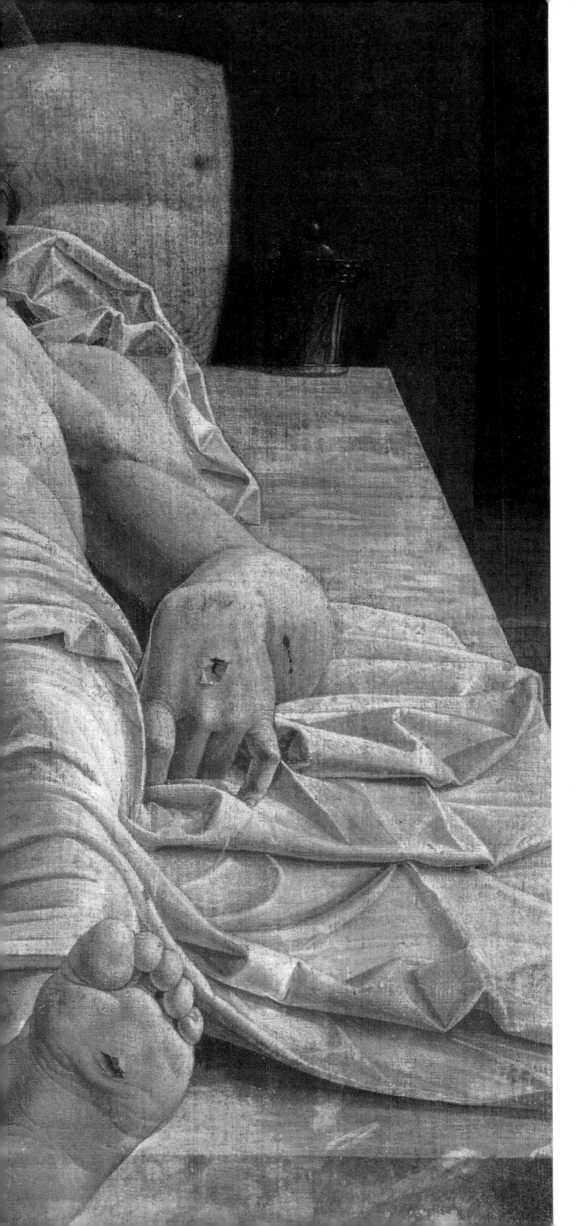

380-381 Andrea Mantegna, Dead Christ, *late 15th century, canvas, Brera Art Gallery, Milan. Notice the bold, harsh foreshortening of this impressive view of the crucified Jesus. A Venetian artist, Mantegna is universally known for his frescoes in the Gonzaga ducal palace in Mantua. There, too, skilled foreshortening and the imaginative use of perspective illustrate a refined and cultured world, filled by a subtle melancholy. In this religious work, on the other hand, everything is dramatically tense. The viewer can read in it omens of further death and crisis which developed following the death of Savonarola at the stake.*

THE IDEALIZATION
OF CLASSICAL ANTIQUITY

382-383 Michelangelo, The Madonna of the Steps, 1490-95, marble, Casa Buonarotti, Florence. Giorgio Vasari, the biographer of Italian artists, called Michelangelo "divine." He was not even twenty years old when he sculpted The Madonna of the Steps *and* The Battle of the Centaurs. *These masterpieces show clearly that sculpture is produced not by placing the material on a surface, as in painting, but by raising it. They show Michelangelo's extraordinary skill, especially remarkable given both his youth and the different techniques used. For* The Madonna, *he follows a technique similar to that used by Donatello. In* The Battle of the Centaurs (a mythological theme suggested to him by Poliziano), *he shows total confidence in producing an energetic tangle of moving and grasping naked bodies, which can be considered a prelude to the themes he developed in his later years.*

384-385 *Michelangelo,* The Battle of the Centaurs, *1490-95, marble, Casa Buonarotti, Florence.*

A WORSHIP
OF NATURE

388-389 *Giorgione*, The Tempest, *1505-10, canvas, Academy, Venice. This painting, showing the moment before the storm actually arrives, is full of symbolism which has not yet been fully deciphered. Like* The Three Philosophers *and* The Concert Champêtre, The Tempest *is a small painting designed for the enjoyment of the buyer in his private home – a type of painting which was to have great success in the future. The ambiguity of the subjects reveals both the personality of the artist and the wish of the buyer for a work accessible to a small circle of cultured and refined friends. Vasari said that Giorgione was born to put the spirit into figures and to illustrate the freshness of the living. He presents us with a new pictorial language. The landscape absorbs the horizon and the human figure tends to reflect the smoothness of the natural space. The wavering forms of his work, the warm and soft colors, the melancholy mood which runs through figures and landscapes, are all part of an attempt to create a work that is both accessible to the viewer and peaceful to view.*

390-391 Giorgione, The Castelfranco Madonna, panel, 1504-10, Cathedral, Castelfranco Veneto; details with St. Liberale and the Madonna. Compared with the traditional arrangement of the Madonna enthroned among the saints, Giorgione represents her against a natural background, which immediately attracts the eye because of its contrast with the Madonna's green dress and red cloak. The composition is reduced to a simple triangular scheme and the saints – here limited to two – seem lost in their own thoughts.

MOVING BEYOND
MATERIAL LIMITATIONS

392-393 Michelangelo, Moses, 1515-16, marble, San Pietro in Vincoli, Rome. This statue is part of the complex marble group designed by Michelangelo for the tomb of Pope Julius II. This construction virtually obsessed the artist for more than thirty years. At the start of the 16th century, the Pope had entrusted to Michelangelo the task of building his mausoleum. It was to have been placed in St. Peter's for the eternal glory both of the Pope and of the church itself. Michelangelo was forced to interrupt the project several times – for instance, when he was given the commission to decorate the Sistine Chapel. In later years he suggested a new version of the mausoleum, but because he was out of favor with the Pope's heirs, the project was not completed until the 1540s; the scale was much smaller than originally planned and it was placed in the Church of San Pietro in Vincoli rather than in St. Peter's. The superb statue of Moses, dated 1515-16, is at the center of the final version of the tomb. It is the sculptural corollary of the powerful illustrations of the prophets in the Sistine Chapel. These figures symbolize the superhuman force that is necessary to liberate mankind from the material world to reach the spiritual world.

THE DIVINE MICHELANGELO

394-395 Michelangelo, Pietà, 1497-1500, marble, St. Peter's, Vatican City. This well-known Pietà is found in St. Peter's and was sculpted at the end of the 15th century. The tender, sad face of the young mother as she holds her dead son in her arms – just as she held him when he was a child – gives to this work a poignancy that is greater than in anything else by this artist. All the artist's attention here was focused on evoking the ideal of spiritual beauty which was so important in the time of the Florentine Medicis, a period of which Michelangelo is one of the most representative artists.

THE PRIVATE
ROOMS OF JULIUS II

396-397 *Raphael,* Debate on the Blessed Sacrament, *1509, fresco, Stanza della Segnatura, the Vatican, Raphael began decorating the apartments of Pope Julius II with the Stanza della Segnatura, the study and private library where he signed and sealed official documents. The themes were chosen by* the Pope and were worked out with the help of a neo-Platonic philosopher. The intention was to glorify Truth, Beauty, and Goodness through allegories of theology, philosophy, justice, and poetry, using illustrations of historical characters who had distinguished themselves in various fields. Raphael *gave many of these figures the features of the great men of his time; Pope Gregory IX has Pope Julius II's face, da Vinci's face appears on the figure of Plato, and so on. In the second room, the* Heliodorus, *the frescoes show a series of heavenly interventions on behalf of the Church.*

398-399 *Raphael*, The Liberation of St. Peter, *detail, 1514, fresco, the Heliodorus Room, the Vatican, Rome.*

*400-401 Raphael, Parnassus,
1510-11, fresco, Stanze, the
Vatican, Rome.*

TITIAN'S WOMEN

402-403 Tiziano Vecellio (Titian),
Sacred and Profane Love, 1515,
canvas, Borghese Gallery, Rome.
This work did not receive its best-
known title until the 17th century.
It has been interpreted in various
ways, including a reading as an
allegory of pagan and Christian
beauty. It shows the strong
expressiveness of Titian, who was
25 years old when he painted it.
He clearly wanted to work with
the contrast between horizontal
and vertical lines, the reserved
beauty of the clothed woman
and the opulent beauty of the
nude, and the presence of the
sarcophagus as a symbol of death
against the fountain, an equally
strong symbol of life.

404-405 Titian, Danaë, 1545-46, oil on canvas, Naples, Capodimonte Museum. Titian had many powerful clients, including doges and kings, cardinals and pontiffs. Among the most important was Pope Paul III's nephew, Cardinal Alexander Farnese, for whom the painter took up the theme of Danaë. Along with Venus, Danaë was among the mythological subjects he most loved. The skillful use of color, combined with the strongly sensual quality of the large nude, makes this a work of tremendous charm.

MEDITATIONS
ON DEATH

406-407 Michelangelo, tomb of
Lorenzo de' Medici, Duke of
Urbino, 1524-34, the New Sacristy,
St. Lorenzo's Church, Florence,
with statues of Dawn and Evening
at Lorenzo's feet.

THE MOVEMENT TOWARD MANNERISM

408-409 Lorenzo Lotto, Portrait of a Gentleman, c. 1527, canvas, Academy, Venice. This painting is filled with information about the gentleman in the portrait for those who can read it. The masterpiece shows signs of great refinement in the ribbons, compasses, a ring, letters, a lady's soft shawl, and the petals of a withered rose. The art historian Anna Banti has written that the gentleman illustrated must have had an extremely secretive character!

410-411 Raphael, Portrait of Julius II, 1511-12, panel, Uffizi, Florence. At the same time that he was decorating the Vatican Stanze, Raphael was also busy with a series of portraits, which he saw as simple displays of affection for friends and acquaintances or dutiful gestures toward patrons. Among these works is the famous portrait of Julius II, who is shown as a solitary old man still full of energy and dignity. This portrait, of the Pope reveals the way in which the Urbino-born artist saw the human figure. Raphael's figures, unlike Michelangelo's, were not torn between the physical and the spiritual worlds; rather, he saw them as having achieved interior balance. In this portrait, attention was also given to the psychological state of the subject. His obvious energy, wealth, and strength of character displays Julius II's self-confidence despite his great age; his surroundings, from his clothing to his numerous rings, support this impression.

GUIDO RENI AND SENSUALITY

414-415 *Guido Reni,* Atalanta and Hippomenus, *canvas, Capodimonte Museum, Naples. A Bolognese artist who combined the opposing schools of the Caracci brothers and Caravaggio, Guido Reni seems to look back to the Mannerists in this mythological painting. His transparent overlays, the use of cold colors and unusual shades, the crossing lines, and the diagonally traced bodies reveal a uniquely subtle, somewhat nervous style of painting.*

TWO DESCENTS
FROM THE CROSS

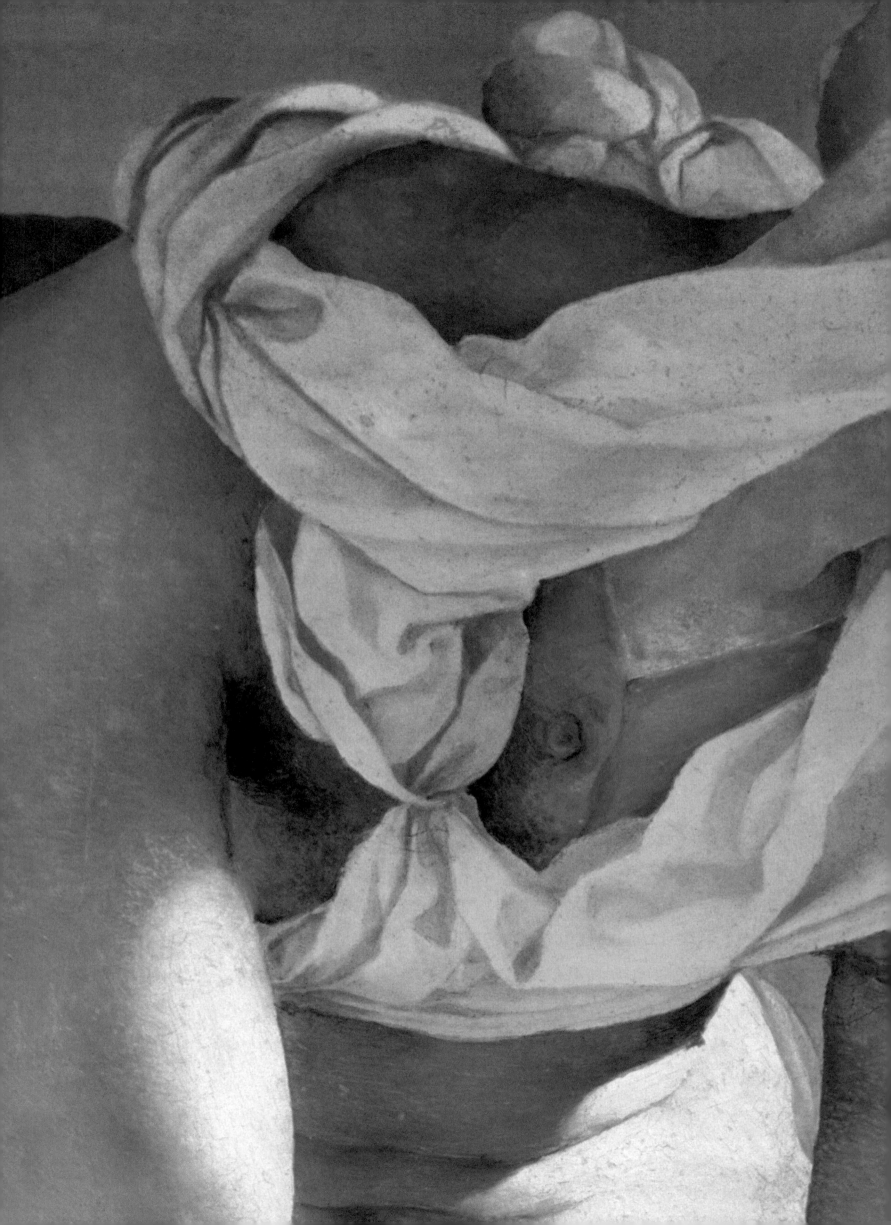

422-423 and 424-425 *Rosso Fiorentino*, The Descent from the Cross, *1521, panel, Pinacoteca, Volterra*.

AMONG LEAVES
AND FLOWERS

426-427 *Antonio Allegri, known as Correggio, decoration of the Abbess's Apartment, 1519, fresco, Convent of St. Paul, Parma. Allegri's first commission, from the cultivated Abbess Giovanna Piacenza, was obtained before he reached the age of thirty. This painter of style and grace decorated an apartment in her convent. Originality, pictorial freshness, and illusionism serve to create a flowering pergola, encircled by putti and cupids in a whirl of colors. More than a place of spiritual retreat, the convent of St. Paul also served as an elegant meeting place for the ladies of Parma's high society. The figurative playfulness of the vault (which becomes a pergola dense with vegetation with openings that enclose sculptures similar to real figures) shows the contrast between truth and fiction, nature and art- art that is a joy for the eyes and an ornament for a noble and exquisite society.*

428-429 Correggio, the Abbess'
Apartment, detail of the vault.

LIGHT AND SHADE IN VENETIAN PAINTING

430 Jacopo Robusti, known as Tintoretto, St. Mark Rescuing the Saracen, *1563-66, for the Scuola di San Marco, oil on canvas, Academy, Venice.*

431 Tintoretto, Removal of the Body of St. Mark, *1563-66, for the Scuola di San Marco, oil on canvas, Academy, Venice. The son of a cloth dyer from whom he took the nickname Tintoretto ("the tinted one"), Jacopo Robusti accepted the teachings of the Mannerist school. He studied the works of Michelangelo and, above all, was fascinated by the theatrical element which became the dominant keynote of his work. With his large canvases for the Scuola Grande di San Marco he became an important part of the Venetian scene. He received praise from discerning critic Pietro Aretino because of his entirely original use of theatricality and spectacular scenes. In the paintings depicting scenes from the life of St. Mark, Tintoretto pursued the theme of supernatural intervention as both a wonder and a miracle, a theme which became dominant in his work. His very dynamic scenes feature strong contrasts of light and oblique flights into the distance, both surprising and emotionally involving the spectator. In this amazing new way of representing the miraculous, Tintoretto heralded some of the favorite themes of the Baroque period.*

434-435 *Paolo Veronese,* The Feast in the House of Levi, *1573, oil on canvas, Academy, Venice. In 1573, Veronese painted a Last Supper for the Convent of San Zanipolo. It met with the disapproval of the Inquisition because of the unconventional images the artist had introduced into the religious picture, and because he was suspected of practicing Lutheran heresy. When asked whether he thought it fitting that the painting should include "buffoons, drunkards, German soldiers, dwarfs, and other similar scurrilities," Veronese answered that painters were permitted the same license as poets and madmen; then he saved his painting by changing its title to* The Feast in the House of Levi. *Anticipating much modern theory on the use of color, Veronese discovered the luminous effect created by juxtaposing complementary shades such as ruby red with emerald green, and yellow with violet, to created a gratifyingly pleasing effect. The greatest example of this method is seen, perhaps, in the frescoes in the Villa Barbaro-Volpi at Maser, near Treviso.*

NEW WAYS OF
SHOWING LIGHT

*438-439 Michelangelo Merisi
da Caravaggio,* The Calling of
St. Matthew, *1599-1600, canvas,
San Luigi dei Francesi, Cappella
Contarelli, Rome.*

439 Caravaggio, St. Matthew and
the Angel, *1602, canvas, San Luigi
dei Francesci, Rome, Capella
Contarelli. In this work, the story
of St. Matthew's martyrdom is set
in the time of the artist; the people
in the picture are dressed in
clothes of the 1600s. Like
Masaccio, Caravaggio used
contemporary settings in this*
*way to enhance the Christian
experience. The light has a new
and strong value, an
expressiveness never before seen.
Similarly, the composition with
St. Matthew and the angel shows
originality in the way in which
the saint is surprised at his work
as the angel dictates to him the
genealogy of Christ.*

440-441 *Caravaggio*, Rest During the Flight into Egypt, *c. 1593, canvas, Galleria Doria Pamphili, Rome. Caravaggio is noted for the tremendous power of his painting and his novel way of avoiding every convention and academic tradition. Nevertheless, he offers a landscape with muted colors, glimpses of nature in the foreground, and an atmosphere of domestic intimacy and tenderness as the Virgin and Child are put to sleep by music played by the angel.*

442-443 *Caravaggio*, Basket of Fruit, *c. 1596, canvas, Pinacoteca Ambrosiana, Milan.*

STATUES FOR THE CARDINAL

444-445 Gianlorenzo Bernini, Apollo and Daphne, 1622-25, marble, Galleria Borghese, Rome. Tremendous energy and a strong view of the world made it possible for this great Neapolitan sculptor and architect, mainly active at the papal court, to bring a new vision to sculpture. With a series of monumental groups commissioned by Cardinal Scipione Borghese (one of the most brilliant patrons of the arts of the time) for his villa-museum, this artist was able to show his skill. Among his works for Borghese are the twisted statue of David and the group of Apollo and Daphne, which takes the verses of Ovid's Metamorphoses and shapes it into marble. Through Bernini's ability, the marble came to seem almost as transparent as alabaster.

446-447 Gianlorenzo Bernini, Apollo and Daphne, detail, marble, 1622-25, Rome, Galleria Borghese.

448-449 Gianlorenzo Bernini, David, detail, 1623, marble, Galleria Borghese, Rome.

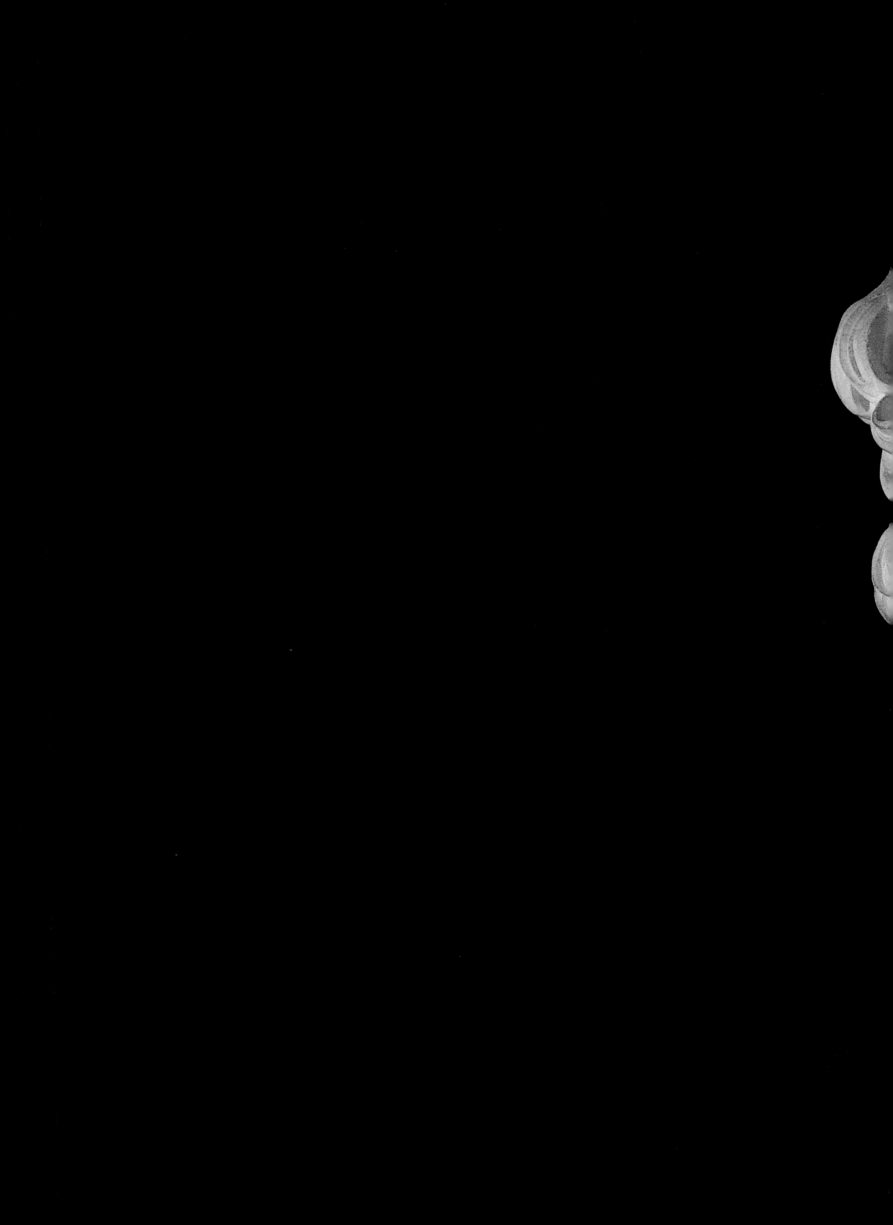

NEOCLASSICAL TASTE

450-451 Antonio Canova, Paolina Borghese Bonaparte as Victorious Venus, 1804-1808, marble, Galleria Borghese, Rome. The Neoclassical ideal of sublime beauty, for which the artist constantly strives, can be seen in this famous sculpture of the sister of Napoleon and wife of Prince Camillo Borghese. Canova put a thin layer of wax over the nude statue to give the marble a pinkish transparency. In addition to this evocation of the softness of flesh (the same which we find in his famous Three Graces), Canova created a slight feeling that the features of the face are actually quivering. The half-closed lips and the softness of the cushions combine to evoke a subtle eroticism.

The appeal of the sacred

There is nothing that equals the continuous historical importance of the Church, which from the beginning of the Christian era brought both culture and art to Italian life. Today it may be difficult to imagine what churches once meant for the people. The building itself was often the only stone building within a wide area, the only building of any importance. Its towers served as a reference point for people traveling from a distance. During religious ceremonies, the citizens of a city would gather in the church; the contrast between the tall building, replete with paintings and sculptures, and the humble homes where they spent their everyday lives must have been overwhelmingly dramatic. One can understand why communities took so much interest in the construction of their churches and why they took so much pride in the richness of their decoration.

The building of a church often took place over a period of years or even decades, and in economic terms transformed an entire city. The quarrying of the stone and its transport, the preparation of scaffolding, the employment of wandering craftsmen who brought not only their skills but also stories of distant lands. . . . all represented an event of real economic importance.

The construction of the first basilicas created the need for a large symbolic repertory from which artists could draw in order that the holy word could be spread to everyone. The Old Testament, with its scope and wealth of events, was from the beginning the source of a great deal of inspiration for Christian artists. It is also believed that the earliest Christian symbols – the dove, fish, and lyre – were borrowed from pagan iconography, with symbolic meanings which often proved difficult to interpret.

454-455 St. Cosmas and St. Damian, *6th century, mosaic in the apse of Rome.*

455

456 *Sacra di San Michele, Susa, 12th century, detail of the sculpted decoration of a window. The Sacra di San Michele, one of the most singular Romanesque buildings in the region, is located at the entrance to the Susa valley. In the Middle Ages, this valley was a busy route for pilgrims and for Crusaders heading for ports before sailing to the Holy Land. Lombard, Ligurian and Tuscan merchants also used this route. According to tradition, the Benedictine Abbey was founded in 988. It was in a strategic position of great importance, and became not only a destination for pilgrims but also the central refuge of the population, as indicated by the walls around it. The church itself gives the effect of a fortress and is built on a very high base which also contains the monastery buildings. The sculptural decoration is of great interest. There is a monumental staircase and a portal sculpted in the first half of the 12th century with doorposts bearing the symbols of the constellations and the signs of the zodiac.*

Pope Gregory the Great, living in the middle of the sixth century A.D., believed that painting could be as great in value to the illiterate as writing was to those who could read. Since many members of the church could neither read nor write, the paintings served the same purpose as an illustrated book can serve a child. The subjects were presented in as clear and simple a way as possible, excluding everything which might distract from their basic religious purpose.

For much of the Middle Ages, Christian iconography consisted of decorated manuscripts and liturgical texts and illustrated books. The creativity of the artist was therefore somewhat limited, until Giotto at Padua and Duccio da Buoninsegna at Siena, viewing the conventional figurative themes from another angle, advanced religious art with their detailed, realistic, paintings.

During the Renaissance, and even more clearly during the Baroque era, the artist became progressively more detached from the subject, and artistic works became more independent of traditional religious iconography. While the formal links are maintained, the content of the work often varies from traditional schemes. In some cases, there is a partial or total extraction of the theological content; this changed the relationship between culture and religion, which until that point had more or less coincided. While the subject of art remained religious, it reflected the problems of the artist and embraced the philosophical, scientific, and cultural elements of the age in which he lived.

Stylistic Developments

After the edict of Constantine in 313 A.D. that decreed the full liberalization of the Christian religion, a standard typology for churches was established. These first churches were basilicas with a longitudinal plan. Various theories have been put forward to explain the choice of such a design, but the most valid, perhaps, is that which suggests that architectural elements from the pagan world were adjusted to meet the needs of the new religion. At the same time, there came in from the Near East churches which had a central plan, originally used for small buildings and later for churches of quite remarkable size. During the Medieval period, the basilica plan was dominant in both Romanesque and Gothic churches, although often in different versions.

Churches with a central plan became increasingly important during the Renaissance. The cultural environment which favored this plan also fostered the emergence of philosophical ideas, studies, and treatises about man and his central role in the order and rationality of nature. Furthermore, a renewed interest in the studies of classicism and a careful study of the works of Vitruvio supported the view that man, enclosed in a circle or square, was the symbol of the universe.

During the seventeenth century, religious building design was subjected to the influence of two different but connected movements. The Counter Reformation movement supported the need for preaching and propagandizing in the renewed church; the other movement reflected a different artistic feeling and an altered spiritual sensibility, and aimed at expressing the church triumphant. This led to an increase in the number of churches which consisted of only a single large area without chapels and excessive decoration; on the other hand, there was a marked preference for centralized or elliptical plans that represented an attempt to open the religion to the people. Bernini's vision of space, for instance, reflects this feeling.

Romanesque and Gothic Cathedrals

After the year 1000 A.D., when the irrational fear of the millennium had passed, Europe saw an exceptional building fervor. This was tied to an increase in population, economic development, and the investment of treasures accumulated over the centuries or brought back from expeditions to the Orient. Cathedrals have been called the first great financial effort of the new Europe. A German monk, Rudolf, addressed this phenomenon. He pointed out that all over the world, and especially in Italy and France, people were rebuilding churches not because it was necessary but rather in a competition to see who had the best buildings. In France alone, eighty cathedrals and five hundred large churches were built over the course of three centuries. Those who took part in the building received religious indulgences.

The enthusiasm for this movement was compared by the twentieth-century architect Le Courbusier to the enthusiasm of the modern world as advances in technology brought countries closer together. Europe, he felt, had at the millennium organized crafts into a search for new techniques which led to both unexpected and unknown forms. A universal language favored the exchange of culture from the West to the East and from the North to the South. In a similar way the twentieth century was able to bring diverse cultures together.

In Romanesque and Norman churches, round arches usually rest on solid pillars. The general impression that these churches give both internally and externally is that of massive power. They have little decoration, few windows, strong walls, and towers reminiscent of medieval fortresses. These huge masses of stone, built by the church in a land of farmers and warriors who had only recently converted from paganism, seemed to express the concept of a militant church. These buildings offered shelter from the assaults of evil; according to this concept, the duty of the church on earth was to fight the powers of darkness until the Day of Judgement, when the hour of triumph for the church would come. The structural revolution of the Romanesque style was based on a technique which must have appeared extremely daring. In Sant'Ambrogio in Milan and in many cathedrals in the Lombardy area, the roof has a system of cross vaults. It is no longer separate from the walls, but joins with them to constitute a unique mass and image.

The cathedrals, built as they were over decades, were active building sites watched enthusiastically by the citizenry. In these hives of activity, architects acted at one and the same time as contractors, urban planners, and engineers. Some of them became heroes in their own days, such as Lanfranco, builder of Mantova Cathedral. He was described as both mirabilis artifex and magnificus aedificator – an admirable artist and a magnificent builder.

459 Lorenzo Ghiberti, the bronze doors of the Baptistery, detail, Florence, 1424-1452.

460 Leonardo da Vinci, The
Last Supper, *1495-97, tempera
on plaster, refectory of the Convent
of Santa Maria delle Grazie,
Milan.*

The basic building materials, chosen from those available in the region, were normally left with their natural surfaces. Only the sculptures would sometimes receive a delicate polychromatic protective covering. The masons, organized into corporations based on secret codes and various degrees of initiation from the apprentices up to the master, met in lodges at the base of the cathedral. This base was a covered workshop where they could continue working during the winter. The building under construction was directly controlled by the Chapter, a group of canons who were independent of the bishop. Normally, the cathedral was not only the guiding center of religious life, but also the center of civic life (along with the town hall and the market square). In the aisles of these religious buildings one could have discussions and do business; during this period, the church drew nearer than it had ever been before to being the multi-functional equivalent of the pagan basilicas.

As well as being the symbol of the bishop and the religion, the cathedral was also the pride of the entire town and came to express strength as well as faith. There were even some fortified churches which, in times of need, could give shelter to the inhabitants of the town. It has been said that every cathedral should be viewed as a safe refuge, representing the military vocation of a feudal society. One commentator said that the Gothic cathedral is bourgeois and urban, while the Romanesque is monastic and aristocratic. The bourgeois aspect of the Gothic cathedral arose because the lay community came to play more and more of a part in the building of cathedrals, which in themselves could never have existed without the wealth of the cities.

From the thirteenth century on, Gothic architecture introduced new techniques which represented more than just technical developments. The pillars alone became sufficient to hold up the ribs of the vault; the stones between only filled the space, making it unnecessary to build massively thick walls. It was possible to build a framework in stone that could hold the entire construction. All that was needed were slender pillars and narrow vaulting ribs – there was no longer any need for heavy stone walls and, indeed, wide windows could be added. Soon, structures in stone and glass could be constructed, unlike anything previously known. This was the inspiration for the Gothic cathedral. Using flying buttresses to complete the ribbing of the vault, the Gothic cathedral was able to appear suspended within its stone structure.

Standing inside a Gothic cathedral, we can see the complex play of compression and tension which sustains the high vault; there are no walls or massive pillars blocking our view. These new cathedrals gave the faithful a vision that almost matched Revelations, with its prophesy of pearl doors, priceless gems, and roads of pure gold and transparent glass. In the Gothic period, it seemed as if this vision had come down from heaven to earth. The walls of these buildings were not cold and unpleasant but rich with beautiful windows which shone like precious stones. The believer who abandoned himself to this beauty could feel close to understanding the mysteries of the Kingdom of Heaven. Even from a distance, these buildings seemed to proclaim the Heavenly Host and the prestige of a triumphant church.

The Central Plan Renaissance Church

The history of science is of basic importance to the story of humanism. When Filippo Brunelleschi became the director of building for the Cathedral of Santa Maria del Fiore in Florence, he was supposed to use the original foundation created by the Gothic architects: an octagonal cupola with equilateral ribs along with the mystical significance of that Marian crown. However, he used a radically new and different method. He was unable to use traditional scaffolding that rested on the ground, nor were specialized craftsmen available. This led to a variety of amazing inventions. The dome was built with suspended scaffolding, and the building site was organized in an almost industrial way.

Aside from Brunelleschi's technological inventions, the political value of the building also upset medieval perspectives. The dome, Leon Battista Alberti said, seemed to cover all the people of Tuscany with its shadow, reflecting the new imperialistic will of Florence. In this aspect, the cathedral revealed itself as "state architecture" beyond feudalism, aiming for both national and regional hegemony.

Despite its being added onto the base of the Gothic cathedral, the dome of Santa Maria del Fiore is the first great temple built upon the central plan as developed by humanism, first in architectural theory and later in actual practice. It was Leon Battista Alberti especially who, in the mid-fifteenth century, codified a new vision of space which changed not only the spatial but also the religious view of the Gothic cathedral.

462-463 *Pavia*, The Charterhouse,
Giovanni Solari, 15th century.

464 *Filippo Brunelleschi, Capella dei Pazzi in Santa Croce, Florence, 15th century, interior.*

The Great Hall Churches of the Counter Reformation

The history of Saint Peter's in Rome reflects the contrast between the styles of churches. The first plans, developed by Giuliano da Sangallo and Fra'Giocondo were, respectively, a cross inside a square and a basilica similar to St. Mark's in Venice. After the actual building had begun a debate started; over the course of the sixteenth century it became a real argument. Numerous plans were presented by many architects, including Raphael, which had the aim of transforming Bramante's temple into a basilica. The nave was finally built by Carlo Maderno. It should be remembered in any discussion of the building of St. Peter's that it was the selling of indulgences for this colossal building which provoked Martin Luther's protest and Rome's reply, changing the course of Christianity.

Following the radical movement led by the German monk against the absurd and almost Babylonian splendor of the Roman church and after the Reformation and the sack of Rome in 1527, the Vatican took a series of countermeasures. These involved the foundation of other new religious orders, a reorganization of other orders through the Society of Jesus (the Jesuits, founded 1534), the revival of the Inquisition, and the setting up of the Holy Office. It was, however, primarily the Council of Trent (1545-1563) which established the strategies for regaining lost credibility through a new way of viewing religion.

At the same time, the church exercised a rigid control over art. Primarily because of the strong Jesuit influence, a new type of hall began to be built. This type of church was considered the most suitable for preaching, and the Council of Trent considered it a way of attracting the masses to the church. The Chiesa del Gesù in Rome (1568-1573) can be considered both the prototype and the conclusion to a debate that had lasted centuries.

The result was reached in the end by the contrasts between the needs of the Jesuits and Cardinal Alessandro Farnese, its powerful commissioner and financier. The Society of Jesus was able to impose the already tried and tested design of the church; the Cardinal, in his turn, was able to ensure that the hall was vaulted like the transept of St. Peter's rather than having the flat roof suggested by the Jesuits. Once this compromise had been reached it was left to the selected architect, Vignola, to give formal definition to a type of church which was to find great favor throughout the entire Catholic world. The history of the Chiesa del Gesù had a significant influence on later architecture; various treatises printed from the middle of the sixteenth century onward praised the design of the church and its construction. Cardinal Borromeo, for instance, urged bishops to consult with an architect in designing churches, and also urged that the building should be in the shape of a cross as in the Roman basilicas. Andrea Palladio pointed out the value of the cross shape as well, saying that it represented the cross on which Jesus was crucified.

467 *Francesco Borromini,
Sant'Ivo alla Sapienza, mid-14th
century, Rome, interior of the
dome.*

The Theatrical in the Baroque Church

In the first quarter of the seventeenth century, Saint Peter's became the backdrop to the Roman church's proclamation of triumph after the struggle of the Reformation. In the transept of the Vatican basilica, sumptuous scenes were created to celebrate the heroes of this war. In 1610 a provisional section was built onto the basilica for the canonization of Carlo Borromeo, and in 1622 Ignatius of Loyola, Teresa of Avila, Filippo Neri, and Francesco Saverio were all proclaimed saints at the same time. In 1623 in Saint Peter's, Gianlorenzo Bernini began work on the baldacchino, or canopy, one of the outstanding features of Baroque architecture. Over the course of several decades he redesigned the basilica with sculptures and many colored statues, culminating in the Cathedra itself. Finally, Bernini built the colonnade, which brought a new urban feeling of space to St. Peter's. The colonnade in St. Peter's Square is not only an entrance to the church but also takes the church further into the city. The two rows of columns represent the church embracing the faithful. Bernini felt that the entrance must show that the church welcomes Catholics with open arms as a mother welcomes a child, while it also welcomes heretics and infidels in order to bring them to the truth faith.

Each of Bernini's works can be viewed as part of a great spectacle. Many of his religious sculptures can be viewed as tragic recitations; his architectural efforts have a theatrical element as well. Consider the "theater within the theater" aspect of the Raimondi Chapel in San Pietro in Montorio and the Cornaro Chapel in Santa Maria della Vittoria, where each chapel is a smaller dramatic stage within the larger stage of the church itself. Sant'Andrea al Quirinale provides a total scene and the Church of the Assumption a backdrop to the story of Christianity.

Every means possible was used to spread the religion. The use of light in architecture was important in this respect. During the Middle Ages and into the age of humanism, light was used in a metaphysical way; then it changed into a physical use of light inside a definite space. For Caravaggio, light was an instrument of meditation and, indeed, redemption. In Baroque architecture light was used with such skill that while true light was reflected from bronze and stucco there was also the impression of additional light coming from within the materials themselves.

From time to time, light was made to take on different characteristics: light being reflected; light coming from above, the side, or the back; half-light or dim light; chambers of light – all part of a plan to create theaters of light and sound. When one enters these churches it is possible to understand how the splendor and ostentation of precious stones, gold, and stucco were designed to evoke heavenly glory in a more literal sense than that of medieval cathedrals. The more the Protestants preached against the ostentation of the church, the more anxiously did the church try to acquire the work of the finest artists. Thus the Reformation and its challenge to the cult of images had a direct effect on the development of the Baroque style.

The Roman Catholic church had realized that art could serve religion more broadly than it had in the Middle Ages, when it was limited to teaching the gospel to the illiterate. It was now viewed as a way to convert those who, perhaps, had actually read too much. Architects, sculptors, and painters were called upon to transform the churches into huge art shows of overpowering splendor. These spaces were perfect frames for the sumptuous rites of the Roman Catholic church.

With the fall of Renaissance philosophy, its morality also collapsed. The once seemingly rational hierarchical structure of the universe became relational, and was replaced by more direct and emotional relationships. A new age was born; the relationship between spectator and work of art was completely changed.

With this, Leon Battista Alberti's view of a rigid law-ordered world, in which everything is clearly defined, was no longer adequate. Everything seemed to be rely upon chance; even the categories of aesthetic pleasure changed.

The contemplation of a fifteenth-century masterpiece is based on a static but delicate balance of emotion and logic. Man, moving from the initial vision, gradually entered into an increasingly subtle world of interpretation, participating psychologically in an interior both secret and harmonious.

In the seventeenth century, man and art lost this balance. In the new forms of architecture, every turn brought a surprise; decoration was based on a variety of perspectives; canvases were loaded with mystery; surfaces formerly a simple white or gray plaster were luxuriously gilded. All these changes were part of a collective turning away from the past. In the seventeenth century, the need for law was felt strongly – but since it could no longer be based on reason it had to be based on consent and on tradition. By insisting on this concept, society was saved from chaos. The art and architecture of the period embody this effort. Beneath the sensuality and rhetoric of religious painting and the splendor of these gilded churches lies the terror of eternal damnation, the need to reinforce the culture, and the desire to create an aura of permanence within the civilization of the period.

Propaganda has never been so much at one with art. At no time since the seventeenth century has the relativity of affirmed values been felt so acutely; nor has the reaction to the dangers of a crisis – the Reformation – been so decisive.

468-469 Rome, Santa Maria Maggiore, façade, 4th and 5th centuries.

LIGHT EXPRESSED
IN STONE

470-471 San Vitale, Ravenna, 6th century, mosaic decoration of the vault, Emperor Justinian, Bishop Maximian, and the court. The extreme simplicity of the external architecture contrasts with the richness of the internal decoration. It also contrasts with the complexity of the plan, which is an octagon around a smaller octagon, all opening into an exedra. The principal elements of decoration are the elegant capitals, the marbles, and the mosaics.

472-473 *Mausoleum of Galla Placidia, Ravenna, 5th century, interior, mosaic over the entrance showing Christ as the Good Shepherd.*

474-475 *Mausoleum of Galla Placidia, 5th century, Ravenna.*

472

THE CHARM OF THE BYZANTINE EAST

476-477 St. Mark's, Venice, 11th century and later. The fundamental architectural nucleus of the basilica, which we can no longer see, was a large building in the form of a Greek cross topped by five domes. This is the third construction of the basilica, made in the 12th century as a visible expression of Venetian power. The decoration uses numerous materials – stone, marble, and bronze – for sculptures, bas-reliefs, and mosaics, and was finished only in the 16th century. It somewhat cancels the effect of the thickness of the masonry structure. In the façade, the Romanesque influence can be seen in the lower part, while the upper arches and crowning statues are Gothic.

478-479 *St. Mark's, detail of the façade*

480 *St. Mark's, four bronze horses which decorate the façade. The gilded bronze horses, pride of the basilica, are over six feet high. They are a Byzantine work dating from the 4th century; along with many other relics and precious objects, enamels and icons, they represent the treasure of St. Mark's. These works are all rich booty of the Fourth Crusade, which was led by the Venetian Republic and ended in the sack of Constantinople.*

481 *Venice, St. Mark's, interior. The interior of the basilica is of incredible richness. Mosaics entirely cover the upper part of the building; precious multi-colored marble and ancient and medieval columns can be found. Here, with the golden light flooding the basilica, it is clear why Emperor Basil II referred to Venice as "Beloved daughter of Byzantium."*

REMEMBERING THE NORMAN KINGS

482-483 Cappella Palatina, Palermo, 1132. Arab-Norman Palermo is represented in all its splendor by the Cappella Palatina, the royal oratory built by Roger II in the Palazzo dei Normanni, an extraordinary example of different moods coexisting in a single building.

The small basilica has three apses and three naves divided by columns which are supported by Arabic arches. The extremely rich mosaic decoration combines the Byzantine and Arab worlds. The mosaics completely cover the walls, domes, and apses and are the work of craftsmen brought from Byzantium. The rich wooden ceiling with its decoration in the central nave is a masterpiece of Arabic craftsmanship.

484-485 *Monreale, the cathedral, 12th century, detail of the capitals, the apse, the choir, and the bronze door by Bonanno Pisano On ascending to the throne, William II wanted to follow his ancestor Roger by building a cathedral worthy of the royal Norman tradition. This was the inspiration for the construction at Monreale of a cathedral based on the one in Cefalù. In this work, the characteristic Norman eclecticism is apparent in works including mosaics and fired polychromatic enamels. Along with those in Venice, the mosaics in Monreale are the most important document of Byzantine mosaic art in Italy. The church is also decorated with two bronze doors of western manufacture. The door in the façade, inserted in a portal with marble decorations, is the work of Bonanno Pisano and dates from 1186.*

FROM ROMANESQUE RIGOR TO THE BEGINNING OF THE GOTHIC

486 *Interior of the Baptistery, Parma, end of the 12th century. The octagonal Baptistery is the most important in north Italy. Begun at the end of the 12th century and not finished until 130 years later, Benedetto Antelami worked on it as both sculptor and architect. He was the first artist to change from the traditional Romanesque equilibrium to the new Gothic style, combining the tradition of Lombardy, his home, with his direct experience of French culture.*

488 Vuolvinio, front of the
reliquary altar, wooden box
covered with gold and gilded silver
leaf, precious stones, and enamels,
9th century, Milan,
Sant'Ambrogio. This golden altar
is one of the most important
works by a goldsmith from this
period. The primitive basilica
of Sant'Ambrogio was built in
the 4th century. In conformity
with the design of paleo-Christian
buildings, it had a longitudinal
plan. Over the centuries its
structure underwent many
complex changes, finally
culminating in the 12th
century with the construction
of the present basilica. This
building is a testament to the
difficult technical progress
which accompanied its
transformation into a
Romanesque cathedral.

489 Milan, Sant'Ambrogio,
12th century, aerial view of
the building.

490 bottom and 491 This basilica, built by Benedetto Antelami, is a typical example of Gothic-Cistercian architecture despite the Romanesque features on its brick and green stone front. The central portal has a lunette sculpted by Antelami himself which shows the martyrdom of St. Andrew.

490 top Vercelli, Sant'Andrea, 13th century, lunette by Benedetto Antelami and interior.

492-493 Vercelli, Sant'Andrea, view of the vaulted ceiling.

RELIGIOUS STORIES

494 Basilica of St. Francis, Assisi, 13th century. This basilica, the center of the Franciscan order, is organized as two churches with single naves and vaulted ceilings. The Lower Church functions as a large, dark crypt while the luminous, slender Upper Church was designed for preaching. This building is one of the best examples in central Italy of the movement from Romanesque forms to the freer interpretation of Gothic forms. On the one hand there is the austere façade and the sturdy bell tower; on the other there is the portal with twin openings, flying buttresses, and ogee windows. In the interior, the life of the saint is illustrated in the stained glass windows, which are among the oldest and most remarkable in Italy. The walls have frescoes by Giotto in the Upper Church and by Pietro Lorenzetti in the Lower Church.

495 Basilica of St. Francis, Assisi, interior with frescoes by Giotto.

496-497 and 498-499 *Basilica of St. Francis, detail from Giotto's frescoes. After 1296 Giotto began the frescoes on the lower part of the nave of San Francesco at Assisi. These works illustrate the life of St. Francis, whose order was expanding rapidly during this period. The saint is represented as an extremely dignified man of his times, in a clear break with traditional ways of portraying saints. Giotto shows the best-known episodes in the saint's life, while continually emphasizing the reality of the objects and animals and the humanity of the people. Moreover, in scenes (such as the saint renouncing worldly goods) the stories are set against precise architectural backgrounds and show personalities who are real and concrete both with regard to their bodies and to their clothes. In this way, Giotto tried to bring the story of this man who embraced poverty to the new bourgeoisie and mercantile reality of his time.*

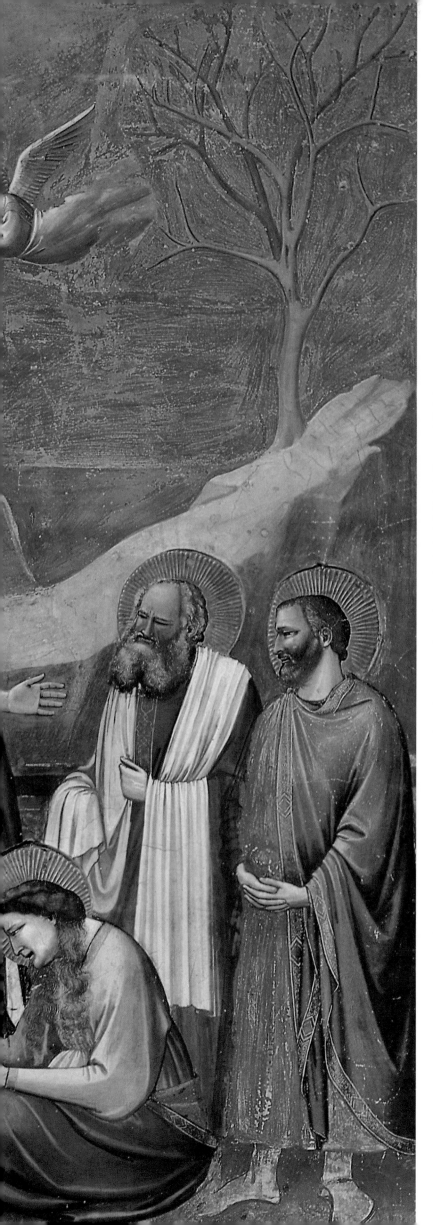

500-501 Scrovegni Chapel, Padua, beginning of the 14th century, frescoes by Giotto. Giotto's paintings, done between 1303 and 1310, cover all the surfaces in this small and simple private chapel of Enrico degli Scrovegni. The paintings define the space, not only in single scenes but also in the general organization of the painted wall and the entire room. The frescoes include the story of the Virgin and Christ; at the rear is a large scene of the Day of Judgment, with a portrait of Enrico degli Scrovegni offering the Virgin a model of the chapel.

MIRACULOUS PISA

502-503 *The Baptistery, Pisa, 12th through 14th centuries. With its green lawns and white marble, Piazza dei Miracoli at Pisa is one of the extraordinary monumental complexes of Italy. It consists of the round Baptistery, the Cathedral, the world famous Leaning Tower, and the large arcades of the cemetery. The Baptistery is built on a Romanesque plan although its final form is more Gothic. Begun in the middle of the 12th century, it was not completed until the end of the 14th, therefore requiring the work of many artists. Nicola and Giovanni Pisano are almost certainly among the creators of the splendid sculptures, placed in niches that run around the building.*

THE CHURCH
TRIUMPHANT

504-505 *The cathedral, Siena, 13th and 14th centuries. Giovanni Pisano participated in the construction of the cathedral at Siena, creating the beautiful façade. This is the only Italian example of this period of an organic relationship between sculpture and architecture. The statues seem almost to speak to one another through their interplay of attitudes and glances.*

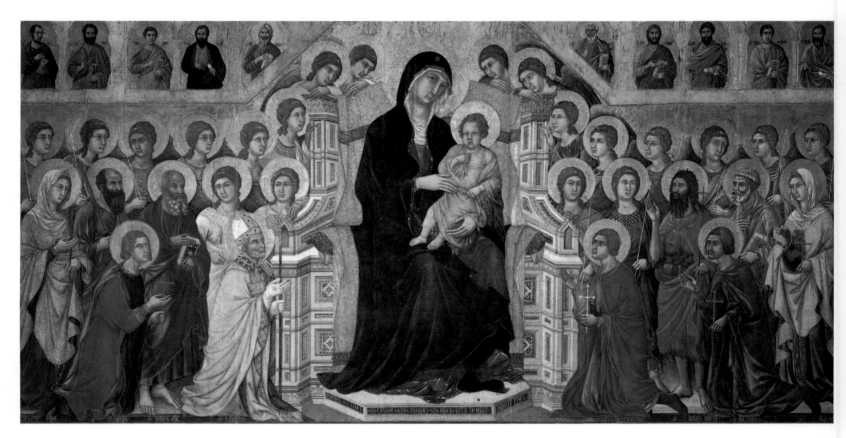

506 *Duccio da Buoninsegna,* Maestà of the Madonna, *1311, panel, Museo dell'Opera del Duomo, Siena. In the Museo dell'Opera del Duomo (Cathedral) is this large work painted by Duccio da Buoninsegna (1308-1311) with* The Maestà of the Enthroned Madonna with the Child, *in the midst of a group of angels and saints. Among the saints is the patron saint of Siena, kneeling in the foreground.*

507 *Siena cathedral, interior view.*

508 Orvieto cathedral, first half of the 14th century. The architect and sculptor Lorenzo Maitani designed the cathedral façade with the delicacy of a goldsmith. He used a wealth of spires and pinnacles, lace-like marble work, and

mosaics. The sculptures are by Maitani, an artist who represented the most elegant Sienese taste.

509 Orvieto cathedral with a view of the Chapel of San Brizio with frescoes by Luca Signorelli.

510-511 Orvieto cathedral, detail of the decoration of the façade.

512-513 Orvieto, Chapel of San Brizio, The Resurrection of the Flesh *from the cycle of frescoes by Luca Signorelli, 1499-1503. Signorelli used apocalyptic visions and terrible images*

to reject false prophecies and bring mankind closer to the Catholic faith. On the eve of the Lutheran reformation, the story of the Antichrist, the Day of Judgment, and the visions of Hell and Paradise in these frescoes reflected the tension of the times.

THE SUPREMACY OF FLORENCE

514-515 *Santa Croce, Florence, façade and details, 13th through 16th centuries. Begun in 1295 by Arnolfo di Cambio for the Franciscan Order, Santa Croce has three naves with wide ogee arches. In the middle of the 16th century, Giorgio Vasari modernized the interior, removing the choir and adding classical altars in the side aisles. Among the many masterpieces in this basilica, a wooden crucifix by Donatello deserves special mention.*

516 Donatello, crucifix, 1425, carved wood, originally polychrome, Santa Croce, Florence.

517 Santa Croce, interior.

518-519 Santa Maria Novello, Florence, detail of the upper part of the façade, 10th century. Leon Battista Alberti, in designing the façade of this church, developed ideas which proved extremely influential. The geometric designs of Romanesque origin are placed within a rational classical structure, combining the traditions of medieval Tuscany with those of ancient Rome.

520-521 Baptistery and Giotto's bell tower, Florence, 11th through 14th centuries. Dedicated to St. John, this baptistery was built in a Romanesque style in the 11th century on the site of a building from ancient times. It has the characteristic octagonal structure and is entirely faced with marble, in a dramatic contrast between the white marble of Carrara and the green marble of Prato. The interior of the dome is covered in mosaics by Venetian masters with Byzantine educations. The floor, with its bi-colored marble insets, is decorated in what can be considered an Oriental style. The gilded and bronzed door, made by Lorenzo Ghiberti at the beginning of the 15th century, is rightfully famous. It is divided into compartments with Bible stories and figures of apostles, sibyls, and personalities of the time. The Baptistery also contains a late work of Donatello (1453-1455) showing Mary Magdalene in a distressing image of the dissolution of a human being.

THE NOBLE FABRIC OF
THE CATHEDRAL

522-523 *The cathedral, Milan, 14th to 19th centuries. Gian Galeazzo Visconti, Lord of Milan, wanted his city to have a cathedral which would show the prestige of Milan both in Italy and north of the Alps.*

524-525 Milan cathedral, windows and two views of the interior. The foundations of Milan's cathedral were laid in 1386. Its design, the result of collaboration by many architects (including foreigners), came from long theoretical discussions on both technical and philosophical matters. Five centuries elapsed between the cathedral's beginning and its completion; nonetheless the architectural style, based on northern European Gothic models, remained true to the original ideas. The interior is divided into five sloping naves covered with groin vaults. The vertical movement in which all the architectural elements combine is made more evocative by the light that shines through the splendid windows.

TITANS AND GIANTS

526-527 Michelangelo, The Creation of Man, from the frescoes in the Sistine Chapel, 1508-12, Vatican City. The program of Pope Sixtus IV for the decoration of the Vatican palaces was intended to celebrate the history of the papacy. At the same time, it was intended to merge the Christian vision with the stories of Moses and the life of Christ. During the first phase of the work, the best artists of the time were engaged, including Perugino, Luca Signorelli, Botticelli, Ghirlandaio, and Piero di Cosimo. In the years between 1481 and 1483, they created a plan filled with symbolic events and crowded with portraits of personalities of the period. This decorative plan was continued by Pope Julius II, with the story of Genesis painted on the ceiling by Michelangelo, and by Leo I, who celebrated the early years of the church with the tapestry cartoons by Raphael. Finally, Pope Paul III concluded this grandiose work with Michelangelo's Last Judgment, completed in 1541.

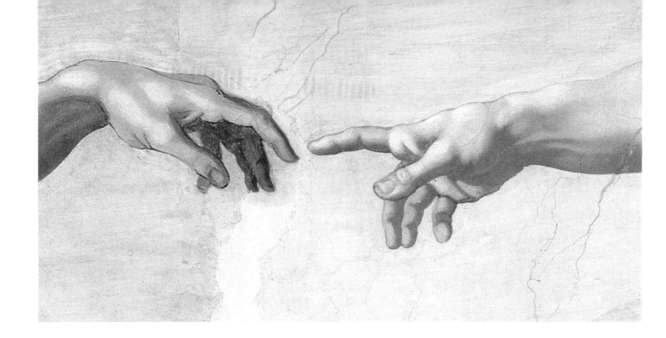

528-529 Michelangelo, *from the frescoes in the Sistine Chapel, detail of the vault.*

530-531 Perugino, The Consignment of the Keys, *from the frescoes in the Sistine Chapel.*

A THANKFUL OFFERING FROM VENICE

532-533 Venice, Santa Maria della Salute, Baldassare Longhena, 17th century. Built by the Venetian senate to thank the Madonna for her intervention in the plague outbreak of 1630, the Salute basilica was started in 1631. It was not consecrated until 1687. Architect Baldassare Longhena placed the grandiose dome on top of a high tambour circle, which in its turn is connected to the lower body of the church, making it one of the most notable features of the Venetian skyline. Using white stone, with a light gray stone for the dome, Longhena fully exploited the play of light and reflection so typical of Venice. A similar play of light and shade is found in the interior of the octagonal structure; the load-bearing parts are of gray stone, and the walls are covered with white plaster.

THE EMBRACE OF THE CHURCH

534-535 St. Peter's Basilica, Rome, 16th and 17th centuries, overall view with the square filled with people, the dome, and the colonnade. Construction of the most famous building in Christianity began in the reign of Pope Julius II, at the start of the 16th century. Over the centuries there were many discussions about the plan and whether to use the conservative Latin cross or the more innovative central plan; the artists Giuliano da Sangallo, Bramante, Raphael, Antonio da Sangallo, Peruzzi, and Michelangelo all worked on the building. In 1547 the job was given to Michelangelo, who decided to follow the central plan originally suggested by Bramante.

536-537 St. Peter's, Rome; three
different views of Bernini's
canopy. At the beginning of the
17th century, Pope Urban VIII
summoned Gianlorenzo Bernini to
complete the long drawn
out construction of St. Peter's.
We owe the canopy, which was
finished in 1633, to him. It
immediately became the prototype
for numerous imitations and
variations. He was also responsible
for the large oval colonnade in the
square in front of the cathedral.
This solution is skillful for more
than one reason. Not only can
it hold large numbers of people,
it also satisfied the Pope's desire
to symbolize the arms of the
church reaching out to the
faithful. The colonnade acts as
the solemn entrance to the most
important church in Rome, and
perhaps the world.

538-539 St. Peter's Square, Rome.

INDEX

A

Abballu di li Giudei (San Fratello), 312c
Abbondanza, Via dell' (Pompeii), 160c, 161c
Abruzzese, Apennines, 30c, 31c
Abruzzo, 17, 120c, 310c
Accademia, Galleria dell' (Venice), 254c, 366c, 367c, 388c, 389c, 408c, 409c, 430c, 431c
Acireale, 136c, 312c
Adamello, 58c, 59c
Adda, river, 32, 58c
Adige, river, 61c, 158, 222c, 223c
Adoration of the Magi, by Beato Angelico, 341c
Adoration of the True Cross, by Piero della Francesca, 348c
Adriatic Sea, 31c, 40, 94c, 95c, 276c, 277c
Aeolian, islands, 42c, 43, 138c, 139c, 142c, 143c
Aesculapius, 154c, 183c
Agnelli, family, 57c
Agostino di Duccio, 268c
Agri, river, 36c, 37c
Agrigento, 156, 156c, 312c, 313c
Aiguille du Glacier, 2c, 3c
Aiguille du Midi, 2c, 3c
Aiguille Noire, 44c
Ailly, Pierre d', 15
Alagna, 56c, 57c, 308c
Alassio, 96c, 97c
Alatri, 156
Alban Hills, 35
Albano, lake, 35
Albaro, 243c
Albenga, 96c
Alberti, Leon Battista, 254c, 323, 457, 462, 466, 518c, 519c
Albertini, villa (Garda), 33
Albo, mountain, 144c, 145c
Alcamo, 134c
Alcantara gorge, 134c
Alexandria (Egypt), 226c, 227c
Alexander VII, pope, 168
Alfieri, Piazza (Asti), 296c, 297c
Alfieri, Vittorio, 250c
Alfonso of Aragon, 336c
Alghero, 285c, 302c, 303c
Alighieri, Dante, 162c, 163c
Alps, 17, 28, 28c, 29, 29c, 30, 32, 36, 50c, 73c, 196c, 197c, 205c, 522c, 523c
Alpini, Via degli (Verona), 223c
Altoatesine, Alps, 72c
Amadeo, Giovanni Antonio, 215c
Amalfi, 40c, 41c, 163, 305c
Amalfitana Coast, 40c, 41c, 130c, 131c
Amati, Carlo, 204c, 205c
Ambrosiana, art gallery (Milan), 442c, 443c
Ammannati, Bartolomeo, 254c
Ampezzane, Dolomites, 67c
Amphitheater (Capua), 223c
Anacapri, 126c, 127c
Anagni, 156
Ancona, 40, 163
Andrea da Bologna, 270c
Andrea del Castagno, 320
Angera, 76c, 77c
Angera, Rocca di, 76c, 77c
Anguillara Sabazia, 35c
Anguillara, family, 35c
Antelami, Benedetto, 203c, 486c, 487c, 490c, 491c
Antermoia, 70c
Antinoös, 158c, 159c
Antolini, Giovanni, 174c
Antonelli, Alessandro, 203c
Antonelliana, Mole (Turin), 196c, 197c, 203c
Antony Abbot, saint, 310c, 311c, 312c
Antonio da Ponte, 232c, 233c
Annunciation, by Leonardo da Vinci, 352c
Annunciation, by Simone Martini, 330c
Aosta, 55c, 158, 160, 199c
Aosta Valley, 48c, 49c, 50c, 51c, 52c, 53c, 54c, 55c, 286c
Apollo and Daphne, by Gianlorenzo Bernini, 444c, 445c, 446c, 447c
Apollo, statue of (Pompeii), 160c, 161c
Apennines, 21, 28, 29, 30, 31c, 36, 39, 107c, 118c, 119c, 120c, 121c, 156
Appia, Via, 40c, 158c, 160
Aprilia, 174
Apuan Alps, 30, 106c, 107c
Apulia, 374c, 375c
Aragona D', family, 145c
Aranci, gulf, 151c
Archivio pubblico (Venice), 230c, 231c
Arco della Pace (Milan), 204c
Arena (Milan), 174, 174c
Arena (Verona), 223c
Aretino, Pietro, 431c
Arezzo, 155, 163, 164, 166, 260c, 261c, 348c, 349c, 350c, 351c
Argentario, 39c, 115c
Argentario, Giuliano, 218c
Argentera, Capo, 148c, 149c
Arno, river, 18, 21, 154c, 155c, 248c, 251c, 305c
Arno valley, 39
Arnolfo di Cambio, 250c, 252c, 514c, 515c
Arrival of the Ambassadors, by Vittore Carpaccio, 366c, 367c
Arsenale, Piazza (Borgo Trento), 222c
Asinelli Tower (Bologna), 244c
Assisi, 119c, 162, 163c, 268c, 296c, 494c, 495c, 496c, 497c
Assumption, church of the (Positano), 131c
Asti, 83c, 296c, 297, 297c
Atalanta and Hippomenes, by Guido Reni, 414c, 415c
Augustus, emperor, 55c, 293
Augustus, Tomb of, 177c
Aurelian Walls, 183c
Aurina, valley, 72c, 73c
Avignon, 330c
Avola, 168
Ayas, valley, 54c, 55c

B

Badia, Val, 70c, 72c, 74c, 75c, 306c, 307c
Baldassini, Via (Gubbio), 263c
Baldo, mountain, 79c
Balmat, Jacques, 45c
Balsamo, Loggia (Brindisi), 276c
Banchi, Loggia dei (Bologna), 162
Banti, Anna, 408c, 409c
Barbagia, 36c, 144c
Barbaro-Volpi, villa (Treviso), 434c, 435c
Barberini, Piazza (Rome), 185c
Barcaccia (Rome), 183c
Bardonecchia, 56c
Bargello, museum (Florence), 322c, 336c, 338c, 339c
Bari, 39, 276c, 277c
Barna da Siena, 258c
Bartolo di Fredi, 258c
Basente, river, 36c, 37c
Basilicata, 36c, 37c
Basil, emperor, 481c
Bassano del Grappa, 90c, 91c
Battaglia delle Regine (Valle d'Aosta), 286c
Battaglia Terme, 90c
Battista Sforza, 336c
Battista Sforza, bust (Francesco Laurana), 336c
Battle of San Romano, by Paolo Uccello, 344c, 345c
Battle of the Centaurs, by Michelangelo Buonarroti, 382c, 383c, 384c, 385c
Beato Angelico, Giovanni da Fiesole, called, 340c, 341c, 342c, 343c
Beatrice d'Este, 202c, 203c
Beccafumi, Domenico, Domenico di Giacomo di Pace, called, 324
Belgioioso, Palazzo (Milan), 206c
Bella, Isola, 32, 33c, 76c
Bellagio, 32, 81c
Bellini, garden (Palermo), 280c, 281c
Bellini, Gentile, 354c, 368c, 369c
Bellini, Giovanni, 354c, 356c, 357c
Bellini, Jacopo, 354c
Beltrami, Luca, 175c
Benaco, lake, 32 (*see also* Garda, lake)
Benato, Marco, 227c
Benedettini, Via dei (Palermo), 278c
Benedetto da Maiano, 259c
Bereguardo, 86c
Bergamo, 163c, 166, 214c, 215c
Berlinghieri, Berlinghiero, 247c
Bernini, Gianlorenzo, 168, 168c, 183c, 184c, 188c, 190c, 191c, 317c, 324, 326, 444c, 445c, 446c, 447c, 448c, 449c, 458, 466, 536c, 537c
Bernini, Pietro, 183c
Berrio Blanc, mountain, 55c
Bettoni, Villa (Bogliaco), 33
Bianchi, Bianca de', 301c
Bianco, Capo, 136c, 137c
Biandronno, lake, 32
Birth of Venus, by Sandro Botticelli, 358c, 359c, 360c, 361c
Bisentina, island, 34c
Bissona (Venice), 298c
Blanche, Vidal de la, 17
Blu, lake (Valtournanche), 32
Blue Grotto (Capri), 126c
Boboli Gardens (Florence), 251c, 255c
Bocca della verità (Rome), 180c
Boccadasse, 243c
Bogliaco, 33
Bologna, 162, 164, 244c, 374c, 375c
Bolsena, lake, 34c, 35
Bon, Bartolomeo, 232c
Bon, Giovanni, 232c
Bonatti, expedition, 44c, 45c
Borghese, Prince Camillo, 450c, 451c
Borghese, family, 444c, 445c
Borghese, Galleria (Rome), 27c, 317c, 402c, 403c, 444c, 445c, 446c, 447c, 448c, 449c, 450c, 451c
Borghese, Paolina, 27c
Borghese, Scipione, cardinal, 444c, 445c
Borgo and Castello, medieval (Turin), 199c
Borgognone, Jacques Courtois, called, 202c, 203c
Bormio, 59c, 308c
Borromee, islands, 32, 33c, 76c
Borromeo, Carlo, cardinal, 465, 466
Borromeo, family, 76c, 77c
Borromeo, Palazzo (Isola Bella), 32, 76c
Borromini, Francesco, 168c, 189c, 201c, 467c
Botticelli, Sandro, 18, 192c, 193c, 358c, 359c, 360c, 361c, 362c, 363c, 364c, 365c, 524c, 525c
Bra, Piazza (Verona), 223c
Bracciano, lake, 35, 35c
Bradano, river, 36c, 37c
Bramante, Donato di Pascuccio di Antonio, called, 210c, 386c, 387c, 465, 534c, 535c
Brenta, 28c, 29c, 60c, 61c
Brenta, river, 90c, 91c, 172c, 173c
Brenva, 46c, 47c
Brera (Milan), 213c
Brera, art gallery (Milan), 326c, 327c, 328c, 352c, 354c, 355c, 380c, 381c, 386c, 387c
Brescia, 166, 214c
Bric di Monviso, 50c
Brindisi, 133c, 276c
Bronzino, Agnolo di Cosimo, called, 324, 412c, 413c
Brunate, 81c
Brunelleschi, Filippo, 17c, 250c, 251c, 252c, 323, 462, 464c
Bruno, Giordano, 184c
Bucintoro (Venice), 298c
Budelli, island, 6c, 7c, 42c, 43c, 150c, 152c, 153c
Buonarroti, house, 382c, 383c, 384c, 385c
Buono, tribune of Malamocco, 226c, 227c
Burano, island, 92c, 93c, 298c
Burlamacco, king, 291c
Busambra, 36

C

Ca' d'oro (Venice), 232c
Ca' Dario (Venice), 239c
Ca' Foscari (Venice), 298c
Caccia, Capo, 148c, 149c
Cadore, 71c
Cagliari, 36c, 42c, 148c, 284c, 285c, 302c
Cagliari, gulf, 43
Cagnola, Luigi, 204c
Caius Cestius, pyramid of (Rome), 183c
Cairoli, Largo (Milan), 206c, 207c
Cala Madonna, 140c, 141c
Cala Viola, 148c, 149c
Calabria, 15c, 28, 36, 144c
Calatafimi, 36, 312c, 313c
Calderone, glacier, 120c, 121c
Camaiore, 164
Camera della Badessa, decoration of the, by Correggio, 426c, 428c, 429c
Cammarata, 36
Cammarata, mountain, 36
Camogli, 102c, 103c, 300c, 301c
Camosciara, 30c
Campania, 21c, 30, 32, 39, 156, 156c, 158
Campidano, pianura, 36, 36c
Campidoglio (Rome), 307
Campidoglio, Piazza del (Rome), 166, 166c, 167c
Campo de' Fiori (Rome), 184c
Campo, Piazza del (Siena), 164, 256c, 257c, 260c, 292c, 293, 293c, 294c
Campo, Piazza del (Siena), 18c
Canal Grande (Venice), 166c, 224c, 232c, 233c, 234c, 235c, 238c, 239c, 290c, 291, 291c, 298c
Canestro di frutta di Caravaggio, 442c, 443c
Canova, Antonio, 27c, 326, 329, 450c, 451c, 452c, 453c
Capitani, Palazzo dei (Todi), 263c
Capitano, Loggia del (Vicenza), 220c
Capitoline Jove, 307
Capo Bianco (Ponza), 124c, 137c
Capo Milazzese, 138c, 139c
Capodilista, Gabriele, 173c
Capodimonte, museo (Naples), 321c, 404c, 405c, 414c, 415c
Cappuccini, monastery (Turin), 199c
Cappuccini, monte dei (Turin), 199c
Capraia, island, 114c, 115c
Caprera, island, 42c, 43c, 150c
Capri, island, 40, 40c, 126c, 127c
Caprolace, 40
Capua, 156, 160, 223c
Capuana, gate (Naples), 174c
Caracalla, baths (Rome), 177c
Caracciolo, Via (Naples), 274c, 275c
Caravaggio, Michelangelo Merisi, called, 326, 326c, 327c, 414c, 415c, 438c, 439c, 440c, 441c, 442c, 443c, 466
Carezza, lake, 32
Carignano, Palazzo (Turin), 197c
Carlotta, villa (Como), 32
Carnival, 290, 291, 291c, 303c, 312c
Carpaccio, Vittore, 366c, 367c, 368c, 369c, 370c, 371c
Carracci, brothers, 414c, 415c
Carraia, ponte alla (Florence), 154c, 155c
Carroccio, 297, 297c
Casale, Roman villa (Siracusa), 281c
Casalrosso, 86c
Caserta, 30, 170, 170c
Caserta Palace, 170c, 171c
Cassia, Via, 160
Castel dell'Ovo (Naples), 274c, 275c
Castel Genovese, 145c
Castel San Pietro, 164
Castel Sant'Angelo (Rome), 22c, 23c, 188c, 189c
Castel Sant'Angelo, National museum (Rome), 188c, 189c
Castelfranco Emilia, 164
Castelfranco Madonna, by Giorgione, 390c, 391c
Castelfranco Veneto, 164, 390c, 391c
Castellammare, gulf, 156c, 157c
Castellamonte, Carlo di, 199c
Castello, Piazza (Turin), 168, 200c, 201c
Castelluccio, 122c, 123c
Castelrotto, 75c
Castelsardo, 145c, 302c, 303c
Castelvecchio, 222c
Castelvittorio, 106c, 107c
Castiglione, Baldassarre, 324
Castor and Pollux, temple (Rome), 180c, 181c
Catania, 168, 169c, 280c, 281c, 312c
Catania, gulf, 43
Catinaccio (*see also* Rosengarten), 28c, 62c, 63c
Catinaccio d'Antermoia, 28c
Catini, mountains, 120c
Cattaneo, Carlo, 155, 174
Cattedrale, Piazza (Asti), 297c
Catullus, Caius Valerius, 33
Cavalcata (Sassari), 303c
Cavalieri, Palazzo dei (Pisa), 249c
Cavalieri, Piazza dei (Pisa), 249c
Cavalieri, portico dei (Brindisi), 276c
Cavallo, mountain, 90c
Cavone, river, 36c, 37c
Cazuffi-Rella, houses (Trento), 163c
Cedrino, lake, 144c
Cefalù, 136c, 282c, 484c, 485c
Cellini, Benvenuto, 338c
Cereto di Spoleto, 119c
Certosa (Pavia), 202c, 203c, 210c, 462c, 463c
Cervinia, 50c, 51c
Cervino, mountain, 28c, 32, 48c, 49c, 50c, 51c
Cevedale, mountain, 58c
Chamoix, 50c
Chamonix, 2c, 3c
Chanson de Roland, 312c
Charles III Bourbon, king of Naples and Sicily, 160c, 161c, 170, 170c
Charterhouse (Pavia), 202c, 203c, 210c, 462c, 463c
Châtelard, castle, 55c
Chia di Luna (Ponza), 124c
Chia, 149c
Chianti, 4c, 5c, 113c
Chigi, Palazzo (Rome), 183c
Christ at the column, by Giovanni Bellini, 355c
Cilento, 40
Cima della Tosa, 60c
Cimabue, 270c, 271c, 273c
Cimini, mountains, 34c, 35, 35c
Cimon delle Pale, 63c
Cinque Terre, 104c, 105c
Circeo, 40, 40c
Circus Maximus (Rome), 307
Cislago, 32
Cisterna, Piazza della (San Gimignano), 164, 258c
Città della Pieve, 162
Cittadella (Padua), 164
Cixerri, 36
Clara, saint, 163c
Clement XI, pope, 189c
Cocullo, 120c, 311c
Coda di cavallo, Capo, 151c
Codex Astensis, 297, 297c
Coducci, Mauro, 239c
Colfosco, 306c, 307c
Colico, 32
Collegiata (San Gimignano), 258c, 370c, 371c
Collegio dei Cambi (Perugia), 296c
Colleoni, Bartolomeo, 215c
Colleoni, chapel (Bergamo), 163c, 214c, 215c
Colleoni, monument (Venice), 164
Colonna, Palazzo (Rome), 183c
Colonna, Piazza (Rome), 168, 183c
Colosseum (Rome), *see* Flavian Amphitheater
Comabbio, lake, 32
Comacchio, valleys of, 41, 95c
Comacina, Isola, 81c
Como, 32
Como, lake, 32, 32c, 33c, 80c, 81c, *see* Lario, lake
Componidori (Sardinia), 289
Comunale, villa (Milan), 206c
Comune, Palazzo del (Udine), 220c
Conca d'Oro, 36
Conca Verde, 147c
Concerto campestre, by Giorgione, 388c, 389c
Conciliazione, Via della (Rome), 190c, 191c
Concord, Temple of (Agrigento), 156c
Condotti, Via (Rome), 176c
Conegliano Veneto, 91c
Conero, mountain, 41
Conigli, Isola dei, 42c, 140c
Consoli, Palazzo dei (Gubbio), 263c
Consoli, Via dei (Gubbio), 263c
Constantine, emperor, 181c, 194c, 210c, 457
Constantine, Sala of (Rome), 194c
Constantine's Arch (Rome), 181c
Constantine's Dream, by Piero della Francesca, 349c
Constantinople, sack of, 480c
Contarelli, chapel (San Luigi dei Francesi, Rome), 438c, 439c
Contarini, fountain (Bergamo), 163c
Coperto, bridge (Bassano del Grappa), 90c, 91c
Corbara, 119c
Corbara, lake, 34c
Cordusio, Piazza (Milan), 206c
Corleone, 36
Cornero, chapel (Santa Maria della Vittoria), 466
Corniglia, 104c
Corno Grande, 30c, 31c, 120c, 121c
Coronation of the Virgin, by Filippo Lippi, 264c, 265c
Correggio, Antonio Allegri, called, 245c, 320, 426c, 427c, 428c, 429c
Correr, Palazzo (Venice), 239c
Corsa dei Ceri (Gubbio), 310c, 311c
Corsica, 42c, 43c
Cortina d'Ampezzo, 32, 75c
Corvara, 306c, 307c
Cosimo I de' Medici, 255c, 322c, 340c, 344c, 345c
Cosimo I de' Medici, monument (Pisa), 249c
Cosimo I, bust by Benvenuto Cellini, 338c
Costantino di Torres, 284c
Courmayeur, 2c, 3c, 45c, 46c, 47c, 49c
Cozie, Alps, 50c
Creation of Adam, by Michelangelo, 524c, 525c

Cremona, 160
Cristallo, mountain, 66c, 67c
Crocifisso, festa del (Calatafimi), 312c, 313c
Croix Noir, arena, 286c
Crotone, 156
Crozzon del Brenta, 60c
Crucifixion, The, by Beato Angelico, 342c, 343c
Crucifixion, The, by Masaccio, 321c
Crucifixion and saints, by Beato Angelico, 340c
Cuma, 156, 160c, 161c
Cumponidori (Sardinia), 18c, 19c
Cuneo, 57c
Cupid and Psyche, House of (Ostia), 158c
Cusio, lake, 32
Cycle of St. Francis, by Giotto, 272c

D

D'Annunzio, Gabriele, 78c
D'Este, Borso, 166
D'Este, Ercole, 166, 167c
Dama col Mazzolino, by Andrea Verrocchio, 336c, 337c
Damiani Almeyda, Giuseppe, 278c
Danae, by Titian, 404c, 405c
Danae, 404c, 405c
Dante, Via (Milan), 206c
Danube, river, 184c
Darsena (Milan), 212c
David, by Donatello, 322c
David, by Gianlorenzo Bernini, 448c, 449c
David, by Michelangelo, 14c, 254c
Dead Christ, The, by Andrea Mantegna, 380c, 381c
Delago, Torre (Vajolet) 62c, 63c
Della Robbia, Luca, 246c
Dente del Gigante, 44c
Deposition from the Cross, by Pontormo, 416c, 417c, 418c, 419c, 420c, 421c
Deposition, The, by Benedetto Antelami, 486c, 487c
Deposition, The, by Rosso Fiorentino, 422c, 423c, 424c, 425c
Desenzano, 33, 78c
Diano Marina, 300c
Diavolata (Catania), 312c
Diocletian, emperor, 226c, 302c
Diocletian, stadium, 16c, 17c, 168c, 185c
Dioscuri, temple of the (Rome), 180c, 181c
Dispute over the Sacrament, by Raphael, 396c, 397c
Doge's Chapel (Venice), 226c, 227c
Dolada, mountain, 90c
Dolomites, 28c, 29c, 32, 60c, 61c, 66c, 67c, 70c, 71c, 144c, 145c, 306c, 307c
Donatello, Donato di Niccolò di Betto Bardi, called, 322c, 323, 382c, 383c, 514c, 515c, 516c, 520c, 521c
Dora Baltea, river, 48c, 202c
Dora Grossa, Via (Turin), 168
Dora, river, 55c
Doria di Passerano, castle (Asti), 83c
Doria Pamphili, gallery (Rome), 440c, 441c
Doria, family, 145c
Douja d'Or (Asti), 296c, 297c
Duca degli Abruzzi, Museo nazionale delle montagne (Turin), 199c
Ducal Palace (Gubbio), 263c
Ducal Palace (Mantua), 380c, 381c
Ducal Palace (Urbino), 263c
Ducal Palace (Venice), 10c, 11c, 166c, 230c, 231c, 239c
Ducale, Piazza (Vigevano), 202c
Duccio da Buoninsegna, 331c, 332c, 333c, 457, 507c
Duomo (Milan), 155c, 204c, 211c, 524c, 525c
Duomo, Museo del (Milan), 204c
Duomo, Piazza (Bergamo), 214c
Duomo, Piazza (Brindisi), 276c
Duomo, Piazza (Milan), 208c
Duomo, Piazza (Orvieto), 266c
Duomo, Piazza (Sassari), 284c
Duomo, Piazza del (San Gimignano), 164, 167c
Duomo, Piazza del (Spoleto), 12c, 13c

E

Efisio, San, festival of (Cagliari), 302c
Egadi, islands, 43, 136c
Elba, Isle of, 39, 114c
Eleonora de' Medici, 255c
Elio, mountain, 35
Elmo, villa (Montecchia), 173c
Elsa, Val d', 258c, 259c
Emanuele Filiberto, monument, 168c, 169c
Emilia Romagna, 17, 38c, 39, 39c, 156, 160, 164, 244c
Emilio, bridge (Rome), 154c
Enna, 281c, 313c
Entry into Jerusalem, by Pietro Lorenzetti, 271c
Entrèves, 49c
Eolo, 42c
Era, 156c
Erbe, Piazza delle (Mantua), 216c, 217c
Erbe, Piazza delle (Padua), 220c, 221c
Erbe, Piazza delle (San Gimignano), 164
Erbe, Piazza delle (Verona), 164, 164c
Ercole, 160c
Erei, mountains, 36, 281c
Eremo delle Carceri (Assisi), 119c
Erice, 283c
Este, Villa d' (Como), 32
Estense, castle (Ferrara), 167c
Etna, 20c, 36, 36c, 135c, 136c, 169c, 280c, 281c
Euganean, hills, 90c

F

Fabricio, bridge (Rome), 154c
Falstaff, 291c
Farnese, Alessandro, cardinal, 404c, 405c, 465
Fassa, Val di, 28c, 64c, 65c, 67c
Favignana, island, 136c
Feast in the house of Levi, by Veronese, 434c, 435c, 436c, 437c
Federico II Gonzaga, 217c
Federico da Montefeltro, duke of Urbino, 336c
Fénis, castle, 55c
Ferdinando IV, 170
Ferentillo, 116c
Ferentino, 156
Ferragosto, 293
Ferraioli, Palazzo (Rome), 183c
Ferrara, 94c, 95c, 164, 167c
Ferret, Val, 45c
Ficogrande, 139c
Fieschi, festa dei (Lavagna), 301c
Fieschi, Opizzo, count, 301c
Figline Valdarno, 164
Filetto, lake, 30c
Florence, 17c, 18, 110c, 154c, 155, 155c, 158, 162, 166, 167c, 170, 250c, 251c, 254c, 255c, 304c, 305c, 322c, 323, 325c, 330c, 331c, 336c, 337c, 338c, 339c, 340c, 344c, 345c, 346c, 347c, 364c, 365c, 382c, 383c, 384c, 385c, 406c, 407c, 408c, 409c, 412c, 416c, 417c, 418c, 419c, 420c, 421c, 459c, 462, 464c, 514c, 515c, 516c, 517c, 518c, 519c, 520c, 521c
Flaminia, Via, 160
Flaminius, obelisk of, 176c
Flavius, amphitheater (Rome), 22c, 23c, 178c, 179c, 181c, 223c
Florian, Caffè (Venice), 239c
Fobello, 308c
Fogliano, 40
Fondi, 156
Fontana, Domenico, 168, 182c, 183c
Fonte Branda (Siena), 162
Fonte Nuova (Siena), 162
Forlì, 164
Foro Bonaparte (Milan), 174, 174c
Fortebraccio da Montone, 35
Fortunato, saint, 300c
Forum (Pompeii), 160c, 161c
Forum (Rome), 22c, 23c, 176c, 177c
Foscari, family, 172c
Foscari, Villa (Venice), 172c *see also* villa della Malcontenta
Foscolo, Ugo, 250c, 252c
Fossa delle Felci, mountain, 142c, 143c
Fra' Giocondo, 465
Francavilla, Pietro, 249c (Pierre Francheville)
Francesco di Rinaldo, 256c
Francesco I de' Medici, 111c
Francigena, Via, 202c, 258c
Francis, saint, 93c, 119c, 163c, 268c, 272c, 273c, 496c, 497c
Frate Elia, 268c
Fraternità dei Laici, Palazzo della (Arezzo), 260c
Frederick II, 163c
Fréjus, tunnel, 56c
Freney, 44c, 45c
Frigimelica, Girolamo, 172c, 173c
Friuli, Venezia-Giulia, 71c, 72c
Fusine, lake, 73c

G

Gaeta, 40, 126c, 127c
Gaeta, gulf, 40, 40c, 124c
Gaia, fountain (Siena), 162
Galla Placidia, tomb, 219c, 472c, 473c, 474c, 475c
Galleria di Arte moderna (Milan), 206c
Gallo, Francesco, 82c
Gallura, 36, 147c, 150c
Ganges, river, 184c
Garda, 33
Garda, Lake, 32, 33, 78c, 79c (*see also* Benaco, lake)
Gardena, Val, 64c, 65c, 67c, 72c, 74c, 75c
Gardone Riviera, 33
Garfagnana, 39c, 107c
Gargano, 35, 132c, 133c
Garibaldi, Giuseppe, 312c, 313c
Garibaldi, Giuseppe, monument (Milan), 206c, 207c
Gela, 156
Gennargentu, 36
Genoa, 39, 40, 96c, 103c, 155, 162, 240c, 243c, 305c
Genova, gulf, 39
George, saint, 310c, 311c
Gesù, church of (Rome), 465
Ghiberti, Lorenzo, 17c, 252c, 323, 459c, 520c, 521c
Ghirlandaio, Domenico, 192c, 193c, 258c, 259c, 370c, 371c, 372c, 373c, 524c, 525c
Giara di Gesturi, 144c
Giglio, island, 115c
Gioia, gulf, 40
Giorgino, 302c
Giorgio Franchetti, gallery (Venice), 232c
Giorgione, Giorgio Zorzi detto, 388c, 389c, 390c, 391c
Giotto di Bondone, 17c, 18, 167c, 221c, 250c, 251c, 252c, 270c, 271c, 272c, 320, 494c, 495c, 496c, 497c, 500c, 501c, 520c, 521c
Giovannelli, Villa (Noventa), 173c
Giovanni, San, festa di (Florence), 304c, 305c
Giudecca, island (Venice), 224c, 225c
Giuliano da Maiano, 259c
Giusti, Palazzo (Verona), 223c
Glory, The, by Gianbattista Tiepolo, 172c, 173c
Gnifetti, punta, 52c, 53c
Goethe, Wolfgang, 18, 286
Gogol, Nikolai, 15
Gonzaga, family, 166
Gorino, valley, 95c
Gozzoli, Benozzo, 258c
Grado, 41
Graie, Alps, 48c, 49c, 51c
Graines, 55c
Grammichele, 168
Gran Cratere, 42c
Gran Madre (Turin), 196c, 198c, 199c
Gran Paradiso National Park, 50c, 51c
Gran San Bernardo, 286c
Gran Sasso, 30, 30c, 31c, 120c, 121c
Grande Disco, by Arnaldo Pomodoro, 207c
Grande, fountain (Viterbo), 162
Grande, Piazza (Arezzo), 260c
Grande, Piazza (Bologna), 244c, 245c, *see also* Maggiore, Piazza
Grandes Jorasses, 2c, 3c, 45c
Grano, Loggia del (Bologna), 162
Grassina, 111c
Greece, 156
Gregory IX; pope, 396c, 397c
Gregory the Great, pope, 457
Gressoney, 286c, 287c
Gressoney, valley, 54c, 55c
Grosseto, 110c, 111c, 115c
Guarini, Guarino, 201c
Guastalla, gardens (Milan), 206c
Gubbio, 163, 263c, 310c, 311c
Guercino, Giovan Francesco Barbieri, called, 202c, 203c
Guglielmo II, 484c, 485c

H

Hadrian, emperor, 21c, 158c, 159c
Hadrian's Villa (Tivoli), 21c, 158, 159c
Handing of the keys, by Perugino, 530c, 531c
Hannibal, 29, 35
Hayez, Francesco, 328c
Heine, Heinrich, 15
Heliodorus, stanza of (Vatican City), 195c, 396c, 397c, 398c, 399c
Henri IV, king of France, 249c
Herculaneum, 158, 160c
Hercules and Antaeus, by Antonio del Pollaiolo, 339c
Holy Family, by Michelangelo Buonarroti, 325c
Hruska, botanical garden (Gardone), 33

I

Iglesiente, 36, 148c, 151c
Ignatius Loyola, 466
Ilaria del Carretto, tomb of, by Jacopo della Quercia, 378c, 379c
Imperial Forums, Via dei (Rome), 180c, 181c
Indipendenza, Via (Bologna), 164
Infiorata, 300c
Ionian Sea, 40, 156
Ischia Ponte, 129c
Ischia Porto, 128c
Ischia, castle, 129c
Ischia, island, 40, 128c, 129c
Iseo, lake, 32, 81c (*see also* Sebino, lake)
Italia, Angelo, 168
Italia, Corso (Genoa), 242c, 243c
Italia, Piazza (Sassari), 303c
Italia, Piazza d' (Sassari), 284c

J

Jacopo della Quercia, 247c, 378c, 379c
John, saint, 520c, 521c
Jove, 216c, 217c
Julius, saint, 32, 32c
Julius II della Rovere, pope, 194c, 195c, 408c, 409c, 524c, 525c, 534c, 535c
Julius II, pope, apartaments (Vatican City), 396c, 397c
Julius II, tomb, by Michelangelo Buonarroti, 392c, 393c
Julius Caesar, 196c
Juno, 156c
Jupiter Anxur, temple of (Terracina), 40c
Justinian, emperor, 470c, 471c
Juvarra, Filippo, 200c

K

Kiss, The, by Francesco Hayez, 328c

L

L'Aquila, 120c
La Corricella (Procida), 129c
La Maddalena, arcipelago, 6c, 7c, 42c, 43, 43c, 150c
La Morra, 84c, 85c
La Peggio, villa (Grassina), 111c
La Salle, 55c
La Scala, theater (Milan), 208c
La Spezia, 39, 104c, 105c, 242c
La Thuile, 49c
La Villa, 306c, 307c
Laigueglia, 96c, 97c
Lampedusa, 42c, 140c, 141c
Lanfranco, 458
Larderello, 17
Lario, lake, 32 (*see also* Como, lake)
Last Judgement, by Michelangelo Buonarroti, 192c, 193c, 524c, 525c
Last Supper, by Leonardo da Vinci, 460c
Last Supper, by Tintoretto, 432c, 433c
Last Supper, by Veronese, 434c, 435c
Latina, 174
Lattari, mountains, 30
Laurana, Francesco, 336c
Laurino, king, 62c
Lavagna, 301c
Lazio, 32, 34c, 35c, 39, 40, 110c, 111c, 120c, 156, 158, 170, 174
Le Corbusier, Charles-Edouard Jeanneret, called, 458
Leaning Tower (Pisa), 248c, 249c
Lecco, 32, 81c
Legend of the True Cross, by Piero della Francesca, 261c
Legend of Saint Fina, by Domenico Ghirlandaio, 370c, 371c, 372c, 373c
Legnaro, 106c
Lente, valley, 110c, 111c
Leo X, pope, 110c
Leonardo da Vinci, 18, 213c, 320, 329, 352c, 396c, 397c, 460c
Lesina, lake, 35
Liberation of Saint Peter, The, by Raphael, 398c, 399c
Libertà, Piazza della (Vicenza), 220c
Ligure, Appennino, 82c
Ligure, sea, 39
Liguria, 18, 38c, 97c, 106c
Limone Piemonte, 57c
Linosa, island, 141c
Lipari, island, 138c
Lipari, islands (*see* Aeolian Islands)
Lippi, Filippino, 246c, 264c, 265c
Lippi, Filippo, 264c, 265c, 320
Livigno, 58c
Livinallongo, 67c, 75c
Livorno, 39
Lizza, gardens (Siena), 170
Locri, 156
Logge, Palazzo delle (Arezzo), 260c
Loggia (Bergamo), 214c
Loggia, Piazza della (Brescia), 214c
Lombardy, 32, 33, 58c, 59c, 86c, 160, 166, 170, 206c, 210c, 458, 486c
Lombardia, Castello di (Enna), 281c
Longhena, Baldassarre, 236c, 237c, 532c, 533c
Longosardo, 147c
Lorenzetti, Pietro, 270c, 271c, 494c
Lorenzo de' Medici (il Magnifico), 110c, 252c, 358c, 359c
Lorenzo de' Medici, tomb of, by Michelangelo, 406c, 407c
Lorenzo di Pierfrancesco de' Medici, 358c, 359c
Loreto, island, 32
Lotto, Lorenzo, 408c, 409c
Louvre Museum (Paris), 249c
Lucca, 155, 158, 164, 246c, 247c, 378c, 379c
Lucchesia, 30
Lucignano, 162
Ludovico il Moro, 202c, 203c
Lugano, lake, 32
Luini, Aurelio, 202c, 203c
Lula, 144c, 145c
Luther, Martin, 465

M

Machiavelli, Niccolò, 250c
Macrino d'Alba, 202c, 203c
Madama, Palazzo (Turin), 200c
Maddalena, island, 42c, 43c, 150c, 151c
Maderno, Carlo, 168, 465
Madonie, 36, 134c
Madonna with the long neck, by Parmigianino, 412c
Madonna del Monte, (Venice), 298c
Madonna dell'Assunzione, 292c, 293c
Madonna della Scala, by Michelangelo Buonarroti, 382c, 383c
Madonna di Provenzano, 292c, 293c
Madonna Verona, fountain di (Verona), 164c
Madonnina (Milan), 204c, 205c
Madre, Isola, 32, 33c, 76c
Maestà, by Duccio da Buoninsegna, 332c, 333c, 334c, 335c, 507c
Maestro of San Francesco, 270c
Maggiore, fountain (Perugia), 162, 164c
Maggiore, Lake, 32, 33c, 76c, 77c, *see also* Verbano
Maggiore, Piazza (Bologna), 184c, 165c, 244c, 245c, *see also* Piazza Grande
Magnano, 83c
Maiella, 30, 31c
Maitani, Lorenzo, 267c, 508c
Majorana, Centro scientifico (Erice), 283c
Malcesine, 33, 33c, 78c, 79c
Malcontenta, Villa (Venice), 172c *see also* Villa Foscari
Mamoiada, 303c
Mamutones, 303c
Manarola, 104c, 105c
Manfredi, king, 164
Manfredonia, 164
Mangia, torre del (Siena), 16c, 256c
Mantegna, Andrea, 354c, 380c, 381c
Mantua, 155, 156, 216c, 380c, 381c, 458
Manzoni, Alessandro, 32
Marano, 41
Marca Trevigiana, 90c
Marche, 17, 118c, 119c, 171c, 263c
Marcus Aurelius, 183c
Marcus Aurelius, statue of, 166c, 167c
Maremma, 39, 108c, 109c
Maria Carolina of Austria, 170c
Marie-Louise Bourbon, 245c
Mary Magdalen, Saint, by Piero della Francesca, 260c
Marittime, Alps, 57c, 82c
Marittimo, theater (Tivoli), 158c, 159c
Mark, saint, 431c
Marmilla, 36c, 145c
Marmolada, 62c, 66c
Marmorata, 147c
Marmore, falls, 116c
Marriage of the Virgin, by Raphael, 386c, 387c
Marsicano, mountain, 120c
Martana, island, 34c
Martinelli, mountain hut, 59c
Martini, Simone, 267c, 271c, 330c
Martinière, Bruzen de la, 15
Martyrdom of Saint Andrew, by Benedetto Antelami, 203c
Marzabotto, 156
Masaccio, Tommaso di Ser Giovanni di Mone Cassai, called, 321c, 439c
Maser, 434c, 435c
Maso di Bartolomeo, 263c

Massa Marittima, 166
Massaia manna (Sardinia), 289
Massaiedas (Sardinia), 289
Matitone (Genoa), *see also* Torre Nord
Matterhorn, mountain, 28c, 32, 48c, 49c, 50c, 51c
Maxentius, emperor, 181c
Maximian, emperor, 226c
Maximian, bishop, 470c, 471c
Mazzorbo (Venice), 298c
Meda, Piazza (Milan), 207c
Medici, family, 110c, 111c, 394c, 395c
Medici-Riccardi, Palazzo (Florence), 252c
Mengari, Giuseppe, 208c
Mengoni, Giuseppe, 208c
Mera, river, 32
Mercanti, Loggia dei (Bologna), 162
Mercato, Piazza del (Lucca), 246c, 247c
Mergellina (Naples), 274c, 275c
Messina, 174, 312c
Messina, Strait of, 36, 40
Metamorphoses, by Ovid, 444c, 445c
Mezzojuso, 312c
Michelangelo Buonarroti, 1c, 14c, 166, 166c, 167c, 191c, 192c, 193c, 250c, 254c, 318c, 319c, 320, 324, 325c, 329, 382c, 383c, 384c, 385c, 392c, 393c, 394c, 395c, 406c, 407c, 408c, 409c, 431c, 526c, 527c, 528c, 534c, 535c
Michelangelo, Piazzale (Florence), 251c
Michelozzi, Michelozzo di Bartolomeo, called, 252c
Milan, 9c, 155, 155c, 170, 174, 174c, 175c, 204c, 205c, 206c, 208c, 209c, 210c, 211c, 213c, 275c, 326c, 327c, 328c, 352c, 354c, 355c, 380c, 381c, 380c, 381c, 386c, 387c, 442c, 443c, 458, 460c, 488c, 489c, 522c, 523c, 524c, 525c
Mincio, river, 32, 216c
Minerva, Piazza della (Rome), 182c
Minuccio di Rinaldo, 256c
Miracoli, Campo dei (Pisa), 248c, 250c, 251c
Miracoli, Piazza dei (Pisa), 502c, 503c
Miramare, castle (Trieste), 221c
Miseno, Capo, 128c, 129c
Misteri, Villa dei (Pompeii), 160c, 161c
Misurina, lake, 32
Modena, 155, 170, 201c
Molo Angioino (Naples), 274c
Monaci, 40
Monate, lake, 32
Mondovì, 82c
Monferrato, 82c, 83c
Monreale, 278c, 484c, 485c
Mont Blanc, 2c, 3c, 28c, 30, 44c, 45c, 46c, 47c, 48c, 49c, 50c, 51c
Montalcino, 106c, 110c
Monte di Pietà (Brescia), 214c
Monte Rosa, 30, 48c, 49c, 52c, 53c, 54c, 55c, 56c, 57c, 86c, 87c
Monte San Savino, 162
Monte Sant'Angelo, 133c
Montecchia, 173c
Montelargius, 148c
Montenapoleone, Via (Milan), 209c
Monteriggioni, 162c, 163c
Monterosso, 104c, 106c
Montisola, island, 32
Monviso, 50c
Morazzone, Pier Francesco Mazzucchelli, called, 202c, 203c
Mori (Venice), 226c, 239c
Moroni, Giovan Battista, 214c
Moses, by Michelangelo Buonnaroti, 14c, 318c, 319c, 392c, 393c
Murazzi (Turin), 198c, 199c
Museo civico d'Arte (Borgo Trento), 222c
Museo civico di Arte antica (Turin), 200c
Museo nazionale di Ravenna, 218c
Museo nazionale di Reggio Calabria, 15c
Mussa, torrent, 213c

N
Nanni di Banco, 323
Napoleon Bonaparte, 174, 174c, 204c, 242c, 245c, 450c, 451c
Naples, 17, 39, 155, 156, 160c, 167, 171c, 174c, 274c, 275c, 321c, 336c, 404c, 405c, 414c, 415c
Naples, gulf of, 17, 30, 40, 40c, 41c, 128c, 129c, 170c, 171c
Navigli (Milan), 212c
Navigli, Cerchia dei (Milan), 212c, 213c
Naviglio della Martesana (Milan), 213c
Naviglio Grande (Milan), 212c, 213c
Naviglio Paderno (Milan), 213c
Naviglio Pavese (Milan), 212c, 213c
Navona, Piazza (Rome), 16c, 17c, 168c, 184c, 185c
Naxos, 156
Nazionale, Villa (Stra), 172c, 173c
Nebida, 148c
Nebrodi, mountains, 36
Nemi, lake, 35
Nera, river, 116c
Neri, Filippo, 466
Nestore, river, 35
Neptune, Fountain of (Bologna), 164
Neptune, Fountain of (Florence), 254c
Neptune, Fountain of (Trento), 221c
Neptune, Temple of (Paestum), 21c, 156c
Nettuno, Piazza (Bologna), 184c, 165c
Niccolò dell'Arca, 374c, 375c, 376c, 377c
Nicholas V, pope, 166
Nile, river, 184c
Nirone, torrent, 213c
Nola, 30, 156
Noli, 96c
Nora, 157c, 302c
Normanni, cappella dei (Palermo), 482c, 483c
North Tower, by Skidmore, Owings and Merryl (Genoa), 174c
Noto, 168, 169c
Nova Siri, 36c, 37c
Novara, 86c, 203c
Noventa, 173c
Nuovo, Ponte (Verona), 223c
Nurra, 36

O
Obelisk (Rome), 182c
Oglio, river, 32
Olivo, island, 78c
Oltrepò Pavese, 38c, 39c
Oneglia, 243c
Opera del Duomo, Museo dell' (Siena), 257c, 332c, 333c, 507c
Opi, 120c
Orbetello, 39
Orcia, valley, 110c, 112c, 113c
Oristano, 36c, 157c, 288c, 289, 289c
Orobie, Alps, 58c
Orologio, Palazzo dell' (Ravenna), 219c
Orsanmichele, oratory (Florence), 162, 323
Orta, 77c
Orta, Lake, 32, 32c, *see also* Cusio
Ortisei, 72c
Ortles, 58c
Orvieto, 266c, 507c, 508c, 509c, 510c, 511c, 512c, 513c
Orvieto Cathedral, 8c
Ossaia, 35
Ossuccio, 81c
Ostia, 158, 158c
Ostuni, 133c
Otranto, 39
Otranto, Strait of, 40
Octavian Augustus, 180c, 196c, *see also* Augustus, emperor
Ottiglio, 82c, 83c
Ovid, 444c, 445c

P
Paccard, Michel-Gabriel, 45c (mountain climber)
Padellata (Camogli), 300c
Padua, 17c, 90c, 155, 160, 220c, 221c, 457, 500c, 501c
Paestum, 21c, 156, 156c
Palatina, Porta (Turin), 196c
Palatine, hill (Rome), 176c, 177c, 180c
Palau, 42c, 43c, 146c, 147c
Palazzo Te, Museo civico di (Mantua), 217c
Pale di San Martino, 63c
Palermo, 36, 39, 43, 155, 278c, 482c, 483c
Palestro, Via (Milan), 206c
Palinuro, Capo, 40
Palio (Asti), 296c, 297, 297c
Palio (Siena), 18c, 164, 256c, 257c, 292c, 293, 293c, 294c, 295c
Palladio, Andrea, 90c, 91c, 172c, 173c, 465
Pallanza, 32
Pallavicino, Villa (Stresa), 32, 76c
Pallone, Via (Verona), 223c
Pamphili, Palazzo (Rome), 168c
Pan, 290
Panarea, island, 138c, 139c
Pantalone, 291
Pantelleria, island, 43
Pantheon (Rome), 180c
Paolina Borghese Bonaparte as Venus the Conqueress, by Antonio Canova, 450c, 451c, 452c, 453c
Paolo Uccello, Paolo di Dono, called, 320, 344c, 345c
Paradiso, baia del, 38c
Parco Nazionale d'Abruzzo, 30c, 120c, 121c
Parco Nazionale di Panaveggio-Pale di San Martino, 63c
Parma, 155, 170, 245c, 426c, 427c, 486c, 487c
Parmigianino, Francesco Mazzola, called, 324, 412c
Parnassus, The, by Raphael, 400c, 401c
Paul III, pope, 166, 404c, 405c, 524c, 525c
Pasquali (Bormio), 308c
Pavia, 38c, 39c, 86c, 160, 162, 202c, 203c, 210c, 213c, 462c, 463c
Pazzi, Cappella de' (Santa Croce), 464c
Pazzino de' Pazzi, 304c
Pecetto Torinese, 199c
Pedro de Toledo, don, 278c
Pelagian Islands, 42c, 43, 140c
Peligna, valley, 310c
Pellegrino, mountain, 279c
Pelmo, mountain, 71c
Peloritani, mountains, 36
Pennine, Alps, 28c, 48c, 49c
Perego, Giuseppe, 204c [maquette del duomo d MI]
Perugia, 35, 162, 163c, 164c, 268c, 296c
Perugino, Pietro Vannucci, called, 202c, 203c, 269c, 524c, 525c, 530c, 531c
Peruzzi, Baldassarre, 534c, 535c
Pesaro, 263c
Pescallo, 32c, 33c
Pescatori, Isola dei, 32, 33c, 76c
Peschiera, 33
Petronio, San, 164
Philaretes, Antonio Averulino, called, 323
Piacentini, Marcello, 174
Piacenza, Giovanna, abbess, 426c, 427c
Piano delle Fumarole, 42c
Piazza, Torre di (Vicenza), 220c
Piazza Armerina (Siracusa), 281c
Piccolo San Bernardo, hill, 49c
Piccolo, Teatro (Milan), 206c
Piedmont, 32, 38c, 39c, 50c, 51c, 52c, 53c, 57c, 86c, 199c
Piermarini, Giuseppe, 206c, 208c
Piero della Francesca, 260c, 261c, 346c, 347c, 348c, 349c
Piero di Cosimo, 524c, 525c
Pietà, by Giovanni Bellini, 354c, 356c, 357c
Pietà, by Michelangelo Buonarroti, 14c, 394c, 395c
Pietà, by Niccolò dell'Arca, 374c, 375c, 376c, 377c
Pietrasanta, 164
Pilotta, Palazzo della (Parma), 245c
Pinacoteca (Volterra), 422c, 423c, 424c, 425c
Pincio, gardens (Rome), 176c, 185c
Pino Torinese, 199c
Pinturicchio, Bernardino di Bette, called, 192c, 193c
Pippia de maiu (Sardinia), 289
Pirelli, skyscraper, 174c
Pisa, 39, 103c, 155c, 164, 166, 250c, 251c, 305c, 502c, 503c
Pisani, Almorò, 172c, 173c
Pisani, Alvise, 172c, 173c
Pisani, villa (Stra), 172c, 173c
Pisano, Andrea, 17c, 267c
Pisano, Bonanno, 484c, 485c
Pisano, Giovanni, 502c, 503c, 504c, 505c
Pisano, Nicola, 502c, 503c
Pistoia, 164, 166
Pitti Palace (Florence), 154c, 155c, 166, 251c, 254c
Piz Boé, 63c, 67c
Pizzo Roseg, 59c
Pizzomunno, 40c
Plato, 396c, 397c
Plebiscito, Piazza (Naples), 275c
Pliniana, Villa (Como), 32
Po, river, 38, 41, 82c, 86c, 94c, 95c, 198c, 199c, 208c
Po valley, 32, 32c, 38, 39c, 50c, 160, 162
Po, Via (Turin), 168
Podestà, Palazzo del (Bologna), 184c, 165c
Poggia a Caiano, 110c
Poli, Palazzo (Rome), 186c, 187c
Policastro, gulf, 40
Politeama Garibaldi, theater (Palermo), 278c
Poliziano, Angelo, 362c, 363c, 382c, 383c
Pollack, Leopold, 206c
Pollaiolo, Antonio Benci, called, 339c
Pollaiolo, brothers, 320
Pomodoro, Arnaldo, 207c
Pompa triumphalis (Rome), 307
Pompeii, 158, 160, 160c, 161c
Pontian islands, 124c
Pontine plain, 40, 40c
Pontine, islands, 40
Pontino, archipelago, 40c
Pontormo, Jacopo Carucci, called, 324, 329, 416c, 417c, 418c, 419c, 420c, 421c
Ponza, island, 124c, 125c
Popolo, Palazzo del (Todi), 263c
Popolo, Piazza del (Orvieto), 266c
Popolo, Piazza del (Ravenna), 219c
Popolo, Piazza del (Rome), 168, 176c
Popolo, Piazza del (Todi), 263c
Porto Maurizio, 243c
Porto Pino, 148c
Porto Quartu, 147c
Porto Venere, 39
Portoferraio, 114c
Portofino, 38c, 39, 98c, 99c, 100c, 101c
Portofino, fort, 98c
Portofino, mountain, 98c, 102c, 103c
Portovenere, 104c, 105c
Poseidonia, 156
Posillipo, 174c, 274c, 275c
Positano, 131c
Posta Fibreno, lake, 35c
Postumia, Via (Roman period), 160
Pozzolana, Cala, 141c
Pozzolo Formigaro, 83c
Pozzuoli, 17
Praiano, 131c
Prato, 166
Presanella, mountain, 58c, 59c
Pretoria, Piazza (Palermo), 278c
Pretorio, Palazzo (Trento), 163c
Previtali, Andrea Cordegliaghi, called, 214c, basilica di Bergamo
Priaro, district (Camogli), 103c
Prima Porta (Rome), 180c
Priori, Palazzo dei (Perugia), 163c, 164c, 296c
Priori, Palazzo dei (Todi), 263c
Prisons (Venice), 239c
Procida, island, 40, 128c, 129c
Promessi sposi (The Betrothed), I, by Alessandro Manzoni, 32
Prospero, bishop of Tarragona, 98c
Provinciale, Palazzo (Sassari), 284c
Pubblico, Palazzo (Siena), 256c
Puglia, 28, 35, 39, 40c, 133c, 276c, 277c
Pula, 144c, 36c
Pula, Capo di, 157c
Punta Chiappa (Camogli), 301c
Punta del Mesco, 106c
Punta della Dogana da Mar (Venice), 224c, 235c

Q
Four Doctors of the Church, by Giotto da Bondone, 272c
Quattro Novembre, Piazza (Perugia), 164c
Quirinale, Palazzo del (Rome), 182c, 183c

R
Radda, 113c
Ragione, Palazzo della (Mantova), 216c
Ragione, Palazzo della (Padua), 220c, 221c
Ragusa, 282c, 283c
Raimondi Chapel (San Pietro in Montorio), 466
Ranieri, Luminaria di San (Pisa), 305c
Ranieri, San, 155c, 305c
Rapallo, 103c
Rape of Proserpina, by Gianlorenzo Bernini, 317c
Raphael, 194c, 195c, 320, 324, 329, 386c, 387c, 396c, 397c, 398c, 399c, 400c, 401c, 465, 524c, 525c, 534c, 535c
Raphael, Logge (Vatican City), 194c 195c
Ravegnana, Porta (Bologna), 184c, 165c
Ravello, 130c, 131c
Ravenna, 41, 155, 218c, 470c, 471c, 472c, 473c, 474c, 475c
Razzoli, island, 42c, 43c, 150c
Reale, Palazzo (Turin), 201c
Reale, Piazza (Turin), 201c
Regata (Pisa), 305c
Regata (Venice), 298c
Reggio Calabria, 15c
Reggio Emilia, 164
Regia, Via (Viareggio), 291
Regina della Scala, 208c
Regio, Teatro (Parma), 245c
Reni, Guido, 414c, 415c
Rest during the flight into Egypt, by Caravaggio, 440c, 441c
Resurrection of the Flesh, by Luca Signorelli, 512c, 513c
Retiche, Alps, 58c
Rhêmes, Valley, 50c
Riace, 15c
Riace bronzes, 15c
Rialto Bridge (Venice), 224c, 232c, 233c
Rimasco, 56c
Rimini, 156
Riomaggiore, 105c
Portrait of Battista Sforza, by Piero della Francesca, 346c
Portrait of Dorian Gray, The, by Oscar Wilde, 329
Portrait of Federico da Montefeltro, by Piero della Francesca, 347c
Portrait of a gentleman, by Lorenzo Lotto, 408c, 409c
Portrait of Julius II, by Raphael, 408c, 409c
Portrait of Lucrezia Panciatichi, by Agnolo Bronzino, 412c, 413c
Riva degli Schiavoni (Venice), 235c, 239c
Rivers, Fountain of the (Rome), 168c, 184c
Rizzoli, Via (Bologna), 244c
Rodolfo, monk, 458
Roman Villa (Siracusa), *see* Casale, Roman villa,
Rome, 14c, 16c, 17c, 22c, 23c, 35, 39, 40, 154c, 155, 158, 158c, 159c, 166, 166c, 167c, 168, 168c, 171c, 176c, 177c, 178c, 179c, 180c, 181c, 183c, 185c, 186c, 187c, 188c, 194c, 223c, 291, 317c, 318c, 319c, 398c, 399c, 400c, 401c, 402c, 403c, 440c, 441c, 444c, 445c, 446c, 447c, 448c, 449c, 450c, 451c, 465, 467c, 468c, 469c, 518c, 519c, 534c, 535c, 536c, 537c, 538c, 539c
Rome, Via (Turin), 168
Rome, Via (Verona), 223c
Romano, Giuliano, 216c, 217c
Rosa, Spiaggia (Budelli), 152c, 153c
Rosario Fiorito, procession (Alagna), 308c
Rosengarten, 28c, *see also* Catinaccio
Rosselli, Biagio, 167c
Rossellino, Antonio, 323
Rossini, Gioacchino, 250c
Rosso Fiorentino, Giovanni Battista di Jacopo, called, 324, 416c, 417c, 418c, 419c, 420c, 421c, 422c, 423c, 424c, 425c
Rotonda (Vicenza), 172c
Rotto, Ponte (Rome), 154c
Roverti, Matteo, 232c
Rucellai Madonna, by Duccio da Buoninsegna, 331c
Rufolo, Villa (Ravello), 130c, 131c
Ruggero II, king of Sicily, 278c, 282c, 482c, 483c, 484c, 485c
Rustico da Torcello, 226c, 227c
Rutelli, Mario, 278c

S
Sabatini, mountains, 35
Sabaudia, 40, 174
Saccargia, 284c
Sacra, Via, 156c
Sacred and profane love, by Titian, 402c, 403c
Sacro cuore di Gesù, festival (Val Badia), 306c, 307c
Saint Mark saving a Saracen, by Tintoretto, 430c
Saint Mark's Basilica (Venice), 26c, 224c, 226c, 227c, 228c, 229c, 298c, 465, 476c, 477c, 478c, 479c, 480c, 481c
Saint Mark's Lion (Venice), 226c, 231c
Saint Mark's Square(Venice), 10c, 11c, 166c, 224c, 226c, 238c, 239c, 291
Saint Mark's Treasure (Venice), 226c
Saint Matthew and the Angel, by Caravaggio, 439c
Saint Peter's Basilica (Vatican City), 24c, 25c, 191c, 392c, 393c, 394c, 395c, 465, 466, 534c, 535c, 536c, 537c
Saint Peter's Square(Rome), 168, 168c, 190c, 191c, 466, 538c, 539c
Saints Mary Magdalen and Catherine of Alexandria, by Simone Martini, 271c
Salaria, Via, 160
Salento, 40
Salerno, 30, 163
Salerno, gulf, 30, 40
Salina, island, 142c, 143c
San Bernardino, oratory (Perugia), 268c
San Brizio, chapel (Orvieto Cathedral), 509c, 512c, 513c
San Carlo, Piazza (Turin), 168c, 169c
San Carlo, Teatro (Naples), 275c
San Fedele, school of (Albenga), 96c
San Francesco, district (Pisa), 305c
San Francesco nel Deserto, island, 93c
San Francesco, church (Arezzo), 261c, 348c, 349c, 350c, 351c
San Francesco, church (Assisi), 268c, 269c, 270c, 271c, 272c, 494c, 495c, 496c, 497c
San Francesco, church (Gubbio), 263c
San Francesco, lower church (Assisi), 270c, 271c
San Francesco, upper church (Assisi), 270c, 271c, 272c, 273c
San Fratello, 312c
San Frediano, church (Lucca), 247c
San Fruttuoso, 98c
San Galgano, abbey, 260c
San Gaudenzio, church (Novara), 203c
San Giacomo, island (Venice), 298c

San Giacomo, church (Isola Comacina), 81c
San Gimignano, 162, 164, 166, 258c, 259c, 370c, 371c
San Giorgio di Piano, 164
San Giorgio Maggiore, island (Venice), 225c, 233c, 238c, 239c, 432c, 433c
San Giorgio, castle (Capraia), 114c, 115c
San Giorgio, castle (Mantua), 216c
San Giorgio, island, 10c, 11c
San Giorgio, island, 32
San Giorgio, Palazzo (Genoa), 240c
San Giovanni Battista, church (Gubbio), 263c
San Giovanni Battista, church (Parma), 245c
San Giovanni degli Eremiti (Palermo), 278c
San Giovanni in Laterano, church (Rome), 189c
San Giovanni Valdarno, 164
San Giovanni, Piazza (Florence), 17c, 250c, 251c
San Giovanni, portico (Udine), 220c
San Giulio, island, 32, 32c, 77c
San Lorenzo Maggiore (Milan), 210c
San Lorenzo, Campo (Venice), 224c
San Lorenzo, church (Portovenere), 104c, 105c
San Lorenzo, church (Turin), 201c
San Lorenzo, church (Florence), 406c, 407c
San Lorenzo, Rotonda di (Mantua), 216c
San Luigi dei Francesi, church (Rome), 438c, 439c
San Marco, bacino, 298c
San Marco, colonna di (Verona), 164c
San Marco, convent (Florence), 340c
San Marco, School of (Venice), 430c, 431c
San Marco, Scuola Grande, 431c
San Martino, district (Pisa), 305c
San Martino, cathedral (Lucca), 378c, 379c
San Martino, festival of, 298c
San Michele in Foro, church (Lucca), 246c
San Michele, church (Alghero), 285c
San Michele, church (Castelrotto), 75c
San Michele, sacra (Susa), 456c
San Miniato al Monte, church (Florence), 251c
San Paolo, convent (Parma), 426c, 427c
San Petronio, church (Bologna), 184c, 165c, 244c, 245c
San Petronio, Piazza (Verona), 164
San Pietro in Montorio, temple (Rome), 386c, 387c, 466
San Pietro in Vincoli (Rome), 14c, 318c, 319c, 392c, 393c
San Pietro, cattedrale (Bologna), 164
San Pietro, island, 43
San Remy, bastione di (Cagliari), 284c
San Romano, 344c, 345c
San Ruffino (Assisi), 163c
San Secondo, church (Asti), 297c
San Vitale, monastery (Ravenna), 218c, 219c, 470c, 471c
San Vittore, church (Isola dei Pescatori), 76c
San Zaccaria, church (Venice), 239c
San Zanipolo, Campo (Venice), 224c
San Zanipolo, convent (Venice), 434c, 435c
Sangallo, Antonio da, Antonio Giamberti, called, 534c, 535c
Sangallo, Giuliano da, Giuliano Giamberti, called, 110c, 465, 534c, 535c
Sangro, valley, 120c
Sanguineto, 35
Sansovinian Library (Venice), 166c
Sansovino, Jacopo Tatti, called, 230c
Sant'Agnese in Agone, church (Rome), 168c
Sant'Alessandro, cathedral (Bergamo), 214c
Sant'Ambrogio, basilica, (Milan), 211c, 458, 488c, 489c
Sant'Andrea al Quirinale, church (Rome), 466
Sant'Andrea, Capo, 136c
Sant'Andrea, church (Mantua), 216c
Sant'Andrea, church (Vercelli), 203c, 490c, 492c, 493c
Sant'Andrea, Via (Milan), 209c
Sant'Angelo (Rome), 190c, 191c
Sant'Angelo, Ponte (Rome), 188c
Sant'Antimo, abbey (Montalcino), 106c
Sant'Antioco, 42c, 43
Sant'Antonio, district (Pisa), 305c
Sant'Apollinare in Classe, church (Ravenna), 218c
Sant'Eufemia, gulf, 40
Sant'Ivo alla Sapienza (Rome), 467c
Sant'Osvaldo, church, 72c
Santa Barbara, fort (Siena), 170
Santa Croce, church (Florence), 250c, 252c, 464c, 514c, 515c, 516c, 517c
Santa Croce, church (Lecce), 276c
Santa Croce, Piazza (Florence), 304c, 305c
Santa Felicità, church (Florence), 416c, 417c, 418c, 419c, 420c, 421c
Santa Giustina, church (Padua), 17c
Santa Lucia, port (Naples), 274c
Santa Margherita Ligure, 102c
Santa Maria, district (Pisa), 305c
Santa Maria alla Scala, church (Milan), 208c
Santa Maria Assunta, cathedral (island of Torcello), 92c, 93c
Santa Maria Capua Vetere, 156
Santa Maria dei Miracoli, church (Rome), 176c
Santa Maria del Fiore, church (Florence), 167c, 252c, 462
Santa Maria del Monte, church (Turin), 199c
Santa Maria della Salute, church (Venice), 224c, 235c, 236c, 237c, 238c, 532c, 533c
Santa Maria della Vita, church (Bologna), 374c, 375c
Santa Maria della Vittoria, church (Rome), 466
Santa Maria delle Grazie (Milan), 210c, 460c
Santa Maria di Leuca, 40
Santa Maria di Montesano, church (Rome), 176c
Santa Maria in Cosmedin, church (Rome), 180c
Santa Maria in Trastevere, church (Rome), 188c
Santa Maria Maggiore, church (Rome), 468c, 469c
Santa Maria Novella, church (Florence), 254c, 304c, 305c, 518c, 519c
Santa Maria, island, 42c, 43c, 150c
Santa Reparata, 147c
Santa Rosalia, sanctuary (Palermo), 279c
Santa Tecla (Catania), 136c
Santa Teresa di Gallura, 147c
Santa Trinità, church (Saccargia), 284c
Santa Trinita, bridge (Florence), 154c, 155c
Santi Cosma e Damiano, church (Rome), 454c, 455c
Santi Ildefonso e Tommaso da Villanova, church (Rome), 185c
Santo Spirito (Rome), 190c, 191c
Santo Spirito, Via (Milan), 209c
Santo Stefano, island (Sardinia), 42c, 43c, 150c
Sarca, river, 32
Sardara, 36c
Sardinia, 6c, 7c, 18c, 19c, 28, 29, 36, 36c, 39, 42c, 43, 43c, 114c, 133c, 144c, 145c, 146c, 148c, 149c, 150c, 151c, 157c, 174, 285c, 289, 302c, 303c
Sartiglia (Oristano), 18c, 19c, 288c, 289, 289c
Sass Pordoi, 70c
Sassari, 284c, 303c
Sasso delle Nove, 70c
Sasso Nero, 72c, 73c
Sassolungo, 67c, 70c, 71c
Saturnia, 17
Sauris di Sotto, 72c
Saverio, Francesco, 466
Savoia (Savoy), family, 145c, 150c, 151c, 199c, 200c
Savona, 96c, 242c
Savonarola, Gerolamo, 380c, 381c
Scala, Cangrande della, 222c
Scala, della, family, 78c
Scala, Piazza della (Milan), 208c
Scaligero Castle (Sirmione), 78c
Scaligero fort (Malcesine), 33, 33c
Scardovari, 95c
Scarpagnino, Antonio di Pietro Abbondi, called, 230c
Scrovegni Chapel (Padua), 221c, 500c, 501c
Scrovegni, Enrico degli, 500c, 501c
Segesta, 156, 156c, 157c
Segnatura, Stanza della (Vatican City), 396c, 397c
Segni, 156
Sele, river, 156
Selinunte, 20c, 21c, 156
Sella, group of mountains, 64c, 65c, 67c
Sella, pass, 70c
Sempione, Corso (Milan), 174
Sempione, Parco (Milan), 204c, 206c
Senales, valley, 68c, 69c
Sepolcri, I, by Ugo Foscolo, 252c
Sepoltaglia, 35
Serbelloni, villa (Como), 32
Sermenza, Val, 56c
Serpari, procession, (Cocullo), 311c
Serra di Ivrea, 83c
Sesia, river, 56c, 86c
Sestri Levante, 103c
Sestrière (Lapis Sixtra), 56c, 57c
Sette Comuni, plateau, 90c, 91c
Seveso, torrent, 213c
Sforza, family, 59c
Sforzesco, castle (Milan), 174, 174c, 175c, 206c, 207c
Shelley, Percy Bysshe, 18
Sibari, 156
Sibillini, mountains, 31c, 118c, 119c, 122c, 123c
Sicani, mountains, 36
Sicily, 17, 20c, 21c, 28, 36, 36c, 39, 42c, 43, 114c, 134c, 135c, 136c, 140c, 156, 156c, 168, 280c, 281c, 282c, 312c, 313c, 336c
Sicily, sea of, 43
Siena, 16c, 18c, 106c, 110c, 111c, 112c, 155, 162, 162c, 163, 163c, 164, 166, 170, 256c, 257c, 260c, 292c, 293, 293c, 294c, 295c, 297c, 301c, 332c, 333c, 344c, 345c, 457, 504c, 505c, 506c, 507c
Signorelli, Luca, 192c, 193c, 267c, 509c, 512c, 513c, 524c, 525c
Signori, Piazza dei (Vicenza), 220c
Signoria, Piazza della (Florence), 250c, 251c, 254c
Similaun, glacier, 68c, 69c
Sinni, river, 36c, 37c
Siponto, 164
Siracusa, 156, 281c
Sirino, mountain, 36c, 37c
Sirmione, 33, 79c
Sirotti, Raimondo, 240c
Sistine Chapel (Rome), 1c, 192c, 193c, 392c, 393c, 524c, 525c, 528c, 529c, 530c, 531c
Sistina, Teatro, 185c
Sistina, Via (Rome), 185c
Siusi, Alpe di, 70c, 71c, 75c
Sixtus IV, pope, 192c, 193c, 524c, 525c
Sixtus V, pope, 166, 168
Smeralda, Costa, 146c, 147c
Solari, Giovanni, 462c, 463c
Solari, Guiniforte, 210c
Solaro, mountain, 126c, 127c
Sole, Val di, 58c, 59c
Sorano, 110c, 111c
Sorrento, Gulf of, 40c, 41c
Sorrento, peninsula, 126c
Sighs, Bridge of (Venice), 239c
Sottile, Capo, 131c
Spagna, Piazza di (Rome), 176c, 183c, 184c, 185c
Spanish Steps, 184c, 185c
Spargi, island, 42c, 43c
Spello, 118c, 119c
Sperlonga, 127c
Spiga, Via della (Milan), 209c
Spinalonga (Venice), 225c
Spoleto, 12c, 13c, 116c, 160, 262c, 264c, 265c
Spring, by Sandro Botticelli, 358c, 359c, 362c, 363c, 364c, 365c
Squillante, gulf, 40
SS. Giovanni e Paolo, Piazza (Venice), 164
Stabeler, Torre (Vajolet), 62c, 63c
Stampace (Cagliari), 302c
Stealing of the dead body of Saint Mark, by Tintoretto, 431c
Stendhal, Marie-Henri Beyle, called, 245c, 320
Stories of Saint Ursula, by Vittore Carpaccio, 366c, 367c, 368c, 369c
Stories of Saint Fina, by Domenico Ghirlandaio, 259c
Stra, 172c, 173c
Stresa, 32, 76c
Stromboli, island, 43, 138c, 139c
Sturla, 243c
Sulcis, 36, 148c
Sulmona, 310c, 311c
Supper at Emmaus, by Caravaggio, 326c, 327c
Susa, 456c
Susa, Val di, 56c, 456c
Switzerland, 32c, 50c, 51c, 59c

T
Taddeo di Bartolo, 258c
Taormina, 20c, 134c, 136c
Taormina, Capo, 136c
Taormina, theater, 20c
Taranto, 36c, 37c
Taranto, gulf of, 40
Taranto, Villa (Pallanza), 32
Tarvisio, 73c
Tavarone, Lazzaro, 240c
Tavoliere della Capitanata, 132c
Te, Palazzo (Mantua), 216c, 217c
Teano, 156
Tempest, The, by Giorgione, 388c, 389c
Temple G (Selinunte), 20c, 21c
Teresa d'Avila, saint, 466
Terminillo, mountain, 120c
Terracina, 40c, 127c, 162
Testa, Capo, 147c
Teulada, capo, 42c
Tharros, 157c
Thoms, W. J., 286
Tiber, river, 22c, 23c, 39, 154c, 183c, 190c, 191c
Tiberina, island (Rome), 154c, 183c
Tiberius, emperor, 127c
Ticinese, porta (Milan), 212c
Ticino, river, 32
Tiepolo, Gianbattista, 172c, 173c, 214c, 215c
Tigullio, gulf, 38c, 39
Tindari, 137c
Tintoretto, Jacopo Robusti, called, 231c, 324, 430c, 431c, 432c, 433c
Tires, Val di, 28c
Tiro della Balestra (Gubbio), 310c, 311c
Tirolo, 72c
Tivoli, 21c, 158, 158c, 159c
Titian, 402c, 403c, 404c, 405c
Toce, river, 32
Todi, 163, 164, 263c
Tofana di Rozes, 67c
Tofane, 67c
Tonale Pass, 58c, 59c
Torcello, island, 92c, 93c
Turin, 56c, 155, 158, 168, 168c, 169c, 196c, 197c, 198c, 199c, 200c, 203c
Torre Abate, 94c
Torre Civica (Trento), 163c
Trajan's Forum (Rome), 180c
Trajan's Market, (Rome), 180c
Transfiguration of Christ, by Beato Angelico, 341c
Trapani, 36, 136c, 283c
Trasimeno, Lake, 35, 35c
Treatise on Painting, by Leon Battista Alberti, 323
Three philosophers, by Giorgione, 388c, 389c
Tremezzo, 32, 81c
Tremiti, islands, 41
Trenta Chapel (Lucca), 247c
Trentino Alto Adige, 33, 33c, 58c, 59c, 68c, 69c, 74c, 75c
Trent, 163c, 221c
Trent, Council of, 163c, 465
Tresa, river, 32
Tresenta, 36c
Trevi, 116c, 117c
Trevi Fountain (Rome), 186c, 187c
Treviso, 91c, 162, 164, 434c, 435c
Tribuna (Verona), 164c
Tribunale, Palazzo del (Arezzo), 260c
Trieste, 221c
Trieste, gulf, 41
Trinità dei Monti (Rome), 176c, 184c, 185c
Tures, Castello di, 72c, 73c
Turrite Secca, 107c
Turrite, river, 107c
Turuddò, mountain, 144c, 145c
Tuscany, 4c, 5c, 16c, 18, 39, 106c, 111c, 112c, 113c, 114c, 115c, 156, 162, 170, 246c, 247c, 462, 518c, 519c
Tyrrhenian Sea, 31c, 40, 115c, 126c, 130c, 156

U
Ubaldo, saint, 310c, 311c
Uccellina, mountains, 115c
Udine, 165c, 220c
Uffizi Gallery (Florence), 325c, 330c, 331c, 344c, 345c, 346c, 347c, 364c, 365c, 408c, 409c, 412c
Umberto I, gallery (Naples), 275c
Umberto I, Piazza (Capri), 126c
Umbria, 34c, 35c, 116c, 118c, 119c, 120c
Umbro, Appennino, 118c, 119c
Unknown Soldier, Monument of the (Rome), 176c
Urbano VIII Barberini, pope, 183c, 536c, 537c
Urbino, 194c, 408c, 409c
Ustica, island, 43

V
Vaccarini, Gian Battista, 168
Vaiolet, Torri del, 28c, 62c, 63c
Valcamonica, 21, 32
Valentino, castle (Turin), 199c
Valentino Park (Turin), 198c, 199c
Valley of the Temples (Agrigento), 156c
Valnerina, 116c
Valsavarenche, 48c
Valsesia, 56c, 57c, 308c
Valtellina, 58c, 59c, 308c
Valtournanche, 28c
Vanvitelli, Carlo, 170c
Vanvitelli, Luigi, 170, 170c, 171c
Varano, lake, 35
Varese, lake, 32
Varotari, Dario, 173c
Varro, Marcus Terentius, 156
Vasari, Giorgio, 154c, 155c, 249c, 250c, 260c, 320, 382c, 383c, 388c, 389c, 514c, 515c
Vatican City, 1c, 190c, 194c, 394c, 395c, 396c, 397c, 398c, 399c, 400c, 401c, 524c, 525c
Vatican Stanze (Vatican City), 400c, 401c, 408c, 409c
Vatican Museums (Rome), 194c, 195c
Vecchio, Palazzo (Florence), 154c, 155c, 252c, 254c
Vecchio, Ponte (Florence), 154c, 155c, 251c
Velino, river, 116c
Venere, Castello di (Erice), 283c
Veneto, 32, 33, 33c, 39, 71c, 90c, 160, 166, 170
Venezia, Piazza (Rome), 176c
Venice, 10c, 11c, 18c, 26c, 41, 92c, 155, 162, 166, 166c, 224c, 233c, 234c, 235c, 238c, 239c, 290c, 291, 291c, 298c, 305c, 366c, 367c, 368c, 369c, 388c, 389c, 408c, 409c, 430c, 431c, 432c, 433c, 465, 476c, 477c, 478c, 479c, 480c, 481c, 484c, 485c, 532c, 533c
Venice, gulf of, 41
Ventimiglia, 39
Ventiquattro Maggio, Piazza (Milan), 212c
Ventotene, island, 124c
Veny, Val, 46c, 47c
Verbano, 77c
Verbano, lake, 32
Vercelli, 39c, 86c, 87c, 88c, 89c, 203c, 490c, 492c, 493c
Vermegnana, Val, 57c
Vernazza, 104c
Verona, 158, 160, 164, 164c, 222c, 223c
Veronese, Paolo Caliari, called, 434c, 435c, 436c, 437c
Verrocchio, Andrea, 323, 336c, 337c
Versailles, 170, 170c
Vescovile, Palazzo (Brindisi), 276c
Vespasian, 178c, 179c
Vesuvius, volcano, 17, 30, 158, 160c, 161c
Vetra, Piazza della (Milan), 210c
Vettore, mountain, 31c, 122c, 123c
Viareggio, 291, 291c
Vicenza, 172c, 220c
Vico, lake, 34c, 35, 35c
Vicoforte, 82c
Vicoforte, sanctuary, 82c
Vieste, 132c, 133c
Vigevano, 202c
Villasor, 36c
Visconteo, fort (Milan), 206c, 207c
Visconti, Bernabò, 208c
Visconti, family, 59c, 78c
Visconti, Gian Galeazzo, 155c, 202c, 203c, 204c, 205c, 522c, 523c
Viterbo, 162
Vittoriale (Rome), 176c
Vittoriale degli Italiani (Gardone), 78c
Vittorio Emanuele I, Ponte (Turin), 196c, 199c
Vittorio Emanuele II, Corso (Turin), 197c
Vittorio Emanuele II, Galleria (Milan), 208c, 209c, 275c
Vittorio Emanuele II, monument (Milan), 205c
Vittorio Emanuele II, king of Italy, 176c
Vittorio Veneto, Piazza (Turin), 196c, 198c, 199c
Vocation of Saint Matthew, by Caravaggio, 438c, 439c
Volsini, mountains, 34c, 35
Volterra, 107c, 422c, 423c, 424c, 425c
Vomero, 174c
Vulcano, island, 42c, 43

W
Wilde, Oscar, 329
Winckelmann, Johann Joachim, 329
Winkler, Torre (Vajolet) 62c, 63c

X
XX Settembre, Via (Genoa), 240c

Y
Yeats Brown, Montague, 98c

Z
Zanoia, Giuseppe, 204c, 205c
Zermatt, 28c, 50c, 51c
Zorzi, Palazzo (Venice), 239c

PHOTO CREDITS

Alinari: page 495.
Stefano Amantini/Atlantide: pages 126 top left, 250 top, 250-251, 253.
M. Amendola/Franca Speranza: page 126 bottom left.
Antonio Attini/Archivio White Star: pages 8, 32 top, 32-33, 34 top left, 34-35, 35 center, 35 bottom, 40 top, 76-77, 78 left, 78 top right, 78 bottom right, 78-79, 79 top, 81 top right, 81 bottom right, 81 top left, 81 bottom left, 119 top right, 126 top right, 127, 197 top, 197 center, 198 bottom, 199 top, 199 center, 199 bottom, 200, 201 center, 258 top, 258-259, 456, 459, 464, 494, 502 top, 502 bottom, 503, 507, 508 top right, 508 bottom right, 510-511, 514-515, 515 top, 515 bottom, 518-519.
Giulio Andreini: pages 291 top, 291 bottom.
Archivio Scala: pages 194-195, 194 bottom, 195 top, 195 bottom, 216-217, 217 bottom, 221 top, 258 bottom, 259 top left, 259 top right, 261, 270 bottom, 271 center, 321, 322, 330, 331, 332-333, 334-335, 336 left, 336 right, 337, 338, 339, 340, 341 bottom, 344-345, 346 top, 346 bottom, 347 top, 347 bottom, 348, 349, 351-352, 354, 355, 356-357, 358-359, 360-361, 362, 363 top, 363 bottom, 364-365, 366-367, 368, 371, 372-373, 374, 380-381, 386, 387, 388, 390, 390-391, 394, 395, 396, 397, 398, 399 left, 399 right, 400-401, 402-403, 404-405, 408-409, 412 left, 412 right, 413, 414-415, 422, 423, 430, 432-433, 438-439, 439, 440-441, 444 left, 444 right, 445, 450, 451, 454-455, 460, 462-463, 480, 483, 485 left, 488, 496-497, 498-499, 500-501, 501, 508 left, 509, 512-513, 530-531.
Franco Barbagallo: pages 36 center, 36-37, 134 top, 136 top, 136 center right, 136-137, 137, 138-139, 156 center.
Foto Benini/Realy Easy: page 167 bottom.
Marcello Bertinetti/Archivio White Star: pages 6-7, 18 left, 18 bottom, 21 bottom, 22-23, 24-25, 26, 28 bottom, 28-29, 32 bottom, 33 center, 33 bottom, 39 bottom, 42-43, 44 top, 44 bottom, 44-45, 45 top right, 46-47, 48-49, 50-51, 51 bottom, 52-53, 58 top, 58 bottom left, 58 bottom right, 58-59, 59 bottom left, 60 top left, 60 bottom left, 60 top right, 60 bottom right, 61, 62-63, 62 bottom left, 62 bottom right, 63 top, 63 center, 64-65, 66 top left, 66 top right, 66-67, 67 top right, 67 bottom right, 67 top left, 67 bottom left, 76 bottom, 77 top right, 86 top right, 86 top left, 86 bottom left, 86-87, 87 bottom, 88-89, 92 top, 92 center, 92 bottom, 114 top, 114-115, 146-147, 146 bottom, 147 center right, 150 top, 150 center, 150 bottom, 150-151, 151 bottom, 151 top right, 151 bottom right, 152-153, 154, 157 bottom right, 158 top, 158 center left, 158 center right, 158 bottom, 158-159, 159, 163 top, 166 top left, 166 bottom left, 168 top, 176 top, 176 center, 176 bottom, 176-177, 177 top left, 177 top right, 178-179, 180 top, 180 center, 180 right, 181 bottom right, 183 top right, 183 bottom right, 184 top right, 185 center, 188 top, 190 bottom left, 190 bottom right, 191 top, 191 bottom left, 191 bottom right, 196 top left, 196 top right, 196-197, 197 bottom, 198-199, 201 top, 202-203, 203 top, 226 bottom left, 226 bottom right, 230 left, 230 right, 231 top right, 231 bottom right, 232-233, 232 bottom, 233 top, 233 center, 233 bottom, 234 top, 234 bottom, 234-235, 235 top, 235 center, 235 bottom left, 235 bottom right, 236-237, 238-239, 238 bottom, 239 top left, 239 bottom left, 239 top right, 239 bottom right, 240 top left, 240 top right, 241 bottom, 243 top, 256 top left, 256 top right, 256-257, 276-277, 284-285, 290 top, 290-291, 291 center, 292 top left, 292 top right, 292-293, 293 top right, 293 center left, 293 center right, 293 bottom, 294 top, 294 center, 294-295, 294 bottom left, 294 bottom right, 295 top, 295 center, 295 bottom, 296-297, 296, 297 top, 297 center, 297 bottom, 298 bottom left, 298 top right, 298 bottom right, 299, 300 top, 300-301, 300 bottom, 301 bottom left, 305 bottom right, 308 top left, 308 center left, 308 bottom right, 308 top right, 468-469, 476 top, 476 left, 476-477, 478-479, 490 top, 490 bottom, 491, 492-493, 534, 534-535, 535, 536 left, 536 right, 537.
F. Bertuzzi/SIE: pages 298 top left.
Attilio Boccazzi/Varotto: pages 201 bottom, 201 top right, 201 bottom right.
Livio Bourbon/Archivio White Star: pages 532, 533.
A. Bracchetti/P. Zigrossi - Musei Civici Vaticani: page 1.
Massimo Borchi/Atlantide: pages 130-131.
CameraPhoto: pages 92-93, 93 top left, 93 top right, 206 top right, 224 top right, 224 bottom right, 225, 227 top, 227 bottom, 231 top left, 231 bottom left.
Foto Cautillo: pages 133 bottom right, 276 top, 276 bottom.
Elio and Stefano Ciol: pages 270-271, 271 top, 271 bottom, 272 top, 272 center, 272 bottom, 272-273.
Giuliano Colliva: page 486.
Anne Conway/Archivio White Star: pages 38 left, 96 top, 96 center, 96 bottom, 96-97, 97 top left, 97 top right, 98 top, 98 center left, 98 right, 98 bottom left, 98-99, 99 bottom, 100-101, 102-103, 102 bottom left, 102 bottom right, 103 top, 103 center, 103 bottom, 104-105, 104 bottom left, 104 bottom right, 106 top, 106-107, 174 bottom right, 174 bottom left, 240-241, 241 top, 242-243, 243 bottom left, 242 bottom right, 243 center, 243 bottom, 301 top, 301 bottom right.
Guido Cozzi/Atlantide: pages 39 top, 230-231.
Franco Furoncoli: page 244 top right.
Cesare Gerolimetto: pages 16-17, 33 top, 168 bottom, 182 bottom, 186-187, 190-191, 538-539.
Araldo De Luca: pages 14, 15, 27
FMR: pages 218-219, 317, 318, 375, 376-377, 393, 407, 416, 417, 418-419, 420-421, 424-425, 426-427, 427 top, 427 bottom, 428-429, 436, 437, 446-447, 467, 470, 471, 472-473, 474-475, 486-487.
Granata Press Service: pages 80-81.
Nicola Grifoni: pages 342-343, 352-353, 382, 383, 385, 517.
I.G.D.A.: pages 325, 326-327, 329, 341 top, 368, 368-369, 378-379, 379, 384, 389, 392, 410-411, 431, 434-435, 442-443, 481, 497, 506, 525.
K&B News: pages 406 top, 406 bottom, 448-449, 452-453, 504, 516, 524 right.
Nippon TV: pages 192-193, 193, 526-527, 527 top, 528-529.
Pessina/Realy Easy Star: page 174 top left.
Luciano Ramires/Archivio White Star: pages 28 top left, 28 center left, 30 top, 45 top left, 49 top right, 50 top, 50, 55 top right, 63 bottom, 68-69, 68 bottom, 69 top left, 69 bottom left, 69 top right, 69 bottom right, 70 bottom, 71 bottom left, 71 bottom right, 72 top left, 72 bottom left, 72 right, 72-73, 73 bottom left, 73 bottom right, 74-75, 75 bottom left, 95 top, 95 center, 95 bottom, 119 top left, 119 bottom right, 120-121, 286 top left, 286 bottom left, 286 top right, 286 bottom right, 287, 306-307, 306 bottom left, 306 bottom right, 307 top, 307 center, 307 bottom, 310 bottom.
Guido Rossi/The Image Bank: pages 94-95, 223 top right.
Giovanni Simeone/Marka: pages 171 bottom left, 171 bottom right.
Giovanni Simeone/SIE: pages 167 center, 206 bottom left, 210 bottom, 213, 220 top left, 220 top right.
Giovanni Simeone/Sime: pages 2-3, 10-11, 49 top left, 49 bottom left, 54-55, 55 top left, 55 bottom left, 90 top, 90 bottom, 90-91, 91 top, 91 bottom, 94 top, 172-173, 172 bottom left, 172 bottom right, 173 top, 173 center, 173 bottom, 226-227, 228-229.
A. Tradii: pages 246-247.
Giulio Veggi: pages 76 top, 77 top left.
Giulio Veggi/Archivio White Star: pages 4-5, 9, 12-13, 16 bottom, 17 top, 17 bottom, 18-19, 20 top, 20-21, 21 top, 30 bottom, 30-31, 31 top left, 31 top right, 34 top right, 35 top, 36 top, 36 bottom, 38-39, 39 center, 40 center, 40 bottom, 40-41, 42 top, 42 center, 42 bottom, 48 top, 50 center, 55 bottom right, 56 top left, 56 bottom left, 56 top right, 56 bottom right, 56-57, 57 top left, 57 top right, 59 bottom right, 70 top, 70 center, 70-71, 74 bottom, 75 top left, 75 top right, 75 bottom right, 82 top left, 82 top right, 82-83, 83 top, 83 center, 83 bottom, 84-85, 86 bottom right, 106 center, 106 bottom, 107 top left, 107 top right, 108/109, 110 top, 110 bottom, 110-111, 111 bottom left, 111 bottom right, 112 top, 112 bottom left, 112-113, 112 bottom right, 113 top, 113 center, 113 bottom, 114 bottom, 115 top, 115 center, 115 bottom, 116 top left, 116 bottom left, 116 top right, 116 bottom right, 117, 118-119, 118 bottom left, 118 bottom right, 119 top left, 119 bottom left, 119 top right, 119 bottom right, 119 bottom left, 121 top left, 121 top right, 122-123, 124 top, 124 bottom, 124-125, 125 top left, 125 top right, 126 bottom right, 126-127, 128-129, 128, 129 top left, 129 bottom left, 129 top right, 129 bottom right, 130 bottom, 131 top left, 131 center left, 131 bottom left, 131 right, 132, 132-133, 133 top left, 133 bottom left, 133 top right, 134 center, 134 bottom, 135, 136 center left, 136 bottom, 138 bottom, 139 top, 139 center left, 139 center right, 139 bottom, 140-141, 140 left, 140 bottom, 141 top right, 141 bottom left, 141 bottom right, 142-143, 144 top, 144 center, 144 bottom, 144-145, 145 top left, 145 top right, 147 top right, 147 bottom right, 147 top left, 147 bottom left, 148 top left, 148 top right, 148 bottom left, 148 bottom right, 148-149, 149 bottom, 154-155, 155 top, 155 bottom, 156 top, 156 bottom, 156-157,157 bottom left, 160 top right, 160 center left, 160 center right, 160 left, 161, 162-163, 162, 163 center, 163 bottom, 164 top, 164 bottom left, 164 bottom right, 164-165, 165 bottom, 166-167, 167 top, 168-169, 169 bottom right, 169 bottom left, 170 top, 170 bottom, 170-171, 174 top right, 175, 180 bottom, 180-181, 181 bottom left, 182-183, 183 top left, 183 bottom left, 184 top left, 184-185, 185 top right, 185 bottom, 188 bottom, 188-189, 189 top, 202 top left, 202 top right, 203 bottom, 204 top, 204 bottom, 204-205, 205 top left, 205 top right, 206 top left, 206 bottom right, 206-207, 207 bottom left, 207 bottom right, 208 top, 208 center top, 208 center bottom, 208 bottom, 210 top, 211, 212 top, 212 center, 212 bottom, 212 right, 214 left,214 top right, 214 bottom right, 215, 216 top left, 216 top right, 217 top, 217 center, 218 top, 218 center, 218 bottom, 219 top right, 219 top left, 220-221, 221 center, 221 bottom, 222-223, 222 bottom, 223 top left, 223 bottom right, 224 top left, 224 bottom left, 244 top left, 244-245, 244 top right, 245 center, 245 bottom, 246 top, 247 top, 247 bottom, 248 top left, 248 top right, 248-249, 249 top, 249 bottom, 250 bottom, 251 top left, 251 top right, 252 top left, 252 bottom left, 252 top right, 252 bottom right, 254 left, 254 top right, 254 bottom right, 254-255, 255 bottom, 257 top, 257 bottom, 260 top, 260 bottom left, 260 bottom right, 262, 263 top left, 263 bottom left, 263 top right, 263 bottom right, 264-265, 266, 267, 268 top, 268 center, 268 bottom, 268-269, 269 top left, 268 top right, 274 top left, 274 top right, 274-275, 275 top, 275 bottom, 277 top left, 277 top right, 278 top left, 278 center left, 278 bottom left, 278 top right, 278 bottom right, 279, 280-281, 280 bottom, 281 top, 281 center, 281 bottom, 282 top, 282 center, 282 bottom, 282-283, 283 bottom left, 283 bottom right, 284 top, 284 center, 284 bottom, 285 top left, 285 top right, 288-289, 288 bottom, 289 top, 289 bottom, 302 top, 302 center, 302 bottom, 302-303, 303 top, 303 center, 303 bottom left, 303 bottom right, 304 top left, 304 bottom left, 304 top right, 304 bottom right, 304-305, 305 bottom left, 308 center right, 309, 310 top, 310 center, 310-311, 311 bottom left, 311 bottom right, 312 top, 312 center left, 312 center right, 312 bottom, 312-313, 313 bottom left, 313 bottom right, 314-315, 482-483, 484 left, 484-485, 485 right, 498, 504-505, 505, 520-521, 522 top, 522 bottom, 522-523, 523 top, 524 left.

EDITORIAL DIRECTOR
VALERIA MANFERTO DE FABIANIS

GRAPHIC DESIGN
ANNA GALLIANI - PATRIZIA BALOCCO

WONDERS OF ITALY
TRANSLATION: C.T.M., MILAN

MASTERPIECES OF ITALIAN ART
TRANSLATION: IRENE CUMMING KLEEBERG